'Matthew Johnson's volume will become ... workable international historical archa ... explore the origins of modernization — the Georgian Order. Drawing on important work by Deetz, Glassie, and the members of Archaeology in Annapolis, Johnson comprehensively, and with up-to-date theorization, interrelates landscapes, houses, churches, inventories, maps, how-to-books, technical treatises from the Renaissance, and technologies of the self. He has written a central book in historical archaeology.'

Professor Mark P. Leone, Department of Anthropology,
University of Maryland at College Park

'Matthew Johnson's subtle combination of structuralism, separately tracing the history of individual elements of material culture, and refusing to draw a priori distinctions between physical and mental landscapes demonstrates how archaeology can make important contributions to understanding the perceptual changes involved in the birth of modernity in Britain. His work challenges the credentials of self-serving interpretations of this transformation advanced by scholars of both the political right and the political left.'

Professor Bruce G. Trigger, Department of Anthropology,
McGill University

Social Archaeology

General Editor
Ian Hodder, University of Cambridge

Advisory Editors
Margaret Conkey, University of California at Berkeley
Mark Leone, University of Maryland
Alain Schnapp, U.E.R. d'Art et d'Archéologie, Paris
Stephen Shennan, University of Southampton
Bruce Trigger, McGill University, Montreal

Published

FRAGMENTS FROM ANTIQUITY
An Archaeology of Social Life in Britain, 2900–1200 BC
John C. Barrett

ENGENDERING ARCHAEOLOGY
Edited by Joan M. Gero and Margaret W. Conkey

EXPLANATION IN ARCHAEOLOGY
Guy Gibbon

SOCIAL BEING AND TIME
Christopher Gosden

IRON-AGE SOCIETIES
Lotte Hedeager

THE DOMESTICATION OF EUROPE
Ian Hodder

AN ARCHAEOLOGY OF CAPITALISM
Matthew Johnson

THE ARCHAEOLOGY OF INEQUALITY
Edited by Randall H. McGuire and Robert Paynter

MATERIAL CULTURE AND MASS CONSUMPTION
Daniel Miller

READING MATERIAL CULTURE
Edited by Christopher Tilley

In Preparation

THE RISE OF MESO-AMERICA
Elizabeth Brumfiel

CONTEMPORARY ARCHAEOLOGY IN THEORY
Ian Hodder & Robert W. Preucel

DARKNESS AND HEROES
Ian Morris

ARCHAEOLOGICAL INTERPRETATIONS
Robert W. Preucel

READING ARCHAEOLOGY
Christopher W. Tilley

FEMINIST ARCHAEOLOGY
Alison Wylie

An Archaeology of Capitalism

Matthew Johnson

BLACKWELL
Publishers

First published 1996

2 4 6 8 10 9 7 5 3 1

Blackwell Publishers Ltd
108 Cowley Road
Oxford OX4 1JF
UK

Blackwell Publishers Inc.
238 Main Street
Cambridge, Massachusetts 02142
USA

British Library Cataloguing-in-Publication Data

A CIP catalogue record for this book is available from the British Library.

Library of Congress Cataloging-in-Publication Data

Library of Congress data has been applied for

ISNB 1-55786-345-8
      1-55786-348-2 (pbk)

Typeset in 11 on 13 pt Garamond
by Best-set Typesetter Ltd., Hong Kong
Printed in Great Britain by Hartnolls Limited, Bodmin, Cornwall

This book is printed on acid-free paper

To Becky

Contents

Figures

Preface

This book is an archaeological study of some aspects of landscape and material life in late medieval and early modern England. It has the ambitious aim of understanding many of the changes seen in this period in terms of the shift from medieval to modern, the so-called 'rise of capitalism'. It tries to bring together some recent insights in the theoretical literature and to explore the way they can help us interpret changes in landscape, architecture and material culture. In doing so the book tries to be interdisciplinary: it necessarily cuts across the boundaries of archaeology, economic, social and cultural history, historical geography, architectural history and other related disciplines.

In this Preface I want to sketch out some of the reasons why I came to write this book, so that the reader, perhaps from a different disciplinary background, might better understand some of the peculiarities and biases which are evident in succeeding chapters. In many respects its concerns are embedded in experience of the study of 'medieval' archaeology as an undergraduate between 1982 and 1985. At the time, archaeological theory was in a state of fascinating turmoil. We were being taught a bewildering variety of perspectives on archaeological thinking. Processual archaeology, with its stress on positivism, a social evolutionary framework, reliance on statistical method, systems thinking, and testing, was still very much presented as an orthodoxy. Such an approach was only beginning to be challenged by new ideas of symbolic and structural archaeology (the volume of that title edited by Ian Hodder was published in 1982). New ideas were also filtering in from other disciplinary traditions, in particular structuralism and western Marxism. Whatever one thought of the specific direction archaeological theory was taking, the discipline of archaeology was clearly on the move. We were studying a complex, modern social science on the road to intellectual maturity.

The study of medieval and post-medieval archaeology in England was at that time less engaging. The material itself was as absorbing as the debates sketched out above, but what was written about the material was often less stimulating. Many subjects of intrinsic fascination – castles, monasteries, the complex palimpsests of landscape archaeology – were reduced to what appeared often to be a mind-numbingly dull collection of dates, classifications, and minimal and 'common-sensical' interpretation. Where wider insight did occur, it tended to be in what little reading in the documentary history of the periods was possible: the history of technology, of mentality, and so on (though in fairness the bulk of medieval social and economic history appeared to be of similar character). The few books on medieval archaeology that used any theoretical insights, most notably Hodges (1982), had been castigated as 'premature' by many reviewers. In any case, they dealt with the early Middle Ages rather than the high and post-medieval period.

Studying such a combination of subjects induced a kind of intellectual schizophrenia. Theory essays were written from what came to be known as a post-processual perspective, drawing on many of the ideas at the forefront of the social sciences. At the same time, essays written on the medieval period amounted to little more than tight, hopefully competent reviews of the material to hand. It appeared that other periods had gone through the 'New Archaeology' and beyond; medieval archaeology was still in an innocent, 'pre-processual' phase.

The first notion that it was time to stop grumbling and to do something about this came from two books that turned up on the theory reading lists, Henry Glassie's *Folk Housing in Middle Virginia* and James Deetz's *In Small Things Forgotten*. These two books looked at historic artefacts in colonial North America and attempted a structuralist study of the cultural meanings encoded in those artefacts. They were both readable, exciting, challenging studies in historical archaeology, that dared to say exciting things about historic artefacts. They looked at changes from 'medieval' to 'Georgian' patterns of thought and life through houses, pottery, gravestones, and other classes of ordinary archaeological material. The fact that the two books dealt with material from the other side of the Atlantic engendered a slight feeling of shame. Given that the central transition delineated by both studies was one that started 'back home' in Europe, why couldn't we produce similar work here?

The logical choice for research was therefore to apply and hopefully develop such ideas in relation to late and post-medieval archaeological material, which I tried to do in relation to traditional architecture (Johnson 1993). Inevitably application of structural models to evidence that had previously largely been treated in a traditional manner was fraught with problems, and the final result of the research was a book whose perspective stood at some distance from the theoretical stances of Deetz and Glassie.

It was also unsatisfactory in the sense that it placed one class of evidence – traditional architecture – in a vacuum. In trying in the latter part of that book to understand the changes that happened to houses, it was necessary to refer outwards – to changes in the rural landscape around the houses, in contemporary social and cultural history, in the cultural and social complexion of the household. In short, a wider-ranging, more contextual approach had to be taken.

An Archaeology of Capitalism, then, is in part the product of trying to take that more contextual approach. It is the result of a rather eclectic reading through different topics and subject areas. In so doing I have drawn on a great variety of sources, and have benefited from a wide range of conversations with many scholars of different disciplines.

Ian Hodder first suggested that I write this book, and was full of constant encouragement thereafter. In many ways it was his questioning as a prehistorian of the 'givens' of landscape history – 'why did they need probate inventories? why list things?' – that I have tried to respond to in what follows. Such superficially naïve questions turned out to have very complex and profound answers that led in turn to further questions. Anthony Fletcher read portions of the first draft for historical *naïveté*, and in the process suggested many valuable new ideas. Discussions of the Durham Early Modern Group, Centre for Seventeenth Century Studies and the Centre for the History of the Human Sciences have influenced my thinking in less tangible but just as important ways. Many others read and made comments on the first draft, including Elaine Grummitt, James Whitford, Chris Cumberpatch, Simon Coleman, Mark Edmonds, Martin Millett, and Linda Ebbatson. Discussions with Chris Brooks, Elizabeth Foyster, Sara Pennell, Eric Mercer, Margie Purser, Paul Shackel, Barbara Little, Ed Hood, and Jim Delle also helped in very great measure. My apologies to the many others with whom I have discussed a host of ideas over a pint but who are too numerous to mention here.

Collectively, the staff and students at St David's University College Lampeter and the Dept. of Archaeology, University of Durham, are thanked. David Austin has contributed much, both in the way of critical comment and practical help during the planning stage. Much of the material discussed here was first presented in an undergraduate course at Durham, and the often acute questioning and enthusiasm of the students on that course helped the process along also.

Mark Leone's comments on the initial synopsis turned me away from much tedious repetition of negative critique and I hope made the book less pretentious and more approachable. Other anonymous referees also made valuable comments on the original synopsis. As the book developed, John Davey at Blackwell's showed understanding, patience and practical help in equal measure.

Finally, my largest thanks goes to my wife Becky. Many of the ideas in this book have arisen out of our conversations, but, equally important, her patience, support and forbearance over the last three years have been constant. *An Archaeology of Capitalism* is dedicated to her – with apologies for the boring bits.

Matthew Johnson

1

Introduction

This book is concerned with the archaeology of the late medieval and early modern periods. Archaeology is the discipline that deals with the study and interpretation of landscape and material culture. As an archaeologist, I seek to explore some of the new ideas developed within archaeology, history and the human sciences generally over the last few years in the context of the material record of pre-industrial England and Wales.

The title of the book – *An Archaeology of Capitalism* – thus alludes not just to the subject-matter involved, but also to the theoretical perspectives taken. Post-medieval archaeology in the past has concentrated very much on small-scale, empirical contributions to the study of the period, for example through study of specific industrial techniques and processes or through production and marketing of particular artefact types such as wares of pottery. The approach taken here is wider-ranging and more ambitious. I do not want to draw any initial dividing lines between areas of study, between archaeological and documentary evidence. Drawing loosely on Michel Foucault's use of the term 'archaeology', I want to 'excavate' below the surface of pre-industrial material life; I want to sketch some of the lines of the genealogy, the underlying geology, of certain social, cultural and mental processes that came together in the post-medieval period. I want to understand something of the pathways of the move towards modern ways of life. I want to see these pathways not in a Whiggish or evolutionary sense – that is, in terms of a single 'origin' or one unfolding story – or even in the sense of reducing a diverse and varied set of historical patterns to one massive, unified transition; rather, I want to see the period in terms of a diversity of cultural practices that leave material traces, traces that survive for the archaeologist and that often come to mean different things in different contexts.

Social and material practices – what people do, the way they do it, the meanings they attach to what they do — create and use objects and spaces, material culture and pieces of landscape and architecture, to carry their meaning. We often implicitly assume that as people make their own history, argue out their identities, they leave these objects and spaces in their wake. These objects and spaces remain untouched and adrift, like so much flotsam and jetsam, often forgotten until the time comes for the archaeologist to pick up, record and classify such scraps. This view, however, is simplistic. One of the most exciting aspects of recent archaeological thought has been exploration of the way in which objects and spaces can be picked up again, be reinterpreted in new ways by new groups.

This reappropriation of old familiar things in new ways, carrying new meanings, can even be seen as a necessary process in the case of objects and spaces like old churches, agrarian landscapes and so on. Their mental shape, or the way they are seen by people of succeeding ages and periods, may be changed even as their physical shape remains the same. Even their deliberate destruction and erasure from the surface of the earth can be an act charged with symbolic meaning.

This constant manipulation of material things, this ceaseless war over their meanings, is as much true of everyday objects and spaces as of elite ones. One of the central insights of much of recent social history and historical anthropology is that past systems of thought are entwined as much with the layout of the smallest church or house as with the largest palace; with table manners as much as with formal religious belief; as much with the everyday life of the peasant household, common fields and village community as with the politics of the city and court faction.

In this book, then, I shall look at some of the many classes of objects and spaces from roughly between the height of the Middle Ages to the beginnings of the Industrial Revolution, concentrating on those pertaining to the 'rise of rural capitalism' defined in the very broadest sense. I shall look at their context and history, the way they were classified, used and reused by individuals and groups. I shall use them to try to tell a story about some aspects of the structuring of modernity; that is, how certain aspects of the world we see around us came to be the way they were and are.

Near the centre of this story will be an account of two processes, rather crudely conceived and violently abstracted from their traces in the archaeological and historical materials: enclosure and commodification. The first, enclosure, refers to the changing patterning of mental and material spaces; the second refers to the changing role of objects as loci of cultural, social and economic relationships. I will try to understand these processes as entwined with the everyday actions of men and women. They lie under surface structures of domination and resistance and are renegotiated through human agency.

Enclosure and commodification are emergent structures. That is, they unfold in a period usually seen as pre-capitalist or late medieval, and end in the final culmination of industrial capitalism. They also unfold across different areas of immediate study, in ways that cut across spheres of modern discourse that we often think of as separate, such as 'religious', 'agrarian', 'public' and 'domestic'. Indeed, it can be argued that they culminate in the creation of those spheres as apparently autonomous areas of activity and discourse.

Method of Study

Historical archaeology differs from prehistoric archaeology in many subtle and profound ways, not all of which are worth raising here. There is the question of the relationship between documentary and archaeological evidence; of the social and political resonances of dealing so directly with the rise of modern ways of life; of the arbitrariness of disciplinary boundaries and the dominance of particular traditional forms of historical explanation within medieval and post-medieval archaeology; of the political resonance of doing archaeology at the so-called 'end of history'. Rather than engage in a long and tedious account of where this book stands on these issues, I would rather they emerge through the discussions in future chapters.

What I would like to do is spend a little time explaining the title. The terms 'capitalism' and 'the feudal/capitalist transition' are used here as a necessary shorthand for the changing practices and transitions that have shaped aspects of modern life. In using the word, I do not propose a theory of history. I do not wish to suggest allegiance either to a particular classification of socio-economic formations, or to a suggestion of core or primary features in any such formation, or indeed affiliation to a particular standpoint such as that of Marxism or any other for that matter. Aspects of the theory of the feudal/capitalist transition as defined within more formal traditions are discussed in the next chapter.

The second important word in the title is 'archaeology'. The term 'archaeology' is used in the title both in its generally accepted sense – the study of the material remains of the past – and also in the senses outlined by Michel Foucault (1972). Foucault's use of the term is difficult to pin down, being explicated in terms of metaphors. Very briefly, it refers to looking at the underlying structures of an object and the discourses that created it, of tracing the genealogy of the boundaries drawn round discursive fields in the present.

Even in its more traditional sense the term 'archaeology' conceals ambiguity. I do not mean it solely or even mainly to refer to excavated evidence; archaeology today studies anything physical, from Palaeolithic cave art to twentieth-century beer cans. In this book the archaeological evidence used will include the architecture, whether upstanding or destroyed, of palaces, houses, and other buildings; of the landscape, as interpreted through physical evidence, maps or written accounts; pottery, material goods of all forms, and references to such goods in documents such as household inventories or estate accounts.

The third and possibly most important word is 'An'. First, this book is a strictly provisional study in several senses. Much of the discussion is very much in the form of pointers to potentially interesting areas of analysis or suggestions for future work. It is not intended to be a definitive statement, encyclopaedia or synthesis of everything which is known or has been written about the feudal/capitalist transition. There is a problem of intellectual tactics here: the necessity of looking contextually at the archaeology of the period, of relating different classes of material together, clashes with the degree of expertise needed to deal with any one field in an area of such close and detailed scholarship. The evidence is sparse enough to enable an individual scholar to draw together different aspects of the Neolithic with some confidence; the same cannot be said of the early modern period. I do not pretend to be an 'expert' on such areas as pottery analysis or on most classes of documentary evidence. I have therefore merely tried to draw out links between artefacts and documents in new ways, or merely indicated where future work might be fruitful, rather than make definitive or authoritative statements on complex bodies of material.

Second, only a fraction of the issues usually raised under the heading of the feudal/capitalist transition are raised here; I have concentrated on a certain period (late medieval and early modern; that is, c.1400–1750) before many of the most tangible capitalistic changes (such as large-scale industrialization and creation of a mass urban working class) took place, and on certain bodies of evidence ('agrarian capitalism' in the rural landscape, consumer goods) rather than others (developed colonial landscapes, world trade systems and early industrial sites are barely treated for example). The issues discussed in this book are those that happen to interest me particularly, though the way parallel arguments for other topics of study might be pursued in more detail should be apparent. Some possible avenues for future work are addressed in chapter 9.

The most profound sense of the word 'An' lies in its philosophical resonance. Many scholars influenced by different strands of current theory have argued that the intellectual project of building one grand historical narrative to cover all historical development, whether of the feudal/capitalist transition or human history in general, is looking increasingly doomed. I do not subscribe to such a grand and rather sweeping position without certain qualifications, but if such perspectives have any intellectual validity it is less and less possible therefore to write '*The* archaeology of capitalism'. The understanding presented here tries to be one that links certain objects and themes together in one narrative; there have been and will be other archaeologies, other narratives that have their own validity. I would not wish to attempt to preclude their development by use of the definite article.

The Feudal/Capitalist Transition in Social Theory

The Holy Trinity of social thinkers, Marx, Durkheim and Weber, all had something powerful to say on the feudal/capitalist transition (Giddens 1971: 185), and since their time it is difficult to think of a major theorist who has not addressed this question in some form or another. It has indeed been argued that the origins of modern social philosophy, and of social theory as a discipline, can themselves be traced back to a nineteenth-century conservative codification by de Tocqueville and others of social forms and values such as status, authority and community that were passing away and were increasingly opposed by their respective counterparts of class, power and society (Nisbet 1967).

In the social sciences as a whole, therefore, the transition from feudalism to capitalism has become a classic case study, a key, almost symbolic battleground over which different views of the way the world works have been fought. (More cynically, it has become a well-worn peg on which a series of origin myths justifying or condemning the present nature of things may be hung.) The empirical importance of the questions being addressed have shared the stage with the philosophical resonances of particular explanations. To clarify, theorizing the origins of capitalism is both a task of major importance in understanding the past and present and is also a classic empirical field or case study with which to assess the relative power of competing social theories. The need to avoid confusion of these two aspects, theoretical and substantive, in assessing past thought is readily apparent.

This is seen most forcefully in the parameters of the so-called Protestant Ethic debate. Weber wrote his essay *The Protestant Ethic and the Spirit of Capitalism* in 1905, arguing that the influence of religious radicalism, in particular that of Calvinist Protestantism, was a key factor in changing cultural attitudes, world-views and work practices among certain urban communities in north-west Europe; and that these changes in practices led to the development of nascent capitalism and eventually to the 'iron cage' of industrial society. Religious and cultural factors were thus placed at the heart of any account of the origins of capitalism (Weber 1958). Weber's contribution was therefore twofold. First, as a concrete and major addition to historical scholarship; and second, as a barely coded answer to a classical Marxist conception of social transformation stressing economic and material causality over political and religious 'superstructure'.

The archaeological study of the late feudal/early capitalist period thus has the opportunity to contribute to one of the major debates, 'big questions', of the social sciences. This opportunity rests in large part on the materiality of the transformations under study. Whatever one's definition of capitalism, most agree that it has something to do with material things, how they are produced, circulated and consumed and the social and economic values people place upon them. Most would go further and point out that the changing relationship between things, values and people has a lot to do with the constitution of everyday life under nascent and developed capitalism. So the study of material things in their context, logically, should be able to tell us a great deal about the changing social, ideational and economic patterning attendant upon the feudal/capitalist transition that study of purely documentary evidence alone will not.

This insight is rendered even more powerful if one accepts the premise that material culture is active, that its meanings are manipulated by social actors in maintaining stability and producing change in the rules and norms governing everyday social relations rather than passively reflecting them. We have to consider the ·possibility that the ordinary things the archaeologist digs up or surveys are produced within certain relations such as those between apprentice and master or husband and wife, and are used and maintained within other such relations; that they may help to maintain or change those relations, for example through a thatched roof's need for regular repair by a 'good neighbour' or the use of tokens or jettons in standardizing exchanges of goods previously embedded in systems of 'credit'.

These examples are deliberately obvious ones to make the point; material things, like texts and ideas, often operate in more subtle ways than these. This subtlety makes archaeological study more difficult practically and more problematic theoretically. It also, however, renders archaeological analysis even more potentially productive of profound insight into changing social relations, on the principle derived from cultural anthropology that what is most important is often that which is most implicit and taken-for-granted.

Definitions of Capitalism

Capitalism is not a single, easily defined thing. The term may refer either to a social totality or to specific material or relational elements within a non-capitalist totality (as for example in the statement 'merchant capitalism grew up within the interstices of the feudal structure'). Nor, if one forsakes crude Marxist or functional models of social process, are its visible manifestations or underlying form identical from place to place.

In most theoretical viewpoints, however, capitalism has been associated with merchant and industrial society in general and the factory system in particular. A Marxist view gives us a specific form of social relationship between capitalist and wage labourer in which the latter sells his (alienated) labour, and a mode of production based on capital as opposed to a feudal mode based on land or an ancient mode based on slave labour. Other views also stress the importance of the factory system and mass production (Weber 1947: 158–245). All views also stress the related nature of the factory system and the social practices and ideas that go with it: the need for 'rational' work practices being related to the rise of specific views of time, work discipline and so on; the creation also of a mass working class with attendant ethic (Thompson 1967 and 1963).

Equally important is the principle of market exchange. This is not absent from other social forms as an institution (thus it may exist in the context of feudal borough markets or as an adjunct to a directed economy under the Roman Empire), but what lends exchange its particular flavour under capitalism is linkage with the notion of object or service as pure commodity. Exchange is thus disembedded from society in Polanyi's terms. This linkage raises a series of issues most recently touched on by Miller (1987) and Dodgshon (1985) and will be touched on further below.

Feminists have pointed out that the structure of capitalism is structurally and functionally dependent also on changes in family form and gender roles (as discussed for example in the context of modern industrial society by Coulson et al. 1982). Historically this can be seen in part in the rise of the nuclear family, though recent work has tended to stress that below the elite level nuclear families were the norm for much of pre-industrial Europe at least (Wrightson 1982: 70). What is certainly congruent with the rise of capitalism is the separation of the context of production of material goods and services from the physical and social context of household relations. With this separation has historically come a rise in material living standards, in terms of the purchasing power of the household and the goods found within it; also, many have argued, comes a diminution of women's roles in formally valued economic activity as the context of work is separated from the context of the domestic (Charles and Duffin 1985; Moore 1988).

If capitalism is structurally dependent on changes within household relations, it is also dependent on the structural transformation of the countryside. In crude Marxist models, isolated communities that are more or less self-sufficient in subsistence goods must give way to a countryside providing a massive agricultural surplus to feed the urban proletariat. Such a transformation is one of structure as well as scale: from self-sufficient peasant farming in which the means of surplus accumulation is extra-economic to a system of farming for profit integrated within large-scale markets.

Weber was careful to stress the ideological factors congruent with economic ones, the 'spirit of capitalism', which he identified as a combination of acquisitive individualism and rational view of the productive process. The other side of this coin, that of the attitudes and discipline of the workforce, is the development of work discipline, itself dependent on changing views of time and precision in its measurement (Thompson 1967).

A final point, obvious yet important to state clearly, is that nascent capitalism, the development of the preconditions of industrial society, is, in nature as well as size, not the same thing as fully fledged capitalism. For example, the presence of mercantilist economic strategies was integral to the rise of early systems of colonial exploitation, but is very different from the free market of later capitalism. Again, patterns of work in seventeenth- and eighteenth-century coal and lead mining were not simply an early, smaller version of those of the nineteenth century (Crossley 1990: 204–13). This point is critical since it suggests that it is difficult to construct progressive, quantitative measures of socio-economic change, of 'degrees of capitalism'. Change may be transformative and dialectic rather than progressive and evolutionary.

From this discussion follow four conclusions relevant to our discussion here. First, definitions of capitalism are problematic, since from different perspectives different features are core and necessary, or peripheral and contingent. Different definitions of the structural character of any social formation will obviously condition which explanations of the form are found intellectually coherent and satisfying. Such different definitions will further specify what evidence is regarded as legitimate or relevant to the argument. However, most agree that capitalism is a total system, a formation whose structure penetrates and embraces all or at least most aspects of economic, social and cultural life. At the same time, its structure is not invariant: particular ideological, social or economic elements of that system may vary from locality to locality without necessarily affecting the core relations that make up that totality. This particular variation may be significant in helping to understand different trajectories of different groups; if so, it is necessary to understand where it came from − in other words the particular historical antecedents of that group.

Second, capitalism is not measurable in coarse terms; there is no single index, evolutionary or otherwise, by which different human groups at different times can be judged more or less capitalistic in nature. For example, as Weber (1958: 19–20) pointed out, acquisitive individualism in itself is a feature of many different social forms; it is only when associated with a particular work ethic and 'rational' attitude to property and capital accumulation that it becomes specifically capitalistic in nature.

Third, if the theoretical conception of capitalism must necessarily be a subtle one, its archaeological dissection must be equally so. Empirical 'measures' of capitalism, if they are at all possible, need to be rigorously thought out and carefully qualified within a careful understanding of criteria, definitions and evidence. In short, they need to be theorized.

Fourth, the form of specific capitalist societies depends at least in part on their medieval or feudal antecedents. In other words, if we are to understand why, for example, the English countryside developed in a certain way, we have to understand not only certain forces of change such as political centralization and integration into national markets but the enduring structures from the historical past that such forces were operating upon and transforming. Such structures were simultaneously material and cultural in form: the Church, medieval systems of landscape and husbandry, old castles. Such structures were also often strongly regional in nature and very ancient in origin, and had a key role in structuring the different development of 'farming regions' and landscape types in the early modern period. This point will be discussed in chapter 2.

In what follows I shall concentrate on some themes that happen to interest me, centring on the transformation of the medieval and early modern rural landscape and the period often classified as that of 'nascent capitalism' prior to the Industrial Revolution. In order to grasp the development of the early modern world out of that of the feudal, we must go back to the late medieval period, the fifteenth century. The geographical area taken is primarily that of England, an area I know best from previous researches, but evidence is also cited from the rest of Europe and the American colonies.

Such bounds leave out some important aspects of any full archaeology of such a broad topic. In particular, an archaeology of colonialist imperialism, of urbanism and of traditional 'industrial archaeology' are omitted. Urbanism in particular has been a central theme in the origins of capitalism; both Marx and Weber indicated that they saw the medieval town as playing a central role as a developing capitalistic enclave within the interstices of the feudal system. Certainly towns played a leading role in the transformation of the feudal world. I am not however going to take the view that any one key subsystem or institution was causally central in the dynamics of transformation.

Similarly, colonial expansion and colonialism goes with urban growth. Said has shown how, in later periods, the colonial experience underpins cultural life to a very great extent (1993), and a historical account of the genealogy of such attitudes is clearly necessary. I will discuss some aspects of the emergence of colonial landscapes in the sixteenth- and seventeenth-centuries in chapter 4; and try to show how their genesis is in part related to existing, ancient landscapes and mentalities; but a full consideration of colonialism and its archaeology is a topic that others have begun to explore (McGuire and Paynter 1991; Schrire 1991; Falk 1991). Similarly, traditional accounts of the 'industrial revolution' and its antecedents are omitted, though some comments on the need for a theorized industrial archaeology are made in chapter 8.

Space, Things and People

I now want to look at existing approaches to landscape and material culture in the period 1400–1750, approaches taken both by 'archaeologists' in the traditional sense of the term and by scholars in other disciplines. I want to indicate how aspects of different approaches will be drawn upon in future chapters to sketch the outlines of a method for an archaeology of capitalism.

What is striking about work on the period conducted by scholars trained in different disciplines is its varied nature, particularly in terms of the discursive background – in simple terms the assumptions made, the way the argument proceeds, what qualifies within the scholarly community of that discipline as a strong or a weak understanding, the silences, and in terms of the material used (or not used) as legitimate evidence. Such variation makes synthesis or review difficult. It also makes for difficult argument when what constitutes a strong or weak understanding of a particular issue will vary from audience to audience. In this respect the current insistence on the centrality of rhetoric to historical argument (White 1987) is a lesson best demonstrated not from theoretical persuasion but from the experiences of presenting research drawing on different traditions to different disciplinary communities.

In Britain, archaeological study is classified into 'medieval' and 'post-medieval' archaeology, the former running up to c.1500, the latter usually taken as covering the period 1500–1750. 'Post-medieval archaeology' as a formal sub-discipline with its own academic objectives and criteria is still in its infancy. The journal *Post-Medieval Archaeology* was only set up in 1967, few university appointments specifically targeted at this area have been established, and it is difficult to point to syntheses which lay out an agenda for the archaeological study of the post-medieval period. The most notable general survey that has yet been written (Crossley 1990) has pointed to elucidation of industrial processes in the post-medieval period as its main achievement, if it is felt that the study of traditional architecture and of landscape are considered separate sub-disciplines.

On either side of the 'post-medieval' period as thus conceived two other archaeological periods and sub-disciplines sit uneasily. Medieval archaeology has reached more maturity, though the more wide-ranging and provocative syntheses that have contributed to an understanding of the period as a whole have tended to be confined to the early Middle Ages, before c.AD 1000 (for example Hodges 1982). Within the study of the centuries after 1066, synthetic study has tended to be along thematic rather than chronological lines (Clarke 1984; it is striking that the most notable exception to this rule, Platt's *Medieval England* [1978], was written by a historian). Such thematic divisions echo the establishment in the 1950s and 1960s of 'special interest research groups' on such diverse topics as pottery, small finds, moated sites, villages and so on. Such a classification has resulted in a vast harvest of primary research, but one does not have to belong to the theoretical avant-garde to suggest that this has perhaps hindered the development of holistic approaches to medieval archaeology;

as indeed one self-confessed traditional scholar has suggested, 'life in medieval England did not seem to run along such well regulated lines' (Clarke 1984: 62).

Industrial archaeology is a rapidly developing field of study, particularly in England where it has been prompted by the conservation demands of the great monuments of the Industrial Revolution. So far, however, most work in this area has concentrated on archaeological elucidation of the development of the technologies involved rather than on the social and cultural parameters of industrial development; recent work has begun to question this (Clark 1993). It is also caught between a thematic and chronological definition of its interests; that is, between that of material culture after 1750 or the archaeology of industrial processes from the Middle Ages onwards. If, as is the argument of this book, the archaeology of capitalism can be traced into all areas of landscape and material culture change, and that different spheres of change cannot be so easily distinguished, the implications for the constitution of a coherent, delimited 'industrial archaeology' are threatening.

As a general rule, the disciplinary fields outlined above were constructed in response to the demands of research questions and priorities that were being generated by debates within traditional history. The study of deserted medieval villages, for example, is a major component of medieval rural archaeology. Its study developed in response to quite specific questions being asked by Maurice Beresford, an economic historian, about the existence and chronology of desertion; Beresford enlisted the help of the archaeologist John Hurst (Beresford and Hurst 1990: 19–35) in early archaeological fieldwork. Consequently, the basis of medieval and post-medieval archaeology, and of industrial archaeology as a discipline in its own right, has been fragmented. As repeated discussions have shown (Austin and Thomas 1990; Johnson 1991) this fragmentation has led to a lack of confidence on the part of many archaeologists in any possible active role in the interpretation of history in the later and post-medieval periods. Underlying this lack of confidence are both practical and disciplinary problems. In particular, many archaeologists complain of a perceived junior status to particular forms of traditional history.

It is therefore interesting to note that since the time when medieval and post-medieval archaeology was set up in such obvious subservience to the categories imposed by traditions of those historical disciplines, historians themselves have begun to break down many of the disabling barriers between social, economic and cultural matters and moved on to a more fruitful and exciting plane. The Annales School of historians has always viewed the material world as of prime importance. In *Capitalism and Material Life*, Fernand Braudel (1973) surveyed the material world as part of the enduring 'structures of everyday life' seeing them within a determinist mode as 'the limits of the possible'. More recent Annales writers have moved beyond Braudel's largely materialist view of artefacts and space to the examination of the mentalities of past peoples, and the way the physical world encoded those mentalities.

This shift in patterns of historical thinking has also occurred in English and American scholarship. Annales thinking resonates with the stress on landscape and material culture in recent British work on social history as well as the 'New Cultural History'. Much of the work on early modern England dealing with everyday life and locality, though not dealing directly with material culture, has clear material references that will be picked up in the chapters that follow. In *Revel, Riot and Rebellion* and *Fire From Heaven*, for example, David Underdown (1985 and 1992) contrasts different patterns of community and everyday life in different areas of the West Country. These had clear material referents in distribution of community types across the landscape and in clear landscape and settlement forms. Again, in *Salem Possessed* (Boyer and Nissenbaum 1974) patterns of witchcraft accusation are explained in terms of community faction by looking at their spatial distribution across Salem. Both studies, and a plethora of others, take care to root very wide-ranging questions such as the origins of the English Revolution and eighteenth-century mercantile capitalism in the everyday and small-scale interactions of people within communities, stressing the interdependence between different scales of history. Some of the most fruitful discussions leading to ideas in this book have been with social and cultural historians of early modern England working on a day-to-day level with people dealing with material things, rather than with the theoretically avant-garde.

All this historical work shows patterns of everyday life relating to wider cultural conflict, leading in turn to fundamental long-term change in the social and economic structure of the English countryside (Wrightson 1982; Fletcher and Stevenson 1985). In addition, its influence is being felt in more traditional historical circles. Even in the established journal *Economic History Review*, articles on social and cultural history are included in the annual review, while interdisciplinary historical studies abound.

I suggest that the disciplines most closely related to archaeology are already well into a period both of increased stress on interdisciplinary work and of a reconsideration of what disciplinary boundaries mean. Put very crudely, in researching this book I found myself looking, for example, at how scholars in English literature are looking at the material and historical context of writing (Barker et al. 1991; Leslie and Raylor 1992; Greenblatt 1982; 1993); at historians using material culture in new ways (Burke 1992; Schama 1987); at geographers recognizing the complexity of past landscapes and the importance of history in those landscapes (Gregory 1991 and 1994); at art historians engaging in 'cultural criticism', seeing pictures as complex artefacts that are analogous to texts and that renegotiate and restate cultural meanings (Barrell 1992; Pointon 1993).

Increasingly, then, historians and scholars in related disciplines are using the evidence of material culture – art, architecture, landscape – in ways that acknowledge its actual and potential importance as a source. There is a paradox here. As many forms of history have taken on a 'linguistic turn', stressing the many meanings of the past and the document as a piece of text rather than as raw evidence, so at the same time the practice of historical writing has opened itself to forms of evidence other than the document and other ways of telling stories about the past than traditional narrative texts. So the linguistic turn has opened up new and exciting opportunities for archaeologists to contribute to current historical debates, a widening of scope for the study of the material world.

A further irony is one of the geography of modern scholarship. The American colonies appeared to England in the seventeenth century as a remote colony, of peripheral importance in contemporary affairs let alone in the development of capitalism. In the later twentieth century however a much more theoretically developed body of archaeological scholarship has been developed on the east coast of the United States. In many respects the work of American historical archaeologists has shown in practical terms the way forward for Old World medieval and post-medieval archaeology more than any other school of thought.

American Historical Archaeology

By far the most powerful and integrated school of archaeological thought on the transition to capitalism has emerged from the United States: that of a minority of predominantly East Coast historical archaeologists concerned with the transformation of social life in the colonies in the seventeenth- and eighteenth-centuries (for example Leone and Potter 1988 and Little 1992). Not all scholars working in this field make an explicit linkage of their work with the study of capitalism, though the themes discussed are clearly related if not identical, as we shall see, and the link between their

work and such shifts is made by others (Leone 1988: 19; Shackel 1993). I
want to consider some aspects of the work of this school as a springboard
for a wider consideration of the theoretical demands raised by an archaeology of capitalism.

The key work of this school is that of Henry Glassie, *Folk Housing in
Middle Virginia: A Structural Analysis of Historic Artifacts* (1975). In the
later chapters of this book, Glassie claims to observe a transition in ordinary rural housing in middle Virginia between the earlier and later parts of
the eighteenth century. The earlier period was one of 'hall-and-parlour'
houses, a type related to English antecedents and contemporaries and
discussed in terms of traditional, open patterns of family and community.
Glassie then charts a period of innovation and compromise leading to the
wholesale adoption of the Georgian house, symmetrical in plan and façade,
dominated by a central hallway and two rooms deep (figure 9.1). The two
house types, Glassie argues, correspondingly have English antecedents and
contemporaries: the transition between the two marked a shift to a more
segregated, private lifestyle. The strength of Glassie's work is that this
shift is delineated via a subtle structural analysis not just in ground plan
but through façade, decoration and carpentry detail. It thus combines close
and detailed analysis of small pieces of material culture with closely argued
linkages to wider patterns of social and material life.

These strengths are repeated in James Deetz's influential study *In Small
Things Forgotten* (1977), which carries and extends Glassie's observations of
housing into diverse realms of material culture such as pottery and gravestones. Deetz attempts to show that changes in material culture reflect a
deeper shift in the mentalities of its users. Thus pottery moves from being
colourful and non-standardized to being white and mould-made; the food
preparation it is associated with moves from undifferentiated stews to the
segmented, 'Georgian' meal of meat and two vegetables. In this and other
classes of evidence we see a shift to order, symmetry, segmentation and
standardization; away from 'pre-Georgian' towards 'Georgian'. Deetz thus
moves elegantly through close observation of detailed patterns of material
culture to patterns of everyday behaviour outwards, towards long-term
social and ideational shifts in the culture of colonial America, with a clarity
and attention to detail.

It is an obvious next step to take the mental transition thus delineated
and link it to wider factors. In particular it is possible to see a change from
pre-Georgian to Georgian world-view in materialist terms – that is, in the
context of emergent practices of capitalism. Though this move is not one
taken by either Deetz or Glassie, it has been advanced particularly by Mark

Leone and his students (Leone and Potter 1988). In this perspective the reflection in material culture of Georgian principles is seen as an expression of a dominant ideology. For example, the principles encoded in Georgian architecture of symmetry, order, segmentation and balance are seen as legitimating a world in which the use of these principles in linking time and work discipline is increasingly important. Georgian principles, in this view, act to gloss over a fundamental contradiction: between assertions of human equality as expressed in the Enlightenment and American Revolution on the one hand, and the realities of slavery and class and gender inequalities on the other. Thus, for example, Leone delineates the abstract symmetry and lines of perspective of the formal garden of William Paca, lawyer and American revolutionary, seeing its design as an ideology, papering over the cracks of Chesapeake society (Leone 1984).

The power of this body of work is twofold. In linking 'Georgianization' to a materialist account of incipient capitalism, it has given a fuller and more powerful understanding of change in the period. We see Georganization not as some latest abstracted stage in a Nature/Culture transformation *à la* Glassie, with all the difficulties in critical acceptance that entails if one is not fully prepared to adopt a structuralist outlook, but as part of a much more concrete shift in social totalities. Second, the necessary and inevitable role of such an account in a contemporary critique of late industrial capitalism is far more evident, as Leone and Potter have themselves made clear (Leone and Potter 1988: 19). The materialist historical archaeology of the United States has thus pointed the way forward in its stress on ideology and changing world-view as well as economic changes. It has been extended in other colonial contexts, most notably in South Africa (Hall 1991 and 1992).

Another school of thought that needs to be mentioned in this context is the study of architecture of the eighteenth and nineteenth centuries as embodying power relations of the 'panoptic' state (Foucault 1979; Markus 1993; Hooper-Greenhill 1989). By studying the genealogy of different building types a link has been made between patterns of institutional authority, the organization of knowledge and the patterning of space. In particular the parallels between the layout of factories, prisons, hospitals, museums and so on offer a striking and obvious commentary on the link between power and knowledge in the 'disciplinary society'. This theme and its early modern antecedents will be taken up in chapter 5.

All these studies demonstrate that spaces and objects take on cultural meanings and relate to human action and perception in very different ways in different historical periods. Much of the early literature in post-processual archaeology was animated by the idea that the archaeological record could be understood in terms of past cultural meanings. Familiar or not in other disciplines, such an idealist notion was novel to a generation of archaeologists brought up on traditions stressing adaptation and environmental determinism. Consequently, discussions of meanings tended to consist of assertions such as 'material culture is meaningfully constituted' or 'meaning is actively negotiated by social agents' which had a cross-cultural flavour to them.

I suggest that this assertion was necessary for polemical purposes. It has tended to obscure, however, the *way* in which historical change may be as much about the different *way* in which spaces and objects come to carry meaning as the changing meanings themselves. The degree of alienation from the material world, the degree to which self is stressed and hence the individual's ability to renegotiate meaning, the way in which objects are produced and consumed; all these things change from context to context. The *relation* between things, people, and meanings therefore also changes as much as the things, people, and meanings themselves change. This is a point that has been grasped particularly by Danny Miller (1987), and his work will be discussed in chapter 8.

Conclusion

Most of the central themes facing late and post-medieval archaeology – the role of material culture in nascent capitalism, changing forms of space use and settlement, the relationship between the meanings of things and their changing place as commodities, the common discursive forms underlying document and artefact – have rarely been approached let alone systematically tackled by the discipline of archaeology itself. Rather, they have been tackled more comprehensively and in more depth by scholars in other disciplines or by archaeologists in the former colonies.

Historians in search of the demographic, economic and material 'base' of pre-industrial societies have no shortage of evidence in the late and post-medieval period, as the copious outpourings of the early years of the Cambridge Group for the History of Population and Social Structure demonstrate. Therefore, the traditionally cited role of archaeology in historic periods, in filling out the economic/subsistence gaps in the story supposedly omitted by the textual ramblings of a few monks, may be true for earlier periods but holds little credibility after the early Middle Ages. There are no such gaps in late and post-medieval Europe; if it confines itself to economy and environmental concerns in these periods, archaeology really will remain an expensive way of finding out what we know already.

Archaeology's opportunity, to summarize, lies in the insight that the 'linguistic turn' in history makes spaces and objects just as ideological, just as laden with meaning, as any historical text. The opportunity for exciting and fruitful archaeological study is therefore in the world of cultures and mentalities rather than in what sometimes seem to be the rather stale and tired spheres of demography, economics, and the elucidation of specific industrial processes.

So far, I have discussed the possibility of an archaeology of capitalism as a general project. In the rest of this book I shall look more specifically at different aspects of such a project, by looking at different pieces of evidence and different approaches taken to that evidence.

Chapter 2 will clear the ground by looking at enduring structures in pre-industrial England and Wales, drawing on both landscape and docu-mentary evidence. This is necessary background for those not familiar with the documentary history of the period, but may be skipped by some archaeologists and historians. Chapter 3 will consider the phenomenon of enclosure as part of a narrative of change in the countryside. It will argue that existing understandings of enclosure in terms of economic progress or class conflict are inadequate, and we should rather seek a wider process of closure spanning agrarian, domestic and cultural life. Chapter 4 tries to trace what such an archaeology of closure might look like, relating to-gether the different social practices of enclosing fields, writing and reading agricultural treatises, creating and using maps, and ordering the natural world in the widest sense.

Chapter 5 addresses the archaeology of texts. It argues that by treating texts as artefacts rather than as source material, a fuller and deeper under-standing of changes in mental and material landscapes can be achieved. Closure is seen here to extend to ways of describing and listing the landscape as well as ways of farming and living in it, and to order people as well as landscape.

Chapter 6 addresses another key component of the breakdown of medi-eval and the rise of early modern systems of authority in terms of elite architecture and landscapes. It suggests that new architectural ideas were not simply styles or fashions but rather new ways of encoding authority in terms of knowledge and 'rationality' through the principle of the gaze.

Chapter 7 examines the archaeology of the household and the individual. It reviews recent work on domestic architecture, everyday furniture and other material culture, in an attempt to rethink the 'rise of comfort' in the early modern period. Housing and material culture is seen in a much more complex way than hitherto. Chapter 8 continues these themes with respect to material culture and commodification, looking at the way objects take on meanings in different contexts and the development of new patterns of consumption in the early modern world. Chapter 9 will then look at alternative ways of thinking about the period, and consider ways in which the archaeological analysis presented could be extended to other spheres of evidence. In particular, it will summarize the relationship of the arguments presented here to those of 'Georgianization' put forward by Deetz, Glassie, Leone and others. In this way the book ends not with a rounded thesis, but with a look forward to future debates and new patterns of thought. It is only through such debates, through the clash of ideas and through research generated by that clash, that the archaeology of capitalism can be taken forward.

2

Enduring Structures and Historical Understanding

Having outlined the theoretical background to this study, I now want to turn to the enduring structures, the historical background, of 'pre-industrial' England. In this chapter I shall try to trace a path through some of the background to this period for the non-specialist, both in terms of its historical understanding and its historiography. Historians of late medieval and early modern England may skip what follows. I shall first examine briefly some of the enduring structures of landscape and society in the period, before going on to look at the development and current state of the historical debate over the feudal/capitalist transition. The conclusion to this chapter will ask why it is that there is such a marked disjuncture between these two themes, given that they deal with the same area, period, and, apparently, subject matter.

The Pre-Industrial Landscape

Between 1400 and 1700 the landscape of England was predominantly rural and local. Roughly 90 per cent of the population lived outside urban centres; of these, a small though increasing number of people travelled regularly outside their locality. A literate man like Richard Gough, considered by many to be a gentleman, had travelled extensively from his home county of Shropshire to London in his youth in the later seventeenth-century; towards the other end of the social scale, many servants in husbandry spent their lives moving around a 10–15 km radius (Kussmaul 1981: 38).

The size of this population fluctuated widely. The estimates of demographers vary, partly because most estimates are based on documentary sources related to tax purposes. They therefore tend to list only male householders and/or leave out certain categories such as the poor exempt from taxation. Most scholars working with this difficult material come to a figure somewhere between two and five million for pre-industrial England. The medieval population had been decimated by the long-term economic and demographic crisis of which the plagues and famines of the fourteenth century were in part symptoms. After a mid-fifteenth-century low, the population level appears to have risen in fits and starts before 'levelling off' in the late seventeenth century. One set of population estimates for England (Wrigley and Schofield 1981) gives a population low in 1470 of two million, rising to three million by 1550 and four million or more by 1600. This population rise levelled off around the figure of five million in the late seventeenth and early eighteenth centuries, before exploding as never before from 1750 onwards.

These falls and rises in population level were very broadly typical of western Europe as a whole, which saw a rise in population up to 1350 and between 1450 and 1650, with economic and demographic stability or contraction between these dates (Braudel 1973: 31). Nevertheless the British Isles can be seen as exceptional; both contemporary commentators (such as foreign visitors to England) and modern historians have suggested that England in particular enjoyed a higher general standard of living after c.1400. It is certainly the case that diseases directly related to famine and general dearth were relatively rare after this date (Wrigley and Schofield 1981).

This rising population inhabited part of an island off the north-western corner of mainland Europe that can be seen as a complex mosaic of different overlapping physical and human landscape types. These types are of such diversity that it is difficult to talk of the landscape of 'England' as a natural unity. This is true in both cultural and physical terms. A Kentish farmer in the middle of a densely occupied lowland landscape of fertile arable fields and orchards may have had more in common in terms of lifestyle and level of material affluence with his northern French counterpart as with his contemporary in the northern counties of Northumberland or Cumbria; the Cumbrian farmer might be farming sheep and cattle across a much larger tract of grassland running across the valleys and hills, very much like his Scottish counterpart. 'A yeoman of Kent with one year's rent could buy out the gentleman of Wales and knight of Scales and a lord of the north country' ran a popular proverb (Morris 1949: 136). The Kentish yeoman would also be much closer to the capital of London, a factor which had implications for all spheres of life. Political, economic and cultural centralization, particularly at upper social levels, were increasing forces in the

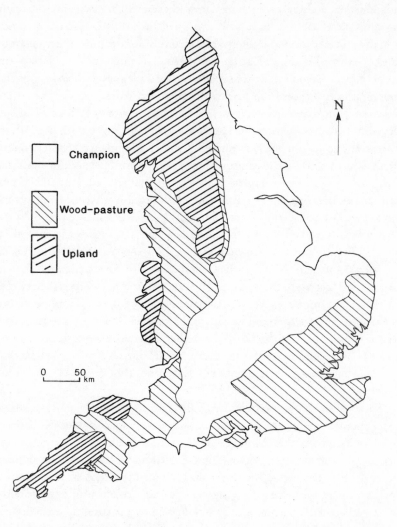

Figure 2.1 The distribution of wood-pasture, champion and upland landscape in England (after Williamson and Bellamy 1986). The diagram is necessarily oversimplified, but does show the way champion landscapes run in a central belt from north to south, with wood-pasture areas on either side and the uplands confined to the north and west. There is no generally accepted explanation for the distribution of champion versus wood-pasture landscapes.

seventeenth and eighteenth centuries that will be discussed in future chapters.

It is also important to stress that variation between different communities and landscapes could be very sharp within regions. Within the north-east of England, for example, the development of coal-mining and rise of Newcastle as a major urban centre gave rise to some very 'advanced' social and economic features, such as the progress of enclosure and other agricultural improvements (Hodgson 1979). At the same time, many communities within the area remained materially poor and traditional in nature. So there is no one index such as distance from London by which we can measure social and economic 'development'.

The physical landscape of England can be broadly divided between the more fertile lowlands of the south and east and the colder, wetter, more barren uplands and valleys of the north and west. In terms of human geography, the rural landscape overlying this physical backdrop can be divided into three very broad types: champion, wood-pasture, and upland (figure 2.1). Such a division is of course a huge oversimplification: recent work on English local history has stressed how different areas formed a complex interplay of different physical environments, *pays*, local societies and what Charles Phythian-Adams has called the 'genius' or distinctive character of different regions (1993a).

Settlement within champion landscape (derived from 'champaigne') consisted largely of a network of nucleated villages, with the occasional isolated farm outside these clusters. These villages were of either regular or irregular form, with apparently therefore either planned or organic origins. The broader lines of the layout of these villages were already ancient by the end of the Middle Ages: they had in the majority of cases been set in place several centuries earlier, in shifts in settlement pattern in the ninth to twelfth centuries (Saunders 1990). Typical elements of such villages included a parish church, manor house and rows of peasant houses. Such houses were usually placed within sub-rectangular plots of land or tenements termed 'tofts', with the narrow frontage onto the street. To the rear of the toft, such holdings often had rectangular strip-like areas termed 'crofts' that often functioned as gardens. The tofts also contained scattered ancillary buildings (figures 2.2 and 3.2). Tenements of this nature were sometimes arranged along a narrow or wide street or streets, or around a village green which could be used as a common, public space.

Around such nucleations would usually be found large 'open' arable fields. The term 'open' is misleading if taken literally; such large units were divided into strips, with each farmer holding a number of strips scattered

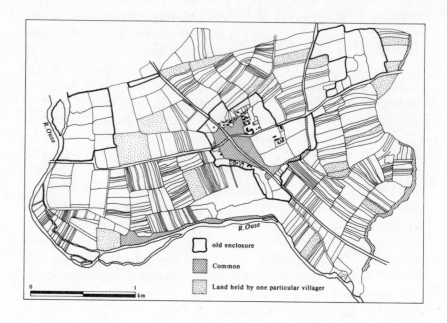

Figure 2.2   The village of Goldrington in Bedfordshire before enclosure of the open fields (after Emmison 1965: 12–13). The nucleated village has houses ranged around a central common, each house in its own tenement. Each village householder has strips scattered across the surounding landscape. In many Midlands villages neighbours would also have adjoining strips in the fields.

across the landscape. Rights of use in these fields did not necessarily equal rights of ownership. The use of open fields would be governed by a complex system of by-laws and 'customary' practices. These practices were usually governed by the manor court which included a wide range of everyday activities within its jurisdiction, and whose documents are often therefore invaluable as a minute record of everyday activities.

Some open fields were arranged in planned two- or three-field systems, where one field would often be left fallow in any given year. This happened most classically in the Midlands of England; other 'champion' areas with large nucleated villages were nevertheless without such tightly organized field systems, as for example in western Norfolk. Beyond the fields, or often between them, lay tracts of land that were held 'in common'. These might be woodland, pasture, marsh and so on. Common ground was subject to common rights; that is, subject to customary practice, any member of the community could graze a number of sheep, gather firewood, and so on.

Champion landscapes often tended to house more traditional, conservative communities with tighter social bonds and more emphasis on 'neighbourliness' than wood-pasture regions. This distinction however is a very broad one and should not be over-emphasized (Razi 1987). The economy of champion areas was invariably mixed; that is, farmers would combine arable farming with pastoral husbandry, keeping cattle and sheep as well as growing cereal crops. The use of manure and the consequent need for a balance between arable and pasture was a key factor in successful open-field farming. Champion communities nevertheless had a relative stress on arable agriculture as opposed to pastoral, a stress that may well have increased during the period in question.

'Wood-pasture' or 'woodland' landscape is so named after its appearance, having many small areas of woodland interspersed with the fields. Large nucleated villages were relatively rare in wood-pasture landscapes, though small nucleations were common enough. Settlement was not necessarily less dense in any given region of wood-pasture landscape than in champion areas, but it was generally clustered in smaller hamlets, apparently loose 'ribbon' clusters or dispersed altogether (figure 2.3). The morphology of such settlement systems has been less closely studied archaeologically than champion areas, and surface appearances of wood-pasture settlement being less regular or 'planned' than that of champion areas may be partly illusory. Dyer has argued for example that the wood-pasture parish of Pendock in the West Midlands shows distinctive elements of regularity in its layout (1990: 116). Houses here were less regularly placed in tofts and crofts; they could often be strung out around very large greens or pieces of common ground (Warner 1987). Churches are often still found in isolated locations in wood-pasture landscapes, at the end of a loose string of farmsteads, with just two or three houses nearby, or in a totally separate location from any settlement cluster in the parish.

Fields in wood-pasture areas had never been laid out in the large-scale open-field systems characteristic of Midlands champion landscape. In other words, open field systems and nucleated villages seem to go together, though the degree of exact correlation and the wider question of why this

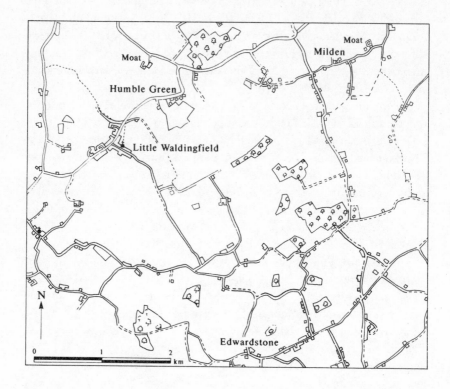

Figure 2.3 Wood-pasture landscape in southern Suffolk. The rarity of large nucleated villages, loose pattern of roads with apparent 'dead ends' at isolated farmsteads, presence of moated sites and irregular patches of woodland are all characteristic of this form of landscape.

should be the case is a continuing debate amongst archaeologists studying the eighth to thirteenth centuries. Whatever the case, in many areas of wood-pasture communities often termed 'ancient landscape' it appears that many of the lines of field boundaries that can be traced off nineteenth-century or even modern maps had survived from the Roman period or even earlier (figure 2.4). Wood-pasture farming practices were therefore much more diverse and less community-based than in champion areas. Instead, wood-pasture communities utilized a variety of smaller open fields, areas laid out in strips, or areas that were not 'open' in any sense.

The mixed economies of wood-pasture areas often had a relative stress on pasture and dairy products, while socially they tended to house rela-

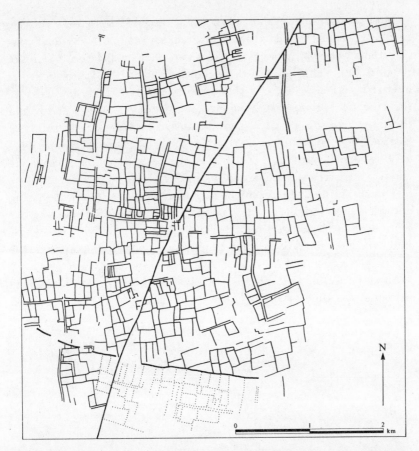

Figure 2.4   Ancient landscape around Yaxley in Suffolk, taken from a nineteenth-century map (after Williamson 1988: 41). An apparently planned system of field boundaries is clearly cut by a Roman road, and seems to be of early or pre-Roman date. Its survival here through the medieval and early modern periods, when contrasted with the wholesale reorganization of settlement and landscape in the Midlands, shows the importance of understanding history and antecedent in the development of the countryside.

tively looser communities. There was less stress on manorial control and more scope for individuals to innovate and introduce new farming practices. Wood-pasture landscapes were often perceived by sixteenth- and seventeenth-century commentators as being more prosperous than champion areas, though the reality is more complex and difficult to ascertain with any certainty. It is certainly true that between the fourteenth and sixteenth centuries England saw a shift in the regional distribution of wealth away from champion towards wood-pasture areas (Platt 1976: 107).

Most areas of the uplands again had a dispersed settlement pattern, though settlement in such a harsher environment was much less dense than in lowland wood-pasture areas. Parishes were often much larger in terms of physical area. Valley areas such as the Dales in the Yorkshire Pennines often had isolated farms scattered along the brows of the hills. In the climatic optimum and population expansion of the twelfth and thirteenth centuries medieval period many areas of the upland had been 'assarted' or brought under cultivation, often for arable; these marginal areas were frequently abandoned after the demographic and economic crises of the later medieval period (figure 2.5).

Though the upland economy became more concentrated on the raising of cattle and sheep in the early modern period, much arable farming did continue in such areas. As a result, small pockets of fertile land upon which arable products could be grown were disproportionately important to the subsistence economy of the uplands.

Socially, upland areas distant from London were perceived by many writers of the time as 'dark corners of the land', relatively lawless and

Figure 2.5 An upland landscape: Swaledale, the most northerly dale in Yorkshire. The valley bottoms have been used for high-quality pasture since the early Middle Ages, the upper slopes for rough grazing of sheep. Some arable cultivation on the slopes in the high Middle Ages was rapidly abandoned after the fourteenth century. This area was owned by Marrick Priory, sited further down the dale; after the Reformation it fell into the hands of local farmers who built a series of isolated farmsteads on the brows of the valley.

housing an ignorant and backward population. Such a stereotype concealed a more complex truth. The uplands remained largely culturally and politically 'conservative', often continuing to be dominated by local magnates deriving their power from old feudal ties. In many areas of the north and west of England a prosperous class of middling tenant farmers was slow to develop, while the great landowners remained correspondingly powerful. In other upland areas such as much of the southern Pennines the 'middling sort' did prosper, however. Kin ties were often still important in upland communities, and proximity to the Scottish border made cattle rustling or 'reiving' by both English and Scots an endemic activity before the seventeenth century.

As I have noted, this threefold classification into three different landscape types each with distinctive social and economic correlates is an oversimplification. Many areas of England combined elements of all three types, while others cannot be readily classified in this way at all. Areas of marsh such as the Fenlands, the clay or chalk escarpments of the Wolds, or particular 'county communities' were and are important sub-regions in their own right. Nevertheless the different areas can be mapped at a very basic level in figure 2.1.

The broader outlines of different pre-industrial landscape types can still be seen today by consulting a large-scale Ordnance Survey map or simply by walking or driving across the countryside. It should be noted that the boundary between the wood-pasture and champion areas in particular can be very sharp, and need not have any relation to changes in physical landscape. Again, 'pockets' of one form of landscape may be found within another due to historical contingency. For example, the parish of Kelloe in County Durham is surrounded by a nucleated champion landscape now itself overlain by a pattern of coal-mines and villages. Kelloe, however, had a characteristic wood-pasture pattern of a ribbon-like string of farmsteads with the church a little way off. This may be due to its ecclesiastical position within the bishopric of Durham.

The origins of the historical and geographical divisions between different landscape types are ancient, stretching back to the early medieval period at least; different models have been proposed for their origins, the latest being that at some point between the sixth and twelfth centuries the different requirements of lordship led to the creation of villages and fields systems in some areas but not in others (Harvey 1989). This is a complex debate that need not detain us here. These historical antecedents are however important to bear in mind, since these different landscape types and their social, economic and cultural patterning structured in turn the different cultural and landscape development of different parts of England in the fifteenth to eighteenth centuries. We shall find that the story of enclosure in particular, and the forces of cultural and economic change generally, differed in their form and impact in different regions and landscape types. To take one example among many, the area of Suffolk wood-pasture landscape shown in figure 2.3 may well have been socially and economically 'progressive' due to lack of strong community and manorial control relative to, say, areas of the Midlands; and this difference can be traced back to the early middle ages. The understanding of any particular piece of landscape therefore involves a balance between local continuities, regional traditions and wider national developments. In any account of a region of pre-industrial England continuity, antecedent and maintained regional difference must share the stage with agrarian revolution, transformation and political and cultural centralization.

Cross-cutting such physical landscape divisions was the religious and political organization of the landscape. The term 'community' as used above had no automatic relation to a settlement or legal unit on the ground. The ecclesiastical unit, within which all parishioners would worship at the same church, was the parish. The civil unit was termed 'the township', while the unit of estate management and court dealing with by-laws and agricultural practices was the manor. Again, the formation of these different units dates back to before the thirteenth century in most areas.

In much of England the physical areas covered by parish, township, manor and village were more or less contiguous; though in every community there was some peculiarity or other (see for example the organisation of Myddle discussed in chapter 5). In much of the north and west, however, several townships might be nested within one large parish, and all over England manorial, township and parochial divides often cut across each other.

Another cross-cutting factor was that of the incidence of rural industries. England had exported raw wool to the Continent for most of the Middle Ages. The later fifteenth century saw the rise of production of finished woollen cloth. In much of Suffolk, Essex, the West Country, and also in the southern Pennines, many rural households combined cloth production with mixed farming, often attracting immigrants into the area. Other industries came a poor second to cloth production before the seventeenth century, though they became increasingly important with the decline of the woollen industry and the rise of coal and metal extraction and trade thereafter. Iron, tin and lead extraction and production played an important part in several regional economies, again on a part-time or shifting basis (Crossley 1994: 244). The Weald of Kent and Sussex played a leading role in iron production, while lead and tin ore was produced from the uplands of the Pennines and Cornwall respectively. Rural industries of this nature were particularly important as time went on, becoming an indispensable supplement to the incomes of agrarian households.

A final factor in the composition of this mosaic of landscape types was the distribution of urban and market centres, above all the social and economic 'pull' of London. Most pre-industrial towns in England were in existence by 1300; they were distributed unevenly across this rural land-scape, with a concentration in the lowlands. By comparison with the Continent, there were many small market towns, often no more than large villages with rights to hold market; few areas of lowland England were outside a day's walk of a market. The inhabitants of these small market towns often combined agriculture with urban occupations. Above these in the settlement hierarchy, county towns served as judicial, political and cultural centres.

The giant of London grew ever larger in the period 1400–1700. London's dominance of the urban and rural landscape cannot be overesti-mated. By the end of the seventeenth century one in ten people in England lived in London. The economy of the 'home counties' of the south and east of England was increasingly geared to production for its markets; the political turmoil of the seventeenth century made the country more conscious of its central position; it even functioned as a marriage market for many in the gentry and aristocracy by 1750. By the eighteenth century London was the dominant cultural, political and social centre for the whole country.

Society and Culture

Within these varied forms of landscape sat equally varied forms of commu-nity and household life. In what follows I shall try to give a portrait of some of the salient features of the pre-industrial society of England and Wales. Like the description of landscape, it will be a necessarily over-general and sweeping statement. The reader is referred to chapter 5 for some discussion of the source material that historians have used to put together the basis for the observations given below, and for an assessment and archaeological critique of the nature of that source material.

An upper-class literate person of the sixteenth and seventeenth centuries might well have described society in terms of 'degrees of people', the relations between different degrees being regulated by a formal conception of status. Early modern writers often conceived of the system as a whole as part of the Great Chain of Being stretching from Heaven through the human to the natural world; consequently, degrees of people and the constitution of society were in this view divinely ordained, part of a God-given order. The classification and description of each link in the chain was open to debate, however, and the whole was perceived to be under threat from the masses; fear of the disorderly multitude was endemic (Hill 1965). We shall deal with each degree in turn.

The monarch was in theory God's representative on earth; in practice he or she was more and more restrained by Parliament. The upheavals of the English Revolution and Glorious Revolution further increased this restraint. By contrast, the power of the State grew tremendously, in terms of a developing bureaucracy, growing power of the centrally organized legal system (Fletcher 1986), suppression of powerful feudal magnates drawing their power from regional bases, greater control by London over the 'dark corners of the land', and the development of a centralized, national political and cultural life. Below the king were the aristocracy: a group of great, titled landowners. Lords often kept large households whose houses and castles were traditionally centres of hospitality; at the start of this period they provided political leadership for local areas through exercise of systems of patronage.

The gentry was a class of landowners below that of the aristocracy. Increasingly through the period under discussion the gentry became the key governing class of pre-industrial England and Wales. Despite being only 2 per cent of the population they owned roughly 50 per cent of the land (Wrightson 1982: 24). In most parishes there would be a gentry family or two, who would serve as Justices of the Peace on the local courts, would look upwards to noble patrons for leadership, and who would in turn be expected to act as the leaders of their communities. Together, the gentry dominated the make-up and complexion of the 'county community', which some historians have interpreted as an increasingly important political and cultural forum for discussion and action.

There have been wide debates over the nature of the gentry as a political community and whether the late sixteenth and early seventeenth centuries saw their 'rise'. It is certainly true that in many counties they came to dominate the scene politically by the early seventeenth century. In Suffolk, for example, the domination of several great landowners had been broken in the middle of the sixteenth century, and by 1600 there was a powerful 'county community' of gentry folk who provided the political leadership and direction for the county (Macculloch 1986). Members of Parliament were largely drawn from the gentry classes; and so, going to London on a semi-regular basis and participating in national debates, they were increasingly drawn into national political life and were a key element of the growing two-way integration between locality and capital.

Yeomen were a socially middling class of tenant farmers of reasonable security and wealth. They were men of 'good credit' within the parish who would occupy its minor offices, and who might in turn look to the gentry for political leadership; but their main activity was in farming. Yeoman households engaged in mixed farming with varying degrees of specialization for the market. Husbandmen were less secure and prosperous working farmers than yeomen. For both yeomen and husbandmen as important a factor in social status and economic security was the form of landholding as much as its size and wealth. Freehold tenure tended to be more secure than copyhold, though legal forms of tenure varied widely (thus, for example, forms of copyhold could be as secure as freehold: Kerridge 1969: 83).

The upper and 'middling sort' (the lower gentry, yeomen and better sort of husbandmen) together made up perhaps a third of the population of England. The other two-thirds were predominantly servants and labourers, about whom inevitably we know much less and who are often portrayed as faceless masses or left out altogether of many traditional historical accounts.

The institution of service was partly an age grade rather than a social class. Adolescent children would be hired out to yeoman or gentry households and remain in service until they saved enough to marry and set up households of their own, usually around the age of 25. They might even employ servants of their own at a later stage in their life. Servants would engage in yearly contracts with masters at 'hiring fairs', moving from household to household. Food and lodging within the house would be provided by the master as well as a cash wage (Kussmaul 1981). Adolescence in pre-industrial England cannot therefore be easily separated analytically from its social and cultural setting, though it can be argued that there was a distinctive world-view associated with adolescence and youth (Ben-Amos 1994). Labourers varied in their social and economic well-being. Though usually holding no land of their own, many had rights to common land and resources of their own to supplement income from work on other's farms.

At the bottom of the social scale was a growing class of people who in the perception of the dominant classes in the sixteenth and early seventeenth centuries posed an increasing perceived threat to social and political order. Classed under the general term of 'masterless men', in other words those who lived outside the formally conceived patriarchal structure of society, these included tramps, vagrants, rogues, vagabonds, tinkers, and other social undesirables in the eyes of literate people of the time.

Others with an ambiguous place in the scheme of things were the urban middling classes: the burgesses and freemen who inhabited the towns. Different social commentators placed urban classes at different points within the ladder of status as articulated above.

Conceptually this social ladder was all held together by a conception of patriarchy. Each household was seen as a little state, a little common-wealth. Legal and political practice required that its wife, children and servants were under the governance and responsibility of its male head; conversely, the monarch was a great patriarch, his people owing him duty and service. In this scheme of things it followed that challenges to author-ity within the household were implicitly challenges to the state and ultimately to God; thus, family and household relations were naturally part of the public sphere and subject to legal regulation, court proceedings and community disciplines of both a formal and informal nature. Such regulation and court proceedings incidentally generated much of the material on which histories of pre-industrial family and household life are based.

The political commentator Bodin was expressing the orthodoxy of the time when he wrote:

A family might be defined as the right ordering of a group of persons owing obedience to a head of household, and of those interests which are his proper concern. The second term of our definition of the commonwealth refers to the family because it is not only the true source and origin of the common-wealth, but also its principal constituent. Xenophon and Aristotle divorced economy or household management from police or disciplinary power, without good reason to my mind . . . I understand by domestic government the right ordering of family matters, together with the authority which the head of the family has over his dependents [*sic*], and the obedience due from them to him . . . Thus the well-ordered family is a true image of the commonwealth, and domestic comparable with sovereign authority. It fol-lows that the household is the model of right order in the commonwealth (Bodin 1576, quoted in Tribe 1978: 37).

It was also held together horizontally by an ethic of neighbourliness and community. Kinship may never have been central to social relations in medieval England, though its importance may still have been underestimated by historians even in the early modern period (Mitson 1993). Even in the 'dark corners of the land' such as the northern uplands, however, the ties of kinship and lineage were being steadily broken down in the sixteenth century (James 1986: 1–16). Vertical principles of patronage and deference were also central. As we have seen, parish communities might look to the local gent for leadership; groups of gentry might align themselves under great aristocratic patrons.

How did this rather normative, static picture of society work in practice? In the first place, there was at least some social fluidity and movement between classes. A prosperous yeoman's children might marry into the gentry classes or a gent dissipate his fortune. It has been argued (Stone and Stone 1984) that such fluidity was perceived by contemporary social commentators rather than existing in any significant measure in reality. This may be so, but the contemporary perception of fluidity and its influence on behaviour may be as important as the reality.

Whatever the case, status distinctions were not simply ones of formal title: they were mobilized through everyday life in an analogous manner to those mapped out by Isaac for colonial Virginia (1983); through seating in church (chapter 5); the goods displayed in one's house, through deference, competition and occasionally ridicule. The studies in Reay (1985b) give some flavour of these.

Class and status relations were cross-cut by those of gender. In preindustrial England reference has already been made to the formal conception of patriarchy. Formally, those who mattered, who existed legally as property owners, who were recruited for political or judicial office, were men. Men were expected to dominate and discipline their wives. It is noticeable that the term 'Man' had a similar ambiguity to its present-day use, referring both to all people on the one hand and male householders on the other. It is also striking that this ambiguity is repeated in traditional historical accounts of contemporary political and cultural norms.

Within this formal legal and political structure of male domination women nevertheless exercised a great deal of power. First, recent work in social history has tended to stress that marriage relations below the upper social levels were more egalitarian and affective than the formal alliances of property and power of the aristocracy and upper gentry (though the idea of companionate marriage has itself been subject to feminist critique: Erickson 1993: 6–8). Second, women exercised power in the household domain. They were responsible for activities such as dairying and brewing in middling households. In some regions in the later middle ages, many women were holders of land as well as being paid at the same rate as agricultural labourers (Hilton 1975: 99–103). In urban contexts individual women could rise to positions of power and influence within a formal patriarchal structure (Howell 1986).

Subordinate perspectives on the formal patriarchal structure of society are difficult to discern, but they do appear. Servants engaged in a constant petty battle against masters. At key moments in women's lives such as childbirth, women exercised control over key domains and excluded men (Wilson 1990). During the brief break in censorship of the English Revolution, all sorts of radical ideas came to the surface though the majority of these still accepted gender subordination as given (Hill 1972).

To conclude, no community in pre-industrial England and Wales had quite the same history, social structure or landscape type as the next, and in this respect the brief account given above is less than satisfactory; endless qualifications could be made to every generalizing statement made within it. Browsing through different detailed accounts of particular regions, parishes or townships, one is reminded of a jazz session in which familiar phrases are repeated endlessly, but in constant variation of pattern and order. Conversely, no community or landscape was absolutely 'typical' of a given type; each area had its own peculiarities.

Similarly, the picture given of social relations in this period has been far too static. Several qualifications need to be made. The first is with regard to the nature of the documentary evidence. Much of the above picture has been put together by social and cultural historians from the evidence of tax records and household inventories, but much also depends on commentaries, personal diaries and other accounts written for and by the literate few. To take one of many examples, much of our evidence for cultural expectations of gender and marriage relations comes from moralistic advice on marital conduct written by male gentry and clerical writers. Such texts were, moreover, written largely for the benefit of middling, male householders; the perspectives of women, of the socially middling male householders themselves, or of the illiterate masses are often far from clear.

On the other hand, much recent exciting historical work has gone into uncovering precisely these subordinate attitudes. Amussen (1988) and Erickson (1993) have used women's wills to look at female perspectives on patriarchy, suggesting a complex picture of women's perspectives somewhere between wholesale acceptance or rejection of dominant male perspectives. Again, the verbatim accounts of court records can be used to indirectly infer 'popular' attitudes to sexuality, religion and culture (Ingram 1990).

There is an underlying theoretical problem here: of how as scholars we make meaningful and wide-ranging statements about mentality, about what people thought in the past, while avoiding the twin traps of making excessively normative statements reflective of dominant views or conversely of fragmenting such an account into a hundred different possible views each unrelated to the next. Relations of power were real in the past, and so were dominant ideologies; society was not an endless carnival. Mah (1991) has made this point in a critique of Darnton's analysis of culture in eighteenth-century France, pointing out the very real conflicts underneath Darnton's carnivalesque views of episodes such as cat massacres. Historians and theorists have yet to confront this problem directly or fully I feel.

Structures of Change

I have tried to give some indication of the present state of scholarship on landscape and social/cultural history of England and Wales. Many aspects of change have already been hinted at: the growth of London, the rise of middling social groups, rural industry, population fall and rise, class polarization, cultural centralization. I want to turn however to one aspect of accounting for historical change; to the way in which that history has been drawn upon by modern thinkers, principally though not exclusively within a Marxist tradition, to create a specific theoretical account of the transition between feudalism and capitalism. This account has also addressed the related question of why Britain was the first country in Europe to undergo agrarian and industrial transformation. I shall review some of the recent historical literature on the rise of agrarian capitalism from the feudal 'economy' as a springboard for archaeological study.

This literature has a genealogy stretching back to Marx and beyond. Marx located the core of capitalist enterprise in the towns, but saw that reorganization of the countryside along capitalist principles was a necessary component of the transition as a whole. Richard Tawney expanded this understanding, stressing that while the 'new spirit' of capitalist enterprise was principally found in urban contexts, changes in the countryside were equally necessary. Tawney further suggested that such a new spirit was seen there in a particularly sharp form, touching as it did on the very core of medieval structures and institutions (1912: 408–9).

Such a view from Marx onwards implied a chronology of capitalist development that, while disputed, has formed much of the background of debate during this period and has been implicitly accepted in part by non-Marxists, as Macfarlane has pointed out (1978). This goes roughly as follows: market capitalism developed in England from the sixteenth century onwards. The early modern period saw the growth of urban centres, the development of class relations in the countryside, and the spread of a market network. These changes created the preconditions for large-scale urbanization and industrialization in the second half of the eighteenth century.

I suggested in chapter 1 that there can be no primary locus or point of origin and identity for capitalism, as it becomes increasingly difficult to locate core versus peripheral features of nascent capitalism or for that matter any other social form. Whatever the case, different traditions of scholarship have increasingly located the pre-industrial countryside as a key arena of social and cultural transformation.

Several important aspects of those institutions and structures conventionally labelled as 'capitalist' have been traced far back into the early modern and medieval periods. Foremost among these is the history of class and class attitudes. Traditional 'class consciousness' of different kinds has been traced back before the industrial setting from which they traditionally stem. Fox (1985: 1–30) has stressed that working-class attitudes as they surfaced in the late eighteenth and early nineteenth centuries have much earlier origins in the experiences of rural artisans and labourers in the pre-industrial period. Thompson and Hobsbawm have examined such attitudes in more detail, showing their antecedents in the protests of rural labourers in the eighteenth century and earlier. The long traditions of radicalism amongst rural artisans stretch back ultimately to the later Middle Ages (Hill 1972; Hilton 1973). Certainly one of the key movements of the seventeenth and eighteenth centuries was one of class polarization and elite withdrawal from 'popular culture' in the countryside; this is a process that will be touched upon in terms of landscape, architecture and material culture in the chapters that follow.

Many scholars have argued that the period 1500–1750 saw a rise in the numbers and political weight of the gentry, yeomen and other middling social groups. Theories of class formation of this kind, whether implicit or explicit, are clearly tied to different conceptions of economic and social development and the theoretical assumptions that underlie such conceptions. This leads us inexorably to the so-called 'Brenner debate' within Marxist historiography. Brenner's argument is that the emergence of agrarian capitalist relations was determined by contingent political processes of class struggle rather than underlying environmental or demographic factors. In other words, scholars must look first to society, politics and culture rather than to any supposed environmental backdrop of the '*longue durée*' for an explanation of the origins of capitalism. Further, they must allow for historical accident and contingency in the story of why, for example, Britain diverged from the Continent in terms of social and economic development in the early modern period. Brenner comments that:

> The original breakthrough . . . was dependent on a two-sided system of class relations: first, the breakdown of systems of lordly surplus extraction by means of extra-economic compulsion; second, the undermining of peasant possession or the aborting of any trend towards full peasant ownership of the land. The consequence of this two-sided development was the rise of a novel social-property system, above all on the land, in which, for the first time, the organisers of production and the direct producers . . . found it both *necessary* and *possible* to reproduce themselves through a course of economic action which was, on a system-wide scale, favourable to the continuing development of the productive forces. In particular, the rise of the landlord/capitalist tenant/wage-labourer system provided the basis for the transformation of agriculture which took place in early modern England. On the other hand, throughout most of the Continent in the same period, the perpetuation of social-property systems characterised by peasant possession and surplus extraction . . . was at the root of continuing agricultural stagnation, involution and ultimately general socio-economic crisis (Brenner 1985: 214–15).

It has recently been suggested that Brenner misinterprets the role of the State in portraying sixteenth-century England as witnessing an unqualified victory of landlord over tenant: Hoyle has pointed out that the State continued to protect tenants' rights in varied circumstances (1990). A broader point is that divergence between England and the Continent cannot be reduced to the role of historical accident. Alan Macfarlane has pointed to different antecedent conditions in medieval England as being important here (1988: 202); though his views are extreme, his stress on a distinctive spirit of 'English individualism' traceable back to the North German forests being highly questionable, the more general point that there were certain long-term structures that conditioned the divergent development of capitalist relations on either side of the Channel is a not unreasonable one.

There was certainly a general European crisis in the later middle ages, of which the population collapse popularly associated with the Black Death was only one symptom (Dyer 1989). Theorists have attempted to draw out from the aftermath of this crisis varying models of structural change in late feudal society and economy leading to nascent capitalism. These models are abstract in nature though they are often embedded in case studies. Guy Bois, for example, drawing on the case of Normandy, has isolated changes in structural conditions in the later medieval period producing what he terms 'centralised feudalism' (1984). Hilton has talked of the transition in later medieval England from an economy based on the relations underpinning feudal estates to one structured around landlord/tenant relations (1985).

One problem with such abstract formulations is that they often appear overly reductionist, attempting to isolate a few critical variables out of a rich and varied record of historical events and processes. There is little indication in such accounts of why particular variables such as the legal terms governing landlord/tenant relations should be critical, unless one has recourse to a priori assumptions from a Marxist or economic/progressive standpoint about which aspects of a social totality govern the nature of social and historical change.

As a result of reducing the argument to such variables, the argument over the feudal/capitalist transition has become an abstract one; historical change becomes a reified process independent of historical agents. This is the point at which the danger occurs of losing contact with the sort of empirical studies discussed above, often pursued at the level of the local community, in which we see medieval and early modern people engaged with their physical and cultural surroundings in an everyday manner. Such studies, in focusing on cultures, values and beliefs, see past communities at least partly in terms of their values and meanings rather than in those of the modern historian.

One of the problems here is the very different nature of historical discourse in the late medieval and early modern periods respectively. This is true in terms both of historiography and of source material. Many of the new approaches in history discussed in chapter 1 have been developed with reference to the early modern period and seventeenth-century Europe in particular, and the period is one of continuing debate. Hence the language of everyday life, cultural conflict and so on is a familiar one to many early modern historians. This is much less the case with medieval English history which as a whole remains much more wedded to a traditional format. In addition, the sources used by early modern cultural historians such as diaries, probate inventories, and so on, either do not exist at all or exist in a very different form for the medieval period.

Thus, historians working from secondary sources attempting to generalize over the late medieval/early modern barrier run the risk of pulling together syntheses put together from very different source materials and whose underlying resonances and positions within the discursive rules of their period specialisms are quite different. Theorists of the feudal/capitalist transition thus end up gluing together syntheses that have been drawn up using very different source materials and that have been written according to different discursive rules and within a different historiographic tradition.

As Glennie has pointed out (1987), part of the problem here is that the objective measures which anchor abstract formulations of late feudal social relations empirically are changeable and mean different things in different contexts. Glennie gives the example of differentiation in the size of farm holdings, which Brenner uses as an index of class relations. He points out that such a simple equation is not tenable: 'on both a priori grounds and on the basis of historical community studies, the economic positions and social behaviour of medieval villagers were related in complex ways' (1987: 298–9).

A related problem is the conflation of quite broad and fluid concepts, ideas and categories like 'power' and 'control', as a prehistoric archaeologist or cultural anthropologist might understand them, with formal economic classificatory terminology derived from medieval and early modern legal concepts such as tenure, ownership, use-rights and so on. To clarify: to an outsider, agrarian historians often seem obsessed with precise legal terms of tenure; the student is deluged with terms like freehold, copyhold by inheritance, and so on, and the often narrow and abstruse legal definitions that go with these. This legal precision is obviously necessary in some contexts. Such stress on legal niceties may however lose its relevance and even obscure the real loci and forms of cultural control when compared with archaeologists' or anthropologists' broader interests in who wielded real power and control in specific social situations. When one realizes, for example, that different legal forms of tenure could change their meaning according to local and historical context, suspicion is sharpened that such narrowly legalistic discussion is missing the broader point about relations between different social groups and their respective power over the land.

A more fundamental and precise way of attacking this problem is to note a contradiction. The often dominant concern within the discourses of economic history are over the formal conditions of land tenure, which are then under the Marxist tradition equated with different forms of control over the means of production. They are thus seen as constitutive of class relations. Such an equation is however rendered deeply problematic when one realizes that the assumptions that drive such a model are derived from a formalist economics resting on categories of rent, value and so on. Such categories derive from a particular view of modern economics and may not be applicable to the lives and thoughts of pre-industrial people at all. Perhaps, rather, they should rest on a substantivist understanding of late medieval and early modern economic practice. It has been argued that even Marx himself did not entirely escape from this contradiction (Tribe 1981: 37–8), and that again we are left with an irony: that Marxist historiography has acted as an ideology, projecting capitalist values (such as division between formal economic value and everyday cultural forms) back into the Middle Ages.

Martin touches on this point from within the Marxist tradition when he suggests that scholars such as Sweezy and Dobb have failed to recognize the interrelatedness of economic and political components of feudal structure. This, he argues, leads to a failure to define feudalism adequately, a speci-fication of infrastructural components (such as political aspects of the relations of production) as superstructural, and an ambiguity regarding the place of commodity relationships in feudalism (1983: 7–14). Martin goes on to propose that the Sweezy and Dobb models of the feudal/capitalist transition are similarly flawed, though his assertion that previous models have ignored the role of class struggle in the historical process is open to debate. Martin suggests that 'traditionally, Marxists have analysed the transition from feudalism to capitalism as a linear succession, making no analytical distinction between mode of production and social formation as concepts. This view of transition generated auto-effective conceptions of change, either in the form of internal dissolution (Dobb) or external dissolution (Sweezy), in which a theoretical linearity corresponds to a linear chronology' (1983: 97). One could go further and suggest that any kind of overarching analytical framework of this kind runs the risk of doing violence to people's own experiences and mentalities in the medieval and early modern past.

Conclusion

This chapter reads in a rather disjointed fashion. The first part was con-cerned with the minutiae of landscape and society, with a more or less practical and empirical account of enduring structures of locality, region and culture; the second, with an account of rather abstract schema of social formations and their mechanisms for transition, focussing on the feudal/ capitalist transition in particular. Sometimes, immersed in the everyday world of household accounts and parson's diaries one day and buried in lineages of the absolutist state the next, it is difficult to believe that the two derive their claims to discursive authority from the same real human actions, the same past. This problem has been noted by others, most obviously E.P. Thompson in his insistence that history was created by real people rather than 'agents'; it means that in terms of concrete historical propositions, the transition from feudalism to capitalism 'remains pre-eminently an abstract problem for Marxist theory rather than a substantive problem for the social sciences' (Glennie 1987: 297). This is a shame. I suggest that one of the things a theoretically informed archaeology can do is to try to bring these traditions together in a concrete fashion. The next chapter will start this process by looking at the archaeology of enclosure, where it is immediately apparent that the use of formal abstract categories, whatever tradition these are derived from, hinders rather than assists the meaningful interpretation of change in culture and landscape.

3

Understanding Enclosure

The green fields of England are famous. They occupy a central place in a myth of ethnic origins: in a narrative of Englishness, of notions of cultural and national identity in a changing world. 'Emotional ruralism' has been seen as an essential constituent of 'Englishness' (Schmied 1992: 71). They are threads of a fabric woven into an unchanging rural idyll, an image formed in opposition to and shaming the squalor of modern industrial cities, Blake's 'Satanic mills'; a rural image that was in part the active creation of landscape painters during and after the Industrial Revolution (Daniels 1993; Shaw and Chase 1989).

Yet, as is so often the case with such images, the placid surface of the rolling countryside is a thin skin over a deeper reality of rupture, of conflict, of human action, of change. Far from being an unchanging constant, much of the pattern of the English countryside we see today was an active creation of the late and post-medieval periods; its creation played a central part in the creation of agrarian capitalism, and thus of the agrarian basis of industrial society. We may like to think of such a landscape as we see it today as a salve for urban alienation, a retreat from the harshness of the modern world. In reality the changing structure and perception of Blake's green and pleasant land played a central part in the constitution of capitalism.

Between 1400 and 1850 much of the rural landscape of England was transformed beyond all recognition: from a land of furlongs and strip fields, of medieval agrarian practices, of a different pattern of everyday work, of a different way of living and thinking, to a modern one, an iron cage whose frame was cast along principles of class relations, of farming for profit. This transformation created a rural landscape capable of feeding the urban masses created by the Industrial Revolution. The pace of this transformation accelerated and its nature took a new form in the later eighteenth and early nineteenth centuries, but its foundations were laid and its path structured several centuries earlier; indeed, much recent work has emphasized the relative importance of agrarian change and 'improvement' prior to c.1750, to the extent that grain exports more than doubled in the century before 1750 (Kerridge 1967; Wrigley 1989: 12–17; John 1976).

Why did this transformation occur? How do we currently understand this transformation as archaeologists and historians? Is this present understanding a limited one, and what other understandings are possible?

The debate over the 'causes' of enclosure and its related phenomenon, settlement shrinkage and desertion, is a classic one in the historiography of late medieval and early modern agrarian history. The debate was also a contemporary one with enclosure itself, sixteenth- and seventeenth-century commentators taking different views of the phenomenon, though many of the 'classic' works on this subject date from the later nineteenth century. It can be seen as a quite fundamental historical debate for a combination of theoretical, methodological, and political reasons.

In theoretical terms, it is not difficult to see that the many 'causes' cited for enclosure as a phenomenon of agrarian change cluster around different spheres of interest; thus, the enclosure debate becomes a battleground for conflicting views of the past according to environmental, economic, social, or Marxist forms of explanation, or indeed any cocktail of these forms one cares to specify. The evidence addressed does play a role in determining the rise and fall of these arguments, though each argument in turn tends to specify which piece of evidence is important (grain prices, arable yields, legal forms and conditions of tenure, depositions before Tudor courts of inquiry) and how that evidence may be legitimately marshalled to form a more or less convincing case (statistically, through distribution maps, by example).

The second, methodological aspect of the debate is that which most immediately concerns archaeologists. How do we, as students of material culture, adequately address or make meaningful scholarly contributions to an ongoing debate where there is not merely textual evidence available, but evidence of a form and a variety of context which in many commentators' views would appear to leave us merely filling in the gaps? One possible move out of this invidious position is to theorize the underlying discourse: that is, to question, to render problematic, to deconstruct the classes of evidence being discussed and the way the style and substance of interpretations are prescribed under existing discursive rules.

The final resonance of the debate over enclosure is a political one. The narratives of enclosure are tied in to a set of wider narratives, of larger stories to do with the creation of 'agrarian capitalism' and thus directly to our own world. It is possible first to observe the dates of writing of the 'classic' texts on Parliamentary enclosure, in the later nineteenth century, and their stress on economic progress as the underlying force. Against this background the socialist Richard Tawney wrote his classic books *Religion and the Rise of Capitalism* and *The Agrarian Problem in the Sixteenth Century*; the former title needs no gloss, while the latter book addressed itself to enclosure as a phenomenon of class conflict. In its memorable conclusion Tawney puts himself in the position of a peasant opposing enclosure:

> True, our system is wasteful . . . Nevertheless, master steward, our wasteful husbandry feeds many households where your economical methods would feed few. In our ill-arranged fields and scrubby commons most families hold a share, though it be but a few roods. In our unenclosed village there are few rich, but there are few destitute, save when God sends a bad harvest, and we all starve together. We do not like your improvements which ruin half the honest men affected by them (Tawney 1912: 409).

This debate continues. Kerridge has made clear his distaste for Tawney's political activities and has linked these to what he sees as his misinterpretations of the evidence. His tone speaks for itself:

> In Tawney . . . a harmful prejudice was all too evident. Tawney the politician barred the way to Tawney the scholar. Time which he might have given to studying history was devoted instead to the Fabian Society and the Labour Party, and he tended to see the world past and present in terms of socialist dogma. Hence his wholly unfair picture of early capitalism as cruel and greedy (Kerridge 1969: 15).

So enclosure is a debate which has resonance at different levels; and it is the interaction of these levels, the way in which theory or the empirical merges into the political, which makes its understanding so interesting and central to an account of the feudal/capitalist transition. It is not possible to give a full review of this debate in traditional terms here; this task is more than adequately performed in standard texts in any case (Yelling 1977). Rather, I will first define enclosure, and examine some of its different forms, for the benefit of non-specialists in this area. I will then go on to examine a range of explanations given, and suggest both empirical and theoretical problems with all such explanations. Out of these problems a wider critique of existing approaches to enclosure will emerge, and the structures of possible alternative understandings will become apparent. It is not possible to claim that a single, more satisfactory explanation for enclosure will be given, for reasons that will become clear.

Definitions of Enclosure

Enclosure can be defined as the replacement of medieval systems of open fields and common farming practices with a private, hedged landscape. We at once see two aspects to any definition of enclosure: the physical aspect of the replacement of unbounded land with a hedged and ditched landscape, and the legal aspect of land with 'common rights' versus 'land held in severalty' free from such rights. These two aspects need to be distinguished both in looking at past practices and in assessing modern scholarship, since the physical fact of enclosure need not imply any change in legal status; conversely, a change in legal rights need not involve physical alteration of the landscape (Kerridge 1967; Butlin 1979: 65). The interrelatedness versus independence of these two aspects is a subject to which we shall return, since it clearly involves questions of how the physical landscape was perceived by contemporaries.

In the vast majority of cases where enclosure was carried out in a physical sense, the immediate action that was involved was that of hedging and ditching a landscape that was previously 'open', however this is de-fined. Large-scale and sudden enclosure has often been interpreted as being associated with desertion, either of villages or of smaller settlements, often by forcible depopulation of settlements by landlords.

Within this very wide definition, differing forms of enclosing activity may be found, with different distributions across England and with differ-ent chronologies and immediate causes. Five forms are discussed here, not to give an exhaustive account of the different varieties of enclosure, but rather to give some indication of the range of actions that may come under this heading.

General enclosure

General enclosure is traditionally associated with depopulation. A wide strip of lowland landscape running up from the Midlands into the north-east of England had been classic 'champion' landscape: that is, it had been characterized in the Middle Ages by a mixture of pasture and arable farming, nucleated settlement and the use of so-called 'Midlands' open field systems. Many settlements in this area, weakened demographically and economically in the later middle ages, were depopulated by powerful landlords, the landscape enclosed and the area turned over to sheep. There appears to have been a peak of such enclosure between the dates of 1450 and 1550. At this time, grain prices were at their lowest after the demographic dip following the Black Death and wool and cloth exports to the Continent were at their highest. There are no known cases of the process reversing itself in full (that is, of villages being repopulated and turned back to open-field agriculture).

Many features surviving in the Midlands landscape seen today can be attributed to this process; the ridge-and-furrow of the medieval common fields underlying the later hedges and ditches, though much has been destroyed by a return to arable since the last war (figure 3.1). Thousands of deserted settlements were created in this process, which are known either solely from documents or which sometimes survive as earthworks or cropmarks on the ground (figure 3.2; Beresford 1954).

The most famous and well-researched example is the famous site of

Figure 3.1 Traces of the 'ridge and furrow' of open fields at Padbury, Buckinghamshire. The open fields were enclosed and the overlying system of field boundaries laid out within the space of one year (1795) by Act of Parliament (Beresford and St Joseph 1958, 135–6). The ridge and furrow survives where the fields have been turned over to pasture, rather than being ploughed up. Cambridge University Collection of Air Photographs: copyright reserved.

Figure 3.2 Hamilton, Leicestershire: the earthworks of a deserted village surrounded by abandoned ridge-and-furrow. Hamilton was enclosed by 1500. The line of the main street and layout of the properties can clearly be seen. Hamilton was one of the first deserted villages to be excavated (in 1948) by W.G. Hoskins and Leicester students (Beresford 1954: 70). Cambridge University Collection of Air Photographs: copyright reserved.

Wharram Percy in the Yorkshire Wolds. This village is shown through tax records to have been declining throughout the later middle ages. It was depopulated in 'about 1500' (Beresford and Hurst 1990: 59), leaving the church and vicarage sitting in an isolated location. The church was reduced in size, but continued to act as the parish church for neighbouring townships. All that is left today is the ruined church and a series of earthworks, set amidst the ridge-and-furrow of the formerly open fields.

To give another typical example among many, tax records show that Welcombe in Worcestershire had 17 tenant households in 1299 and 13 in 1332; there are indications of crisis in the fifteenth century, though the village's fields were still used for arable in the early sixteenth century. This period probably saw the concentration of lands in the hands of one family, the Combes; soon after 1614 the major landowner, William Combe, 'paled and stopped up the common street leading through the town of Welcombe', and according to the depositions of local opposition depopulated the village (Dyer 1980: 254–5).

Such activity continued in spasms, however, according to short-term economic fluctuations up to 1700, as at Clarewood, Northumberland (Wrathmell 1980; figure 3.3).

The draining of the Fens

Another specific form of enclosure quite explicitly linked to contemporary social conflict was the draining of the Fenlands around the borders of Norfolk, Cambridgeshire and Lincolnshire (figure 3.4). This was carried forward by enterprising individuals, 'improvers' or 'projectors' under Royal mandate, who with the help of engineers and ideas imported from the Low Countries drained successive areas, using a combination of straight canals, ditches and embankments, some of which have recently been investigated archaeologically (James 1994). This replaced an economy based on exploitation of the marshland with arable and pastoral farming. They did so in the teeth of bitter opposition from local communities, since drainage involved the destruction of local common rights to the extent of dismantling the whole traditional Fenland way of life at one stroke (Butlin 1990: 62–7). Opposition took both legal and illegal forms, involving petitions to Parliament and full-scale riot.

It is interesting to note that one recent history of this activity suggests that even in raw terms the objective economic gain produced by enclosure was limited at best (Lindley 1982: 12–22). Fenland drainage and enclosure dates principally to the seventeenth century, particularly the earlier period before the English Revolution.

Piecemeal enclosure

A form with less overtly divisive social implications was that of piecemeal enclosure. This form was characteristic of wood-pasture areas in particular, where individual peasants could exchange neighbouring holdings in order to bring together or 'engross' their more scattered strips.

This form is more difficult to pin down archaeologically, since it often leaves many earlier field boundaries intact and thus leaves little physical trace (figure 3.5). This is particularly true in wood-pasture areas where

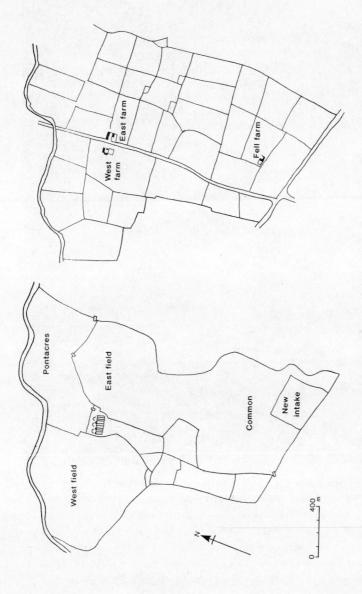

Figure 3.3 Clarewood township, Northumberland, in 1677 (left) and around 1760 (right) (after Wrathmell 1980). Map and documentary evidence suggests Clarewood had only nine houses in the mid-seventeenth century. John Douglas acquired the township in 1686, and the village and its common rights disappeared soon afterwards. Evidence is lacking for formal depopulation but Douglas's notes suggest that he abolished common rights and introduced new, 'improved' farming systems, spending more than £53 on new houses and barns. In 1715 the township was let as two farms standing on the old site of the village; a third new farm, Fell Farm, was created by the 1760s (Wrathmell 1980: 113–19). Douglas undertook a similar depopulation at nearby East Matfen.

Figure 3.4 Fen drainage at the Bedford Level in south-west Norfolk in the Norfolk Fenlands. The Old Bedford River on the right was constructed in 1631; the New Bedford River on the left in 1653. The area between the Rivers could be deliberately flooded to ease high-water levels. The enclosed fields around the system were used for the cultivation of new crops, such as coleseed, rapeseed, hemp, flax, and woad; farmers suffered repeated flooding and drainage problems due to shrinkage of the peat (Glennie 1992: 132–5).

Figure 3.5 Brassington, Derbyshire: here, piecemeal enclosure by agreement between individual farmers has preserved the medieval patterns of furlongs. Such enclosure probably happened relatively early. Cambridge University Collection of Air Photographs: copyright reserved.

large open fields had never been laid out in the first place. For example, in wood-pasture East Anglia the field boundaries in many areas may be traced directly back to the Roman period (figure 2.4), and thus the small-scale engrossing of the late and post-medieval periods left little impact. It is easy to underestimate the scale of this form of enclosure, since it may have been destroyed later: in areas where the whole parish was enclosed by Act of Parliament after 1750, the resulting wholesale reorganization of the landscape may have obliterated such areas of partial enclosure.

In other areas piecemeal enclosure may be more evident, for example where the boundaries of the fields engrossed in this manner run along the lines of the aggregated strips, leaving medieval boundaries 'fossilized' (figure 3.5). This occasionally happened where the community was power-ful enough to resist the encroachment of great landowners.

Piecemeal enclosure is also often difficult to date through documentary sources, since it was a frequently informal process carried out by spoken agreement between farmers. It often therefore left no written trace in the form of court records or other depositions. That being said, the majority of piecemeal enclosure seems to have been completed quite early. For example, in wood-pasture East Anglia the landscape appears to have been fully enclosed by *c*.1600, with the important exception of the commons and greens which though surviving were often encroached upon along the margins (Johnson 1993: 167; Warner 1987).

There were also certain communities in which the landscape was gener-ally or more or less completely enclosed 'by agreement' of the whole community, often through the technical procedure of bringing a fictional case to court. The townships of Sherburn and Shadforth in County Durham were enclosed by agreement between the tenants of the Bishop of Durham, who petitioned the Bishop in 1634 for permission to make a 'partition and division of all there . . . farmeholds landes arrables meadowes pastures and commons of pastures', claiming that their fields were 'for the most part wasted with contynuall ploweing & thereby made bare barren and verie unfruitfull' and that 'if the said lands . . . were divided proportionably by metes & boundes & layde in severalty to the end therefore that that said disired good worke both for themselves & the said commonwealth might be brought to perfection'. Surveyors met with the two communities and drew up maps and other documentation. The general enclosure of 1635 divided the townships completely, within the conditions of common rights over water supply and local stone quarries, and a small area of common for washing sheep (Heppell and Clack 1991).

It is important to note that the term 'by agreement' may be misleading, since all we know in any one case is that opposition to such enclosure did not reach the legal or documentary record. It is quite possible to envisage non-overt or traditional forms of opposition that may not have reached the level of legal action or, in Thirsk's terms, 'riot or revolution' (1967: 200), such as those forms that turn up occasionally in court depositions over other issues. Sharp makes the point in other contexts that the fear of riot was a powerful sanction against potentially unpopular actions (1980; also Bristol 1985). Piecemeal enclosure did have less effect on common rights than did more violent forms of reorganization, and therefore is likely to have attracted less venomous forms of opposition. There were those in early modern communities however who opposed any form of hedging and ditching (see below), and again the attitudes of the lower social orders are less clear.

Enclosure of waste

The term 'waste' did not indicate barren ground: it meant rather ground not under systematic cultivation, though it may have been used for other purposes such as rough grazing, the keeping of rabbits or collection of firewood. Such uses were often subject to common rights. Large tracts of waste were enclosed and even in places brought under arable cultivation in peripheral, marginal or upland areas by farmers working individually or collectively in the centuries before 1300, though these areas were often then abandoned in the less favourable climatic and economic conditions of the later middle ages. Enclosing and reclamation revived, however, from the seventeenth century onwards. Such different waves of activity in upland landscapes could be associated with changes in social structure and tenurial arrangements.

Thus for example the valley of Swaledale in the Yorkshire Dales saw an expansion of settlement from the early seventeenth-century onwards. Here, much of the dale had been owned by Marrick Priory in the Middle Ages; much of the upper reaches of the dale is covered in traces of arable farming that was abandoned in the fourteenth and fifteenth centuries. This land had been sold off after the dissolution of the Priory in the 1530s, and had fallen into the hands of socially middling tenant and *rentier* farmers by the early seventeenth century. A series of dispersed farms set upon the brows of the dale date from this period. They were responsible for the steady enclosure of the valuable lower slopes for a little arable and pasturing of cattle, and piecemeal enclosure of the moors above for rough pasture for sheep (figure 2.5).

Parliamentary enclosure

'Parliamentary' enclosure after 1750 is not the primary subject of this discussion, though it is closely related to the changes being discussed here. In this form the proprietors of land in the community applied to Parliament for an Act, which when passed involved the survey of the parish followed by general enclosure. Parliamentary enclosure was pushed along by the rise in demand for agricultural produce engendered by the Industrial Revolution and the Napoleonic Wars, and again its rate of progress may be shown to relate to the rise and fall of food prices.

Parliamentary enclosure is often found in champion areas where the community was strong enough to withstand the various strains of the fifteenth to eighteenth centuries, the open fields thus surviving till this later date. Much of it is easily recognizable as one travels across the landscape today, the Parliamentary surveyors often drawing the lines of the new large fields ruler-straight across the landscape (figure 3.1). It is important to remember however that many communities enclosed by Parliamentary Act had already experienced centuries of piecemeal enclosure; the general nature and physical result of the Parliamentary Act often belied its nature as the final move in a long-term game. In north Buckinghamshire, for example, half of those parishes enclosed by Act of Parliament were already partly enclosed by 1750 (Reed 1984).

Other forms of enclosure can be argued to exist, and the simple typology given above elaborated according to different nuances of legal terminology. In any case, each rural community experienced its own unique chronology according to specific circumstances. A tiny number of communities were never enclosed: the township of Laxton in Nottinghamshire earns a steady tourist trade through its claims to be an authentic remnant of a medieval past, though its farming practices are not now representative of medieval open-field farming.

But for most if not all people in the countryside enclosure was a one-way experience. Once generally enclosed, very few pieces of land were laid out on an open-field pattern again, however bitter the opposition to enclosure. Occasional examples of enclosure being reversed do turn up, for example in Richard Gough's account of the seventeenth-century parish of Myddle: the encloser of one intake 'was sued . . . for so doing and wars forced to cast it open, and pay costs' (Hey 1981: 68). Again, the depopulator of Chesterton in Cambridgeshire soon went bankrupt and the land was returned to open-field practice (Allen 1992).

Any understanding of enclosure as a process has to grasp this gradual but peculiarly inexorable nature, this ratchet-like mechanism, this apparently complete failure of resistance to a process of enclosure that was at the time hotly opposed by many contemporaries.

Contemporary Debates

The progress of the more visible forms of enclosure caused debate and dissension among literate contemporaries, who expressed their contrasting views on the subject in sermons, pamphlets, court enquiries and other media. The views of the non-literate mass of the population can be gauged indirectly through their participation in rioting and other activity related to protest against enclosure. This explosion of contemporary debate occurred from the beginning of the sixteenth century onwards.

What was apparently important to contemporaries and exercised their pens most was the extinction of common rights; that is, the rights of more than one person to graze sheep or cattle, to gather firewood and so on, on a given piece of land. Opinion could be divided over whether enclosure that did not affect common rights (such as most forms of piecemeal enclosure) was justified or not. 'A hedge in the field is as necessary in its kind as government in the church or commonwealth', argued John Hales in *A Vindication of Regulated Enclosure*, whereas others argued any form of enclosure was to be opposed in any form (Hill 1964: 491; Yelling 1977). The popular reaction to enclosure seems always to have been negative, though whether the lack of reported opposition to piecemeal enclosure was due to popular indifference or bias in the sources is a moot point.

The reaction of the State differed according to context. The late fifteenth- and early sixteenth-century depopulations (see 'General enclosure', pp. 47–50) were viewed as threatening by Royal authority, which established a series of Royal Commissions to investigate the phenomenon. The State in its instructions to the Wolsey Commission distinguished different forms of enclosure thus:

> But first, to declare unto you what is meant by the word 'inclosures'. It is not taken where a man doth enclose and take in his own proper ground where no man hath commons. For such enclosure is very beneficial to the commonwealth . . . but it is meant thereby, where any man has taken away and enclosed any other mens commons, or hath pulled down houses of husbandry [depopulation], and converted the land from tillage to pasture. This is the meaning of this word, and so we pray you to remember it (cited in Tawney and Power 1924: 41).

This is an interesting statement which is worth dwelling on. The distinction so bedevilling modern scholarship, between the physical fact and the legal circumstances surrounding it, is here hard to discern. The concentration on the physical fact, the assumption of identity between the physical landscape and social organization, the embeddedness of the two contexts is a concept that I would argue is integral to medieval mentalities. Here, a medieval mentality is being employed in the service of a newly assertive Renaissance state, in the process of increasing centralization; a phenomenon we shall encounter again in succeeding chapters.

It is also evident in resistance to enclosure. Everyday resistance is a subject to which we shall return, but resistance in the form of riots is well documented (Manning 1988; Sharp 1980). As with many ethnographically documented cases of public disorder, there was a continuum between the activities of revel, carnival, riot and rebellion. Many acts of resistance against enclosure involved elements of symbolic inversion (they were frequently led by women). Villagers engaged in the ritual of 'beating the bounds' of the parish often carried implements for destroying obstacles such as hedges and ditches with them (Kelley 1990; E.P. Thompson 1991: 307–8).

By the sixteenth century, the incidence of enclosure was a routine grievance listed amongst others in petitions from rioting groups. A hostile witness to Kett's Rebellion writing nearly 60 years after the event attributed these views to the rebels: 'Shall they, as have brought hedges about common pastures, enclose with their intolerable lusts also all the commodities and pleasures of this life, which Nature, the parent of us all, would have common? . . . Now that it comes to extremity, we will also prove extremity: rend down hedges, fill up ditches, make way for every man into the common pasture' (cited in Patterson 1989: 42–3). The term 'Leveller', as applied to the radical group in the English Revolution, was first coined in terms of levelling hedges and ditches (Hill 1993: 133). Riots concentrated on the symbolic act of the throwing down of fences and ditches. Again we come back to the changing relationship between the physical fact of enclosure versus legal rights, the embeddedness of farming practices and cultural values in the physical organization of the landscape.

Such complexity of the meaning of and class interests involved in enclosure means that there is no easy, Whiggish political matrix into which contemporary debates and practical action over the issue may be fitted. Puritans, for example, so often seen as socially and politically 'progressive' by English historians, found themselves on different sides of disputes in different contexts. In the specific troubles over the Fenland enclosures, enclosing activity was undertaken by 'projectors' under Royal patent whose activity under the licence of King Charles led directly to opposition from local Puritans including Oliver Cromwell and so to the underlying causes of the English Revolution (Lindley 1982). On the other hand, even the radical Henry Marten felt that 'the keeping of hedges, boundaries and distinctions . . . is a surer way to keep peace among neighbours than throwing all open' (cited in Hill 1993: 134). Enclosure is therefore problematic in terms of at least a narrow view of contemporary politics and culture.

Explaining Enclosure

Just as the views of sixteenth- and seventeenth-century commentators are not easily fitted into a wider framework, so modern explanations of enclosure cannot be summarized and schematized with any ease. There are as many explanations of the causes of enclosure as there are students of it; and each employs environmental, economic, cultural and social variables in a variety of ways. Many such general models of explanation are also implicit rather than explicit in terms of their assumptions and central propositions. Additionally, they are often developed with reference to a specific region, locality or sub-type of enclosure rather than to England as a whole. This all impedes the task of clear exposition of different types of explanation.

The way different explanations might be grouped together under different subheadings is therefore inevitably rather arbitrary: in what follows I have subdivided the different explanations into three groups.

Enclosure and conflict

First, socialist or Marxian explanations linked to class conflict. The most famous exponent of this type of explanation was the early twentieth-century socialist Richard Tawney, most classically in his book *The Agrarian Problem in the Sixteenth Century* (1912).

In Tawney's narrative, settlement desertion and enclosure were the consequences of a shift in the balance of power between landlord and tenant and changing economic conditions. According to Tawney settlements were weakened and shrunken by the Black Death of 1348–9 and the associated economic and demographic decline of the fourteenth and fifteenth centuries, and were easy pickings for acquisitive landlords. At the same time, the landlords' economic interests shifted: they saw that the rise in wool prices and the corresponding fall in those of corn made it economic sense to forcibly depopulate villages, evict the remaining tenants and turn the areas over to sheep farming. The evicted populace are seen in Tawney's account as leaving to swell the urban poor, thus in turn providing a labour supply for urban capitalism and increasing urban demand for rural products, stimulating regional markets and feeding back into the rise of agrarian capitalism.

Such an account in its simplified form has been almost entirely abandoned. In the first place, even Tawney saw that the village community was weakened by economic and demographic shrinkage for more than a century prior to depopulation. Depopulation, enclosure and the turning over of an area to sheep was therefore usually the final act in a long drama of internal decay that is not so simply attributable to class conflict alone.

Further, the work of Rodney Hilton and Christopher Dyer has shown that in many areas the link between enclosure and forcible depopulation is problematic. In some areas enclosure and the turning-over of the landscape to sheep did not follow depopulation as a matter of course, the later action being delayed for as much as 50 years after depopulation. In others, settlement desertion took place against the wishes of the landlords, court records indicating that many landlords sought to restrain tenants from leaving rather than the other way around (Hilton 1985; Dyer 1980). It is nevertheless true that the power of the landlord, which varied from community to community, was a key factor in the nature and progress of enclosure in a region.

Enclosure and climate

An argument strictly applied to medieval settlement desertion but with implications for enclosure is one that stresses climatic change. This view sees landscape change in cyclical form, as a long-term response to cyclical changes in the environment. It makes the valid point that landscape change in general and desertion in particular have had such a cyclical history: that most prehistoric and pre-Conquest settlements were deserted in due course as part of a more or less regular rhythm, and that therefore it is the striking survival of the sites of most villages from the Middle Ages, rather than the shrinkage and desertion of some, that requires explanation in this view. Phases of contraction are characteristic of British prehistory and settlement expansion, shift and desertion may have had at least two phases in the first millenium AD in England (Hodges 1989). More immediately, it has been pointed out that such long-term trends prefigured the economic changes of the earlier fourteenth century. In Norfolk, for example, different soil conditions and the varying effect of climate have been interpreted as conditioning the pattern of settlement and desertion (Davison 1988: 101–5).

In areas of the Midlands and the North, Guy Beresford has interpreted climatic change as central to enclosure. In what he sees as colder and wetter conditions after *c.*1300 he has excavated a series of settlements where peasant tofts were amalgamated into larger farms, fields enclosed and the area turned over from emphasis on arable to pasture. These settlements frequently occur on clayland soils, potentially very fertile in drier conditions but in which the clay packs together and becomes unsuitable for arable in wetter times (Beresford 1975).

Objections to such a view take the classic forms of general objections to environmental determinism. In the first place, there are empirical problems with the relationship between enclosure and climatic change. The climatic evidence does not point conclusively to colder and wetter weather after *c.*1300; rather, a range of interpretations are possible according to which piece of evidence one chooses to stress (Dyer 1989). More specifically Wright has suggested that enclosure preceded climatic change at two key sites (Wright 1976). More generally, it is not clear why cyclical change in environmental background should lead to one of a range of possible specific cultural responses. Thus, a specific prehistoric reaction to harsher conditions might be contraction and abandonment of marginal areas; Anglo-Saxon reaction was a more complex shifting of settlement, nucleation and the creation of open fields; while the late medieval period saw a unique response including the shift from open-field to enclosed landscapes, changes in patterns of land tenure, and social and cultural shifts. It is not sufficient to note the climatic background to explain why this specific response was 'chosen', particularly when the evidence for that background is shaky and contradictory.

Enclosure and 'improvement'

The most common assumption implicit in models of enclosure is that it was the result, among other changes in farming practice, of a drive towards increasing economic efficiency. It is pointed out that enclosure is one of a battery of 'improvements' that meant that agricultural productivity doubled between 1500 and 1750 (Kussmaul 1990; Wrigley 1989). Kerridge was one of the first to point to this phase of improvement, which in his view was more important than the succeeding period and included such diverse changes as 'the floating of water meadows, the substitution of up-and-down husbandry for permanent tillage and permanent grass or for shifting cultivation, the introduction of new fallow crops and selected grasses, marsh drainage, manuring, and stock-breeding' (Kerridge 1967: 40).

Most classically this view of enclosure is found in the early writings of Gray, Chambers and Mingay, who though dealing specifically with Parliamentary enclosure do adopt the general proposition that the open fields were 'inefficient' in whatever sense. The open fields only survived in this view because of 'peasant sentiment', though this sentiment is not theorized or put in the context of peasant social relations.

This view, which takes agrarian 'progress' or technical innovation as an unproblematic phenomenon, is open to the immediate charge that if the open fields were so inefficient why were they laid out in such a form in the first place? With this problem goes the subsidiary one of explaining why, then, enclosure took place at such a gradual pace, varying widely in its impact on different regions. Gray refers to varying soil types in this context, though the evidence is unclear on this point.

This view has been refined by two scholars in a more theoretically explicit way. McCloskey has interpreted open fields as being an important factor in risk reduction in peasant subsistence agriculture. Any one peasant's holding would be distributed in different strips across the landscape and thus less liable to be completely wiped out by some natural disaster. With the development of the market system, and therefore the ability to buy in food in times of hardship, the need for risk reduction is curtailed (McCloskey 1979).

More detailed studies have shown how in certain areas responses to local demand was indeed a key factor. In County Durham enclosure and other agricultural changes, particularly a shift away from arable towards pastoral farming, arose in response to the rising demands of the city of Newcastle and a growing local industrial population needing meat and dairy products. It is interesting that nevertheless 'the system adopted was less rational than physical conditions alone would have suggested since the farmer's perception of soil quality and market conditions tended to overemphasise pastoralism before about 1680 and grain production thereafter' (Hodgson 1979: 43).

The most sophisticated and explicit general model of this sort yet is the model developed by Carl Dahlman (1980). Dahlman's work is valuable in that he is one of the few to discuss the problem in theoretically explicit terms. He starts with several important general points that are valid insights independent of the rest of his analysis.

Dahlman points out first that to understand enclosure it is necessary to understand the nature of the open-field system it replaced in its own terms. That is, we must first understand why the open fields were laid out at some point earlier in the medieval period and why they persisted for so long. Second, he maintains that agricultural innovation alone cannot be seen as the driving force behind enclosure. Many innovations were suitable for introduction by means of cooperation between peasants in the open-field system but were not so introduced. Water meadows, for example, involving large-scale flooding of land in the early spring to warm the ground and thus promote earlier and more lush growth of grass, could have been created and managed in this manner and were certainly a key innovation in the agricultural improvements of the seventeenth and eighteenth centuries (Bowie 1987). Therefore, any explanation must indicate what it was about enclosure specifically that was important. Third, any model of enclosure must explain why, once conditions were right, it was not a sudden event; it must grasp its gradual, protracted nature over three centuries.

Adopting economic assumptions from the formalist school, Dahlman then suggests that the open fields were the result of a need for balance between arable and pasture in the self-sufficient community. In particular, arable fields need manure to maintain productivity. The lack of a market in the feudal countryside made this self-sufficiency necessary. With the rise of urban capitalism and thus of regional marketing systems, this need for self-sufficiency was destroyed. But this penetration of the market into the provinces of England was only a gradual process, and therefore the progress of enclosure was gradual and regionally differentiated according to local factors.

The assumption, however, that enclosure was more economically efficient after the penetration of the market into local regions is open to debate. We have already seen how Fenland drainage was not of unquestionable benefit, particularly in the short to medium term. The relative lack of markets in the Middle Ages can also be questioned. It has been argued that peasant were heavily involved in local markets from the thirteenth century or even before, while commercial life in general was an important feature of medieval England and Wales (Britnell 1993).

More recently Robert Allen has asked the wider question of whether enclosure had any long-term benefits at all, comparing farms in open and enclosed landscapes statistically. It is true that Allen concentrates his arguments on large-scale eighteenth-century enclosures rather than some of the earlier, piecemeal forms discussed above; it is also true that his statistics may be open to alternative interpretations. However, his central conclusion that 'enclosure was not responsible for the growth in yields and labour productivity in England between 1500 and 1800' (1992: 17), if it holds any validity, drives a coach and horses through any argument based on greater economic efficiency.

Alternative Understandings

Enclosure, then, has been the subject of a torrent of scholarly outpourings over the last century. Yet recently there has been an apparent lull in this activity. Since the publication of Yelling's and Dahlman's books there have been few major works on this topic. It has been noted for example that there is no general discussion in Volume Five of *The Agrarian History of England and Wales*, despite the continuing 'abundance of fascinating material' (Habbakuk 1987: 295). Yet few would claim the last word has been said on this subject, and few would dispute the centrality of an understanding of enclosure to the rise of agrarian capitalism in England and Wales. Why this apparent stalemate?

One reason, I suggest, lies in the underlying assumptions of this debate. Figure 3.6 is a rather violent abstraction, a series of flow diagrams that simplify and schematize some of the general models of enclosure that have been discussed above. It is not perfect, nor does it capture more than the salient factors. But the diagram does make an important point, namely that the majority of existing explanations have tended to be no more than different combinations of similar underlying factors: the same variables recur (rise and fall of rent, the relationship between landlord and tenant, the rise of the market, and so on). These variables are related one to another in terms of direct causality, and one or two 'prime movers' are specified.

Now it is something of a theoretical game to construct models of this sort, whether one acknowledges that one is doing so implicitly or explicitly. It is, of course, a game being played for very high political stakes, since the specification of either class conflict or economic progress in whatever form as prime movers involves, by necessity, powerful implications for the negotiation of social and economic change in the present.

Not only is such an exercise a theoretical game, it can also be seen as a myth or narrative, which when connected up to other myths or narratives about the transition between the medieval and modern world form a powerful larger narrative. This larger narrative has assisted in constituting the boundaries of what is considered as legitimate and scholarly in historical discourse, and conversely what is dubious, uncertain and unscholarly. The setting of discursive boundaries in this way has assisted in turn in

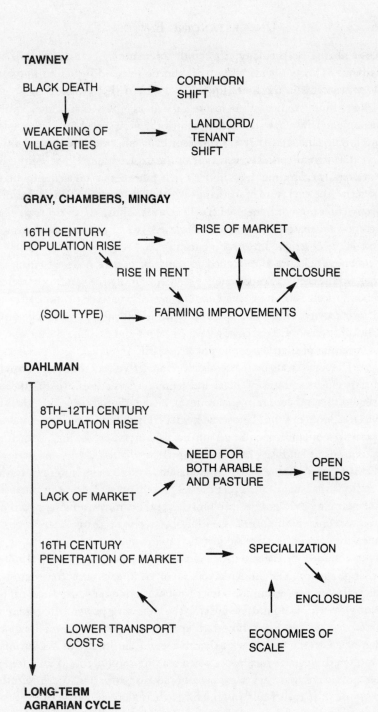

Figure 3.6 Schematic representation of different models of enclosure.

marginalizing archaeology, the study of material culture, within that discourse. This is a wide claim that can be pursued by a scrutiny of the wider problems in the literature on enclosure. I shall isolate four.

First, most studies of enclosure take it as given that it is a unitary phenomenon. We have defined at length the very varied forms that enclosure might take, and the very different class and other interests it might serve in different contexts; yet most of the explanations of enclosure given above tend to subsume these under a general explanation either by taking one form (the enclosure of Midlands open-field systems) as the norm or by simply choosing not to deal with other forms. Thus, 'the enclosure debate' becomes a debate over a series of varied issues that in some sense is artificially constructed from the outset.

Second, enclosure is modelled in terms of passive material culture. In other words, the landscape changes seen are simply the result of social and economic forces: they are the consequence of whatever prime mover one cares to specify. But landscape and material culture, as we have seen in earlier chapters, can be seen as active creations and as such take on a power and meaning of their own, one not necessarily intended by any one social actor. They may thus be related back in an active way to further changes, further transformations of social and economic structures. Pred (1985) has explored this in relation to enclosures in Skane, southern Sweden, showing how changes in physical landscape modelled in turn the work practices and experiences of landscape of agricultural labourers, producing in turn new conceptions of landscape and the material world.

Third, the enclosure debate is modelled in these views in terms of direct causality: what factor or factors caused it to happen? But again, historical understanding does not need to proceed in these terms; a looser relation of ideas to context, of formal parallels between pieces of evidence to an underlying structure, may be just as convincing.

A corollary of direct causality and perceived passivity of material culture is that of agency. The human actors involved in enclosure, for example as landlords, are seen as unified subjects whose actions are clear, rational and unproblematic. Landlords who have the necessary power will enclose to maximize their profits. Those farmers who do not enclose or introduce other new farming methods for that matter are 'backward' or not 'rational'. It is often difficult to remember when reading some accounts that farmers were not aware that they were on a grand road to rational farming practices, just as it is difficult to remember that contemporaries didn't know how political struggles would turn out in Whig interpretations of history. Systematic observation of crop yields and calculations did not appear in treatises on agricultural practices until the later eighteenth century (Tribe

1978: 69–71). In any case, there is some evidence to suggest that ideas that in the modern world are considered as strictly within the domain of the economic were actually socially embedded in the pre-industrial period. Craig Muldrew, for example, has explored how the concept of 'credit' in early modern England was a social rather than economic one; its pursuit did not mean that most people were concerned with self-interest (1993: 169). Rather, it was understood in the sense that most buying and selling was done on 'credit' with varying degrees of formal arrangements; it therefore involved trust between parties based on social standing and reputation. It is this system of 'credit' that one sees in the inventory of a deceased's possessions under the headings 'Debts Good and Bad'. This social and cultural network was a complex one that tied the whole community together; it came under strain in the seventeenth century as class polarization and the breakdown of the community gathered pace.

Fourth, enclosure is seen, again implicitly, as a subsystem, isolated from other subsystems, other spheres of life in the wider social system that was late medieval and early modern England. A casual reader coming to the literature on the history and archaeology of different aspects of medieval and early modern England would find three or four very different pasts being created: one of great men politicking, creating a Renaissance state, and grappling with Protestantism and the Reformation in religious history; one of peasants beavering away at rural industry from post-medieval archaeology; one of carnival mentalities and maypoles from social and cultural history. The fact that the real men and women involved seemed to move easily between these constructed spheres of life apparently worlds apart in the course of their everyday lives, who sat in church, made decisions about whether to enclose, worked in the enclosed fields and farmsteads, and played their part in community politics, while still leading lives that appeared at least to be coherent and unified to them, is lost somewhere between the specialisms of historical and archaeological discourse.

Most discussions of enclosure deal with it as a debate within the specialism of agrarian history, as a purely economic question. It is rare in this literature that cultural questions are closely related to enclosure. Two exceptions prove the rule. Yelling's review of the enclosure debate does include a discussion of 'the local community', but this is placed in the last chapter after earlier and more central discussions of farming systems and productivity (1977). The second exception is the host of references in the work of cultural historians to enclosure, where as we have seen the more violent forms including depopulation emerge as a contentious topic in the pamphlets of the time. But here, it is enclosure being seen as the context for cultural conflict, rather than one being a different form of the other. Only rarely is this relative isolation between different strands of history broken down: most classically in the work of Christopher Hill or in some of the work now appearing under the banner of the New Cultural History.

This assumption of agency and direct causality, of different historical discourses, of a model of society in which divisions into economic, social, religious and political are imposed from the present rather than from the 'insider's' views being examined, is ultimately traceable to the constitution of history in general and to the historical account of the medieval/modern transition in particular as a larger narrative, one that subsumes and overarches the particular narratives of each historical sub-discipline. These economic, social, religious, political spheres are defined as autonomous because that is how modernity perceives them, and because history seeks to account for the causes of the institutions and processes that constitute modernity. These need mean nothing more sinister or conspiratorial than that X, being a High Church Anglican, has a particular interest in writing on church history while Y, being an avid industrial archaeologist, looks for the roots of the industrial revolution by researching on medieval industries. But such mundane and innocent activities nevertheless contribute to such a larger theoretical drive or narrative.

This larger narrative is progressive, teleological and evolutionary; it specifies a gradual transition from pre-modern to modern forms in each of its spheres. It forms the implicit, unspoken backdrop to explanations of enclosure – unspoken because we 'know' it already. The implicit nature of this model allows specific studies of enclosure or any other 'problem' constituted under this narrative to present themselves as atheoretical, 'common sense' or as inductively proceeding from the evidence. Conversely, it allows traditional scholars to condemn anything that questions this narrative as 'theoretical', starting from a preconceived position.

But there is a different way of writing about the past, a way that attempts to dissolve the easy divisions made between different areas of discourse, that does not totalize or seek to render coherent, that does not assume agency and direct causality. It is also one in which the study of material culture may be placed at centre-stage instead of waiting in the wings to be wheeled on; it does so by trying to work through different classes of evidence, looking for common pattern and structure in different classes of material in a formal sense, across traditional discursive boundaries. I am going to borrow Foucault's use of the term 'archaeology' with all its ambiguities to characterize such an approach; but an equally possible way to characterize such a project is as a piece of contextual archaeology, starting with the archaeological material, eschewing external categories as far as possible and exploring its structuring from the 'inside'.

The next chapter will not attempt to specify direct causes for particular forms of enclosure: rather, it will try to sketch out in the broadest manner a genealogy of certain social practices and note parallels across different areas. This is an argument that I suggest qualifies as an understanding since it shows how certain practices 'fitted in' within a certain cultural context. The way this may be done is to work through the evidence in a contextual manner, attempting first to get into the spatial and mental structuring of past communities and then to work outwards across different classes of evidence.

4

Houses, Fields, Maps and Cultures

It is as a link in the development of modern economic relationships and modern conceptions of economic expedience, that the changes which we have been considering possess their greatest interest. The department of economic life in which, both for good and evil, the modern spirit comes in the sixteenth century most irresistibly to its own, is not agriculture but foreign commerce . . . it is nevertheless in transforming agrarian conditions that its nature and characteristics are most impressively revealed, not because it is felt there first or proceeds there furthest, but because the material which it encounters is so dense, so firmly organized, so intractable, that changes, which in a more mobile environment pass unnoticed, are seen there in high relief against the stable society which they undermine. In truth the agrarian revolution is but a current in the wake of mightier movements. The new world, which is painfully rising in so many English villages, is a tiny mirror of the new world which on a mightier stage, is ushering modern history in amid storms and convulsions. The spirit which revolts against authority, frames a science that will subdue nature to its service, and thrusts the walls of the universe asunder into space, is the same – we must not hesitate to say it – as that which on the lips of grasping landlords and stubborn peasants wrangles over the respective merits of 'several' and 'common', weighs the profits of pasture in an economic scale against the profits of arable, batters down immemorial customs, and regarding neither the honour of God nor the welfare of this realm of England, brings the livings of many into the hands of one (Tawney 1912: 408–9).

How do we grasp the meanings of enclosure? How does enclosure as a physical process relate to other, contemporary changes? Can it be related to other transformations in the deployment and use of space in the early modern period?

In any particular context, enclosure was an act, or a series of actions, of creating new forms of boundary. It involved placing hedges, ditches, fences, walls, pales where none formerly existed, or where a different pattern of boundaries was formerly in place.

It has long been a cliché of cultural anthropology that boundaries are not natural and normal things. They can keep out both animals and human beings, or keep animals and human beings in. They can appear to be impenetrable but are in fact pierced, or alternatively can be designed to be invisible to the gaze but actually form a formidable obstacle, as with the ha-ha. Boundaries can be purely legal or mental in nature, not physically apparent on the ground, or can run across former areas of continuous space. Boundaries can be sacred, profane, or as with a church or cemetery wall demarcate the difference between the two.

Boundaries perform different functions and carry different social and symbolic meanings in different contexts. They are rarely purely utilitarian in nature; in pre-industrial England they were not just functional barriers. Boundaries were symbolically loaded in different ways that defy simple schematization. Any gentleman or yeoman familiar with his Bible knew that even the very first fence in Creation separated the garden from the wilderness and would not fail to see boundaries, fences, hedges, ditches, pales as symbolically loaded with a variety of symbolic, religious and political resonances (Hill 1993: 128–35).

The previous chapter noted how the creation or maintenance of physical boundaries was not necessarily the same thing as the alteration of legal and customary rights over the land, though it could have important implications for it. So it is important to note that during the time of enclosure, a complexity and ambiguity of meaning and how it might be assigned to spaces in the fields existed in the minds of contemporaries. This was an ambiguity in part between spaces that were physically unbounded but mentally divided – closed – and bounded spaces that could nevertheless be the subject of common rights. The complexity and subtlety of such divisions was understood by different social groups in different ways. Their understandings could be renegotiated actively through formal, literate discussion of legal and semantic terms or through informal, 'popular' actions such as riot, revel or carnival. The definition and nature of boundaries across physical and mental landscapes thus became a key battleground – a key field – in which different social and cultural interests were played out.

I suggest that if we consider enclosure as a physical process for a moment we may better understand it when we return to discussing the everyday minutiae of medieval and early modern life. At a very basic and obvious level, enclosure transformed the landscape, whether it did so in a particular locality as a single event or over a period of centuries. General enclosure changed not just the shape of the fields but the roads and often the farm locations. Appointed enclosure commissioners thus had a huge range of powers to replan not just the fields but the whole pattern of subjective experience of farming and living on the land. Chapman (1993) has pointed out how little scholarly attention has hitherto been paid to the men who replanned whole landscapes under both Parliamentary and earlier enclosure.

Alan Pred has explored how enclosure transformed in a radical and complete way the subjective experience of landscape in southern Sweden. Here enclosure was often very sudden and across the whole landscape. Pred stresses the restructuring of 'daily paths and projects' of peasants before and after enclosure (Pred 1985: 138–64). In England, where enclosure was a more gradual process when considered within any region as a whole, the more wholesale forms of enclosure nevertheless transformed the everyday, popular experience of landscape very suddenly. It created new forms of social and cultural boundedness. It did so in several different but overlapping ways that are important to distinguish.

First, enclosure went hand in hand with a cultural redefinition of the land. Like the hedges and ditches that bounded it, the land was similarly a resource rich in cultural meaning rather than a morally neutral resource to be exploited. The land was a wilderness to be tamed and brought into cultivation; as such, it was a challenge to 'Man', part of Man's moral duty. In many early modern accounts of agrarian practice and ideals the land was gendered; it was represented in early modern texts and iconography as both female and disorderly. Man's task was in these accounts to order Nature, to make her fruitful and to force her to yield and deliver up her fruits (Merchant 1980: 41 and 128–32).

One way of redefining the land and its boundaries at a literate level was to redefine a series of key words ranging across the domain of cultivation of the land – 'landscape', 'country', 'husbandry', 'terraculture', and so on. 'The cultivated landscape was becoming a key metaphor, and more than a metaphor, in the intersecting realms of national, religious, and individual identity: the indivisibility of political and legal state, physical environment, and social community is captured in the richly ambiguous word country, which, by the sixteenth century had come to mean all three' (Leslie and Raylor 1992: 3). New ways of thinking about cultivation therefore had social and political resonance, just as innovation in science and technology had (Webster 1975: these points are discussed below and in chapter 8).

Macrae (1992) has traced the seventeenth-century battle over the meaning of these words within literate culture, relating it to struggles over control of the land itself. Popular culture had its own terms and means of renegotiating meanings of land and its cultivation. Reay has termed these means 'dramaturgical', outside the bounds of literate culture. They included actions like beating the bounds of the parish, and paralleled actions in other spheres of community life such as charivaris (Reay 1985b: 8). In this sense the observation that we must place the history of enclosure within the context of changing agricultural practices as a whole can be extended; we must consider the whole range of elite and popular cultural practices spanning both landscape and document, of writing and the land.

Enclosure was thus a cultural field that was intimately related to a redefinition of social relations between people. But it was much more than simply a polarization between rich and poor, a dispossession of the masses. Boundaries did not simply distinguish social classes; they could also mediate the tension between neighbours: 'love your neighbour yet pull not down your hedge', ran a popular early modern proverb (Hill 1993: 131).

If enclosure was not simply symptomatic of a polarization of social classes, neither was it a simple introduction or increase in the number of boundaries. We have seen how the medieval landscape was far from unbounded, how the existence of a complex set of common farming practices was not the same thing as communitarian farming. Each peasant householder had his own strips within the open fields and retained certain carefully defined rights and responsibilities over use of common ground. These rights were, however, often defined by an idea that did not rely on maps, surveys, or any of the 'objective' paraphernalia of literate culture. This concept was commonly termed 'custom' that had existed 'since time out of mind'. Customary practice emerges into the discourses of documentary history through its constant citation within medieval records such as manor court rolls. It is cited as justification or precedent for some activity such as the exercise of common rights; it was 'custom since time out of mind' to gather firewood on this piece of land, or to use that piece for grazing, and so on. The idea of custom was associated with the ideas of community and tradition. It was the community that regulated custom; custom itself defined the community. It did so through acceptance of what had always happened, what was traditional. Further, it was an idea associated with everyday practice and the subjective experience of the landscape rather than with abstract, legal concepts of external observers.

Custom, then, was often implicit, a living environment similar to Bourdieu's idea of 'habitus' (E.P. Thompson 1991: 102). Such a subjective experience has been explored by Keith Thomas in terms of popular conceptions of the natural world (1983), and by E.P. Thompson in terms of popular customs (1991). Research by folklorists into more recent rural communities also gives some hint of what was involved in such a conception (Cameron 1984; Ewart Evans 1966). Annual preambulations around the parish boundaries, for example, were taken by the whole community; 'small boys were sometimes ducked in the ditch or given a clout to imprint the spot upon their memories' (E.P. Thompson 1991: 98).

Subjective experience of this kind is rooted at least partly in the body and its corporeal experience of moving through space. This can be contrasted with the way closure places the eye rather than the body at the centre of space, and thus makes the gaze central to the experience of enclosed space (Lefebvre 1991: 261). Gregory has called this shift the 'victory of decorporealization' and has linked it to the eventual production of abstract space under capitalism (1994: 392).

To summarize then, the ideas, definitions and concepts that we observe as codified physically in the open fields and commons, and codified legally in documents such as manor court rolls, were simultaneously embedded in what we would see in the modern world as different spheres of cultural, legal, and economic practice. The physical and utilitarian practicalities of open-field systems were in this way woven into a seamless web with cultural practices, traditional mentalities, ways of seeing the world. They were governed by social institutions (the manor courts) and complex social mores (the ideas of community and tradition).

The suggestions I am putting forward here resonate with recent thought. I am arguing in parallel with E.P. Thompson's argument that we have to see the development of property law in its historical context to accurately see how ideas of custom interacted with formal legalities (1991: 126–43). His incisive comments on the anachronistic nature of much discussion of sixteenth- and seventeenth-century law suggest that we need to stand back a little and see law, custom and its spatial representation in the landscape in its own terms. We need to reiterate and expand Dodgshon's point concerning the historically specific nature of the pre-capitalist landscape. Dodgshon talks of the need for study of what he calls the 'feudal landscape *sui generis*, one whose principles of order set it apart from earlier or later landscapes'; he asserts that under feudalism, social relations were 'anchored to . . . specific spaces' (1985: 116 and 185). Dodgshon sees this system as being gradually dissolved through the penetration of markets. While not accepting Dodgshon's classification of feudalism or his explanation of its dissolution, he has identified the core of

the problem here. Dodgshon's points are congruent with Glennie's observations on the need for a more substantive account of agrarian change that
I discussed in chapter 2. I suggest further that the process of dissolution of
the open landscape was more complex than this and needs to be specified
in greater depth.

What was new about enclosure? Class inequality and differential power
over the landscape was not new. Medieval institutions and landowners had
often thrown peasants off the land to create sheep farms; Cistercian monasteries had in this respect been just as acquisitive as the most rapacious
Tudor landlord (Dyer 1982). More generally the struggle between landlord and tenant over rent, security of tenure and so on was as old as the
Middle Ages, however much the specific terms and balance of the struggle
might change with economic conditions. Enclosure and associated agrarian
changes sharpened such conflict and increased the scale of desertion and
depopulation, but did not in itself mark a radical, qualitative break with
the past. What did mark a break was the number of landless labourers
created in part by enclosure. The Lay Subsidy Returns of 1524 list between
20 and 30 per cent of the population as labourers; this figure had increased
to 60–70 per cent in the estimate of Gregory King in 1688. Enclosure had,
further, robbed these labourers of the chance to keep livestock; this was the
key change in terms of the economic security of the poor (Shammas 1990:
40–2).

What enclosure did do was to create very new forms of boundaries.
These boundaries that cut across old lines and redeployed power over
the land in new ways. The hedges and ditches shifted power over the land
from the manor and community to the individual household. No longer
was cooperation and consent needed to introduce new farming practices;
no longer was the manor court so central to the continuation and renegotiation of agrarian practice. Power over the land was no longer
embedded in common practices that were closely related to the *habitus*,
to socially embedded ideas of custom and tradition; now it was solely
'Man', or more accurately the owner of the estate, or the gentleman or
yeoman farmer, in direct confrontation with Nature. In this sense we can
see the correspondence of enclosure to changing parameters of political
debate, as seen for example in the form of the agricultural treatise (see
below).

Enclosure was also tied up with a change in the nature of this power over
the land. Ownership had existed in the medieval landscape, but its definition was complex as we have seen; there was no necessary equation
between ownership, access and use rights. Enclosure tended to increase the

correspondence between ownership, access and rights, so that what had been a fragmentary, complex and embedded relationship was now a unified, one-to-one relationship between the farmer and the land. It is perhaps not too fanciful to see enclosure as a sort of cultural Protestant Reformation of the land. Just as the Reformation tried to bring 'Man' into a more direct, personal relationship with 'his' God, away from the mediation of priest and community, so enclosure brought the farmer into direct relationship with the land, away from the mediation of manor and village.

Enclosure was also about the way the farmer came to understand the landscape. It was tied up with changing systems of meaning as much as it was with changing power over the land. Closure brings a different way of signifying meaning, a different relationship between elements of the landscape, the social practices carried out within and constituting that landscape, and the everyday and overt symbolic meanings that landscape carries.

To clarify this point, let us take a planned medieval village. It is divided into tofts and crofts, tenements and street, open fields and commons (figure 2.2). Such a landscape is a functional, economic unit. It is arranged the way it is for good economic, utilitarian reasons: the balance of arable to pasture, the reduction of risk to the individual peasant. It is also and at the same time intensely symbolic. It embeds and reflects the cohesion and self-image of the peasant community. The perceptions of the land as tied up with community is open, overt, for all to see. It has been suggested for example that the laying out of earthworks such as ploughing ridges was a way of imposing the structure of the medieval taxation system directly onto the landscape. More broadly, the cultural and political need to inscribe social organisation on to the land may well have been one reason why medieval peasants shifted such great quantities of earth and thus why a twentieth-century landscape archaeologist is able to 'read' in some detail the medieval landscape today from its earthworks (Wrathmell 1994: 187). So in the medieval, open landscape, a distinction between the layout of the landscape and what the landscape means in fiscal, social and cultural terms was minimal or non-existent.

Enclosure, then, saw a change in the way in which landscape signified social meaning as much as *what* it signified. A landscape archaeologist cannot read social organisation from an enclosed landscape with the same facility; neither could a contemporary observer. The divergence between the two made possible and necessary the production of maps, new forms of document, and different genres of writing about the landscape such as the agricultural treatise. All these new forms were created in the increasingly wide space between the physical form of the landscape and what it meant.

Closure was an emergent process: that is, it must be seen as a long-term unfolding of certain ideas. It was not the conscious project of a particular person or social class. The fifteenth-century farmers exchanging and engrossing strips by agreement in a wood-pasture parish were not trying, consciously or otherwise, to actively create a new form of economic rationality or a new view of the land. Nevertheless such actions were active renegotiations of older forms of accepted values, and depended on subtly changing world-views such as those we have already seen embodied in the term 'credit' (Muldrew 1993). Their actions did also have long-term consequences that the farmers probably did not have in mind. It is this lack of a conscious model of what an ideal landscape should look like at any given point at least in the early and middle stages of the process of closure that makes the examples of Ireland and colonial New England, where wholesale replanning of landscapes was at least attempted, so fascinating.

Closure was also a process whose unfolding varied very widely between different regions and contexts. The earls of Northumberland were still creating planned villages and field systems in the fifteenth century, at a time when some Midlands landlords were already engaged in depopulation and enclosure. At the same moment yeoman farmers in many wood-pasture areas were enclosing piecemeal areas by agreement between themselves. There is a tension here: the particular forms and chronologies of enclosure were extremely diverse, as was noted in the previous chapter. They were also profoundly influenced by antecedent conditions such as the nature of medieval lordship and tenurial conditions in the area, or the nature of settlement layout in the earlier and high medieval periods.

Nevertheless, the long-term process of enclosure was a unifying, centralizing one in several senses. First, similar changes can be seen in very different areas. Second, particularly in the later and more wholesale acts of planned enclosure, a model derived from national resources such as agricultural handbooks and manuals can be seen to be imposed on local vernacular landscapes. Third, the long-term result gave expression to uniform notions of economic rationality that suppressed different regional identities. Fourth, enclosure was bound up with integration within an agrarian system and structure of production geared for an ever-wider regional, national and international market. Put very broadly, the enclosing farmer moved away from production for subsistence and limited local markets. The local and regional cultural identities that went with that shifted in parallel, to be replaced by class and national affiliations.

We have seen that with enclosure, no longer does the symbolic merge with the practical. This is important since the end result of closure is the emergence of categories of thought that we consider modern. In the terms of the literate elite writing from the sixteenth century onwards this includes the creation of the 'social', the 'political' and the 'economic' as separate fields of discourse. This can be seen in the disengagement of the state from economic thought (Appleby 1978), a process to be discussed further below.

One aspect of writing the archaeology of enclosure is its implication for the relation of written history to landscape and archaeological study. This implication is that the source materials for both are historically constituted. To clarify, the way people perceive spaces and objects such as houses, fields, maps and lists will vary between culture and culture, social group and social group. Enclosure, as we shall see, involves new genres of writing, new practices of listing, new ways of expressing meaning through written discourse, new articulations and dispersions between social power, landscape and document. This being the case, any attempt to express in ahistorical terms what the relationship between archaeology and documentary study is or should be without reference to the specific historical context being examined is deeply problematic.

Specifically, I am arguing that the late medieval and early modern periods in England saw a reconfiguration of the relationship between written discourse and material culture. In the Middle Ages, the landscape encoded social practice to the point of identity between these two elements; with enclosure, these two elements diverge and it is increasingly possible to draw a distinction between them in the post-medieval period. Indeed, this distinction was in part actively created through the rise of overt, written discourse about the landscape, its economy, politics and meanings. The debate over enclosure mentioned in the previous chapter was one aspect of the proliferation of writing, whatever the specific views of the commentator on the phenomenon. The material presence of that landscape, and the material culture that went with it, thus changed its nature: from being a carrier of meaning in an embedded way, to one which might be drained of meaning, or that might be more freely reassigned meaning, and in which symbolic meaning and practical usage might actually be opposed. (Thus, of course, making it possible for the modern historian to oppose 'symbolic' and 'practical' interpretations of a given piece of evidence.) Closure also sees the creation of autonomous spheres of discourse in areas which were previously more closely related, again to the point of identity.

If we understand enclosure in these terms, working outwards from the physical redefinition of the land, its boundaries and the social relations embedded in its boundaries, we can see enclosure in a much broader light.

We can put enclosure in its context of contemporary mentalities, under-stand it as part of a very wide process of closure. We can do this by reviewing a series of shifts in related cultural practices, some of which have already been mentioned. It must be borne in mind that these shifts do not 'explain' or 'account for' closure in the sense of providing a set of causes; rather, I suggest that as emergent discourses they may be placed alongside enclosure to help understand more deeply a profound set of transforma-tions in mentality and discourse that all these shifts embody.

I am now going to try to ground these suggestions by looking at different classes of artefacts of medieval and early modern life. My argu-ment is that having understood enclosure as part and parcel of a changing set of cultural attitudes and practices, we may better understand and explore its nature by looking at some of those practices. I shall start by comparing fields with houses – that is, open and enclosed 'agrarian' space with open and enclosed 'domestic' space. I suggest that the transformation of the landscape involved in the process of enclosure can be seen to have certain formal parallels with the transformation of domestic and farmstead space seen over much of England at the same time. I shall then go on to consider how agricultural treatises mediated and gave an ideological gloss on the relationship between land, community and individual.

Closure in Houses

In *Housing Culture: Traditional Architecture in an English Landscape* (Johnson 1993). I examined what I saw as a fundamental transformation in the form and use of traditional rural houses and farmsteads between the fifteenth and eighteenth centuries. To summarize its argument, I argued that the late medieval peasant house in much of England and Wales was centred round a central hall open to the roof (figure 4.1). Over time, the hall lost its importance. It was given a ceiling, reducing its aesthetic effect, and a chimney-stack further reduced its size and removed the central open hearth. At either end of the house different rooms proliferated and in-creased in importance as centres of activity in their own right. The doors to the outside world and stairs to the upper storeys of the house were moved away from the hall. An increased stress on the use of upstairs rooms and more centralizd patterns of circulation within the house generally led to acceptance at both upper and middling social levels of the symmetrical 'Georgian' plans of the eighteenth century. In Georgian houses service and kitchen functions had been relegated to the back of the house and social life

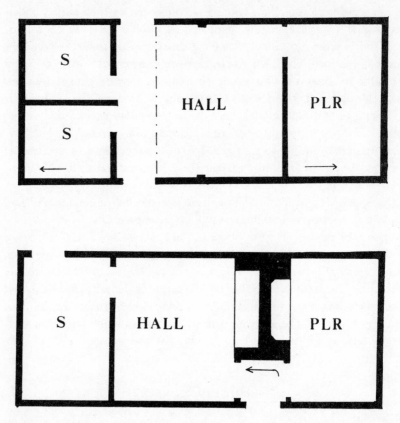

Figure 4.1   Closure in traditional houses (after Johnson 1993: 43). The open-hall house (above) has a central room open to the roof; its key spatial and social divisions are framed around the upper and lower ends of the hall, marked here by the posts supporting the open truss. The seventeenth century 'closed' three-cell lobby-entry house (below) has a smaller, less central hall with ceiling; circulation is now through a lobby with direct access to the upstairs chambers. Social divisions in the closed house are between rather than within rooms.

had moved out of the central hall, with a range of implications for shifting relations of gender and class within the household.

This transformation was more than just a change in the layout of the house. With it came a technical transformation; that is, a parallel change in the way the house was built. The carpentry techniques of the medieval craft tradition gradually gave way to systems that stressed rationality and economic efficiency. At the same time the number of material goods within the house increased, and their form and variation became more complex: there was a shift from the architecture itself towards movable goods as signifiers of social meaning.

Many of the immediate reasons for this set of transformations of the domestic realm may be sought in differing household forms, changing relationships between elements of the household such as master and servant, husband and wife, parent and child. The oft-quoted 'rise of privacy' in the late medieval and early modern periods is thus one symptom of a wider set of changes including the increased stress on the individual, changing patterns of master/servant and husband/wife relationship, and an increased view of the house as commodity and a more commodified view of the household relations within the house (chapter 7 will explore this further).

I suggest that such a long-term transformation of 'domestic' architecture has a series of formal parallels with enclosure of the landscape. We may start by noting similarities between the layout and meaning of space in the medieval open hall and that of the open fields. The open hall was a room that appeared undivided in terms of physical barriers but which was divided conceptually into front and back, upper and lower, high- and low-status ends. Architectural references and markers around the hall (the placing of doors, windows, structural divisions) denoted these areas. As such it 'mapped out' a system of social divisions between different elements of the late medieval household within the same body of space. The hall thus operated as a kind of spatial text, to borrow Henrietta Moore's analogy (1985). It derived its ideological strength and subtlety from being capable of being 'read' in different ways. It asserted the values of household as community, as little commonwealth, as the setting for a family community in a world where servants were considered formally to be part of the family. At the same time it demarcated status differences within that household and combined centralization within the open hall with segregation between the parlour and service ends of the house.

Open fields were usually, as their name implies, undivided in terms of having no hedges and ditches across them (occasionally individuals might fence in their own strips); they did have a 'pale' or fence around the whole. Open fields were nevertheless actually divided into strips, each household farming its own strips or in the case of Midlands systems certain farming practices being done in common. This lack of demarcation could lead to problems in shifting boundaries. Again, in the case of many Midlands field systems, neighbours with adjoining village tenements would have strips of land in the fields adjacent to each other, thus inscribing the social and spatial arrangement of the village in the land.

So an analogous code was at work in both fields and houses. In both, a complex knowledge of space and its customary, embedded meanings was necessary for the observer to be able to 'read' the domestic or agrarian landscape in terms of a set of social and economic relations. Such a code was understood in an analogous way: through the medium of everyday activity. It was as people moved through the hall in the course of their daily lives that its patterning came to appear normal, customary, traditional, along with the social and cultural patterning that went with it. It is the customary and traditional nature of such patterning that makes it so difficult to perceive from documentary evidence. Piers Plowman's complaint that the commensal values of the open hall 'that was made for men to eat in' are being lost, eroded by families dining in private rooms, is notable for its rarity; it is striking that they are articulated only at the point of their dissolution. It was through everyday activity in the fields that the pattern of agrarian social relations reproduced itself: the manor court rolls are full of constant disputes in which appeal is made to tradition, accepted practice, notions of community. These notions, however, are appealed to rather than openly discussed.

The way medieval 'domestic' space was organised, therefore, shows parallels with the constitution of the wider landscape. The processes by which both house and fields were changed also exhibit parallels.

If open fields mapped complex social relations on the ground, the enclosed landscape masked such relations. A contemporary (or a twentieth-century landscape historian for that matter) who knew the code, knew how to 'read' a landscape of open fields arranged around a village, would readily see how they were embedded within medieval social and economic relations. The layout of enclosed fields in a landscape, on the other hand, holds no clues as to their ownership or control. The observer merely sees fields, fields, fields, like so many commodities distributed across the land, interchangeable with one another; as indeed they were interchanged in the act of piecemeal enclosing and engrossing. This or that farm may or may not own this or that piece of land. So whereas medieval society was 'embedded' in the landscape, this embeddedness is lost with enclosure. Fields and social relations can no longer be used as models for each other, at least not without the explication of a guide.

So it was with traditional houses. As the open hall declined in importance, the layout of houses became rationalized, divided according to function. Layout became less a matter of marking social relations within a body of space to be negotiated at a face-to-face level. It became more a matter of segregating, of providing separate rooms for master and servant, or between the world of work and the 'domestic' world. As it did so the meanings of particular spatial elements could be more readily changed; one room in a symmetrical house looked very much the same as the next, the decor and movable goods within those rooms marking their function and relative social position (see chapter 7).

The end of this process saw the eighteenth century 'Georgian' house, with symmetrical identical rooms functionally demarcated, parlour and bedroom of master and wife absolutely separated from 'back' and 'down' space of servant, and with 'male' activities separated from 'female'. The Georgian farmhouse often sat isolated, away from the nucleated village, its site frequently determined by the straight lines drawn by the enclosure commissioners.

Like fields, the interpretation of houses becomes less transparent from the position of the outside observer. It is possible to 'read' the outside of a medieval hall, to judge from the position of the cross-passage and window where, internally, social elements such as lower and upper ends are placed; it is impossible to do so for the symmetrical façade of a Georgian house (figure 9.1).

I suggest therefore that the genealogy of closure in houses and enclosure in fields must be seen in part as a common one. Both closure and enclosure can be seen superficially as a 'rational' process or as a symptom of 'progress'. Enclosed land was generally reckoned more productive than land held in common, both by contemporary commentators (see below) and by most modern economic historians. The prevalence of enclosed fields is seen as one index of 'progress' or 'backwardness' in agriculture, to be set alongside other 'improvements'. Similarly, the changes in house plan have frequently been seen as governed solely by the dictates of comfort and convenience, of domestic improvement; the smaller hall with ceiling and fireplace is warmer and more congenial than the cold, draughty open hall; private rooms satisfy a 'natural' desire for privacy and add to domestic comfort. However, both are, as I have argued, symptomatic of deeper and more fundamental changes in the perception of household and landscape, changes that must be understood in their cultural context.

A consideration of the changing physical layout of houses and fields might therefore suggest that the domestic and agrarian realms were not so separate in the mentality of past worlds as they are today. Such an observation derives support from what we know of attitudes to Nature during this period, which were actively discussed, debated and transformed through the rise of a specific literary genre that appears to have been widely read at gentry and yeoman levels: the agricultural treatise.

Agricultural treatises generally consisted of advice to socially upper and middling farmers on how to run their households and farms. This advice was usually in the form of direct address to the head of household, who was invariably assumed to be male. As is usual with such classes of literature, it is not clear just how far down the social scale they are read and studied. It is similarly unclear how far we are looking at advice that was actively followed or merely a series of homilies that were more often than not honoured in the breach. They were certainly popular, many being printed and reprinted many times (see below).

The picture early treatises paint is of a male gentry and yeoman farmer of sixteenth century England who saw household and farm as part of a continuum which stretched outwards from Man. The task of 'husbandry', as expressed in early treatises on the subject, was good management of all that was within this compass.

An early example of such a treatise is Thomas Tusser's *Five Hundred Points of Good Husbandry*, first published in 1586. *Five Hundred Points* was certainly widely read among the upper and middling sections of society; it ran to multiple editions within a few years and was frequently plagiarized. *Five Hundred Points* was written in rhyming verse, considered by most modern commentators to be poor in quality. Its purpose was to dispense advice on 'good husbandry'. It was addressed to the socially middling farmer and included advice on the treatment of one's wife, family and servants, tips on agricultural practice such as manuring and a host of other matters. Supplementary poems, some of which were added in later editions, included a homily advocating the virtues of 'several' or enclosed land over those of land held in common. Tusser also followed up his success by adding a parallel advice on 'huswifery', the female domain of household management.

This embeddedness in the pre-modern patriarchal mentality of how to govern affairs of family, household and agriculture is perhaps only to be expected. As feminists have pointed out, the notion of the domestic sphere as a 'non-productive' one is an active creation of the later seventeenth century onwards (Amussen 1988). The pre-industrial household was, as with peasant households around the world, 'charged with production', whether that production be for the market or for domestic consumption; household relations were immediately political and economic as well as cultural in nature. The sixteenth-century farmstead in a typical area of mixed farming produced much of its own grain, butter and cheese; larger households brewed their own beer. The immediate question asked by men and women below upper social levels of potential marriage partners was very direct. After the material and spiritual considerations of love and the marriage portion offered by the woman's family, the main criteria were the ability to work hard and maintain the household (Wrightson 1982: 83–4). The farmhouse was thus as much a centre of economy as a domestic setting.

The household was also a political setting. All its members, including servants, were included in the concept of the family; it was a little commonwealth, a little state, as we saw in chapter 2. Thus, the physical setting of the house framed a model of community within which political authority was structured and dispersed as did the open or enclosed fields with regard to that of the village.

Turning to the open fields, we have already seen that contemporary debate saw enclosure as much as a moral and political issue as an economic one. The early concern with the depopulation associated with enclosure had clear moral parameters, as the wording of the preamble to the general Statute of 1489 indicates:

> Great inconveniences daily doth increase by desolation and pulling down and wilfull waste of houses and Towns within this . . . realm, and laying to pasture lands which customarily have been used in tillage, whereby idleness – ground and beginning of all mischiefs – daily doth increase . . . the husbandry . . . is greatly decayed; churches destroyed; the service of God withdrawn; the bodies there buried not prayed for; the patron and curate wronged; the defence of this land against our enemies outwards feebled and impaired; to the great displeasure of God, to the subversion of the policy and good rule of this land (cited in Beresford 1954: 105).

Later sixteenth- and seventeenth-century writings, whether in the form of agricultural treatises, legislation or moral/religious tracts, dealt more specifically with enclosure as opposed to depopulation and the shift from tillage to pasture dealt with in the 1489 Act, but they did so within a continuing moral purpose and framework.

Many contemporary discussions of enclosure looked to the Bible as a source of authority, drawing conflicting lessons that have recently been summarized and explored by Christopher Hill. In the Old Testament fences were symbols of property, and thus of political order; 'a hedge in the field is as necessary in its kind as government in the church or commonwealth', argued the Reverend Joseph Lee in 1656; on the other hand, the radical Traherne associated 'hedges, ditches, limits, bounds' with the Fall. For Puritans the hedge separated the godly church from chaos and disorder: the church is 'planted with a hedge or wall of separation from the world. When God's people neglect to maintain that hedge . . . God hath made his garden a wilderness, as at this day' (Hill 1993: 131, 135, and 140–1).

For Fanshawe, moral, political and landscape order and hierarchy between and within the human and animal worlds were indistinguishable:

> Before the Earth was held in severall
> Twas one great field where all the creatures fedd.
> As in a Common (therefore termed the All)
> Men mixt with beasts together in one shedd
> Upon the ground did take a homely bedd:
> Things were not sorted yet, for then there was
> No Groves where shady trees were billetted,
> Nor grass distinguisht from the corne, butt grass
> And corne and shady trees were shuffled in one Masse.
>   (Fanshawe, *The Progresse of Learning*)

I am not arguing here that all people saw enclosure in the same way, or that all people made identical linkages between the realms of the agrarian, the household and the paternalistic structure of the 'commonwealth' as a whole. Indeed, one of the pleasures of doing historical archaeology in periods such as that of early modern England is that documents do not simply record one dominant discourse; they record debate and dissension, even the views of subordinated or marginal groups on occasion. I am arguing, however, that a recurrent feature of late medieval and early modern mentalities was the lack of modern distinctions between the domestic, the agricultural and the political. This lack of modern distinctions is what we stumble across when we try as archaeologists to 'decode' the organization of open fields and puzzle over the complex and embedded nature: we see that they embed the everyday practices of farming within the social and cultural parameters of the village community, and in the way the open house embeds patterns of household life around a patriarchal ordering of space.

Another way of putting this argument is that patterns of space within the house and the fields both acted as part of the same landscape, albeit at different scales. We have seen with early modern thought, and as recent theorists within the diverse fields of human geography (Gregory 1994; Baker and Biger 1992) and literature (Turner 1979) have argued, that landscapes are not purely physical; they are humanly and mentally constructed, and are at least in part ideological; men and women transform landscapes physically and mentally through different mentalities, different 'ways of seeing'. Further, landscapes are changed by people as an active process, to encapsulate ideas, to actively 'make sense of' the world and in so doing transform it. An extreme example of such a process to which we will return is that of the Palladian landscape, which though a cultural construction involved the physical restructuring of whole regions (Cosgrove 1993). Chapter 8 will consider the general movement of emparkment in such a light. But what happens at such obvious and overt levels happens also at the level of the everyday.

Towards an Archaeology of Closure

The first practice is the rise of 'rational' methods of farming, in the broadest sense. In a direct and obvious way these went with the physical process of enclosure: it was perceived by contemporaries that 'several' land was more productive, whether or not this was actually the case in practice. We have seen that long-term gains from some of the Fenland drainage schemes are problematic to assess. Other advice given within guides to such improving practices as manuring was clearly 'pre-rational' in nature; Hill in *The Gardener's Labyrinth*, published in 1577, advises farmers to dung when the moon was waning and when the wind blew out of the west (Woodward 1990: 257). Thomas Tusser, to take another example, compares different field systems and attributes differences in productivity to the greater convenience of 'several' land. The examples he uses, however, suggest that he is in part confusing field type with quality of soil (thus he compares west with south-east Norfolk). In County Durham, pastoral land appears to have been more highly valued than was 'objectively' warranted before 1650 (Hodgson 1979).

If early agricultural treatises show the embeddedness of agricultural and social relations within their structure as discussed above, they can also be seen as containing the seeds of the dissolution of this embeddedness. Their very existence and growing popularity can be seen to be linked to 'rational' improvement in farming and estate management (figure 4.2). Tribe has charted the discursive development of this form of advice to householders, and some of its problems as a source of evidence have been mentioned above. A genealogy of such advice can be traced back to medieval books on household and estate management as well as to Classical models (Tribe 1978: 53). Written before the printing press was invented, these books were mainly for the benefit of large high-status households and were frequently written by clerics. Nevertheless they defined certain aspects of a tradition, in a way analogous to that identified by Foucault in relation to

Figure 4.2   Frontispiece to an agricultural treatise: Blagrave's *The Epitome of the Whole Art of Husbandry* (1675). Reproduced by Courtesy of The Wellcome Centre Medical Photographic Library.

certain aspects of bodily discipline and control of time in medieval monasteries (1979: 149–50).

Further back, classical models for the running of estates can be found in Cato, Varro and other authors, who many early modern writers used consciously as models for the genre and self-consciously referred to Classical writers for legitimation (Woodward 1990: 254; Fussell 1972). Part of the marked shift in elite attitudes to the land can be traced to the influence of these Classical writers. Joan Thirsk (1992) has shown how the models of such authors prompted a shift in the self-image of many late sixteenth-century gentry landowners, who were encouraged by the image of the Roman villa and its landowner to take an active interest in the land, to pursue estate management and improvement rather than merely viewing it as a source of income. Hence, in part, the market for agricultural treatises and the continuing interest in enclosure and improvement into the seventeenth century.

Tusser's treatise as discussed above showed the 'husbandman' as a solitary figure who through hard work and diligence can tame the land and reap its fruits (Tribe 1978: 60). A marked silence in the text therefore is the landlord/tenant relation. Such relations did appear in other genres such as legal and political discussions of the concept of the manor (in Norden's *Surveior's Dialogue* of 1618 for example). However, Tusser's implied audience, the farmer dealing directly with the land, one of the artefacts of enclosure, is already with us. Nevertheless, in terms of the activity of husbandry, it is not till the early eighteenth century that a different conception of farming is expressed in these books.

Whatever their content, what is interesting about such treatises from an archaeological perspective is their existence and dissemination. For the first time, therefore, the farmer had a book of advice on standard methods of farming. The way that advice was set out, and its underlying cultural parameters, might betray in part a continuing medieval system of values, but its presence and use marks a significant break. Farming practices could now be modelled after a national pattern rather than according to regional practice and custom. They could be discussed with reference to the 'rational' language and order of books rather than purely assigned to custom and tradition. Farmers could read about agricultural innovations rather than hearing about different practices by word of mouth or observing them directly. In all these senses the circulation and archaeology of these books is a more important symptom of closure than, perhaps, what they actually say in terms of practical advice.

What the treatises said nevertheless underwent a profound transformation between the sixteenth and eighteenth centuries. Later eighteenth-century treatises included little reference to Classical authority (Woodward 1990: 259). Instead they stressed rationality, experiment, systematic observation. By 1770 Arthur Young was talking of the need for 'systematised experience' in agriculture (Tribe 1978: 69); by this he meant an accumulation of systematic knowledge from experiment and observation. Macrae (1992) has traced how the values underpinning such a system were victorious in a seventeenth-century battle over the meaning and political structure of agrarian practice, towards a stress on the individual within a free market economy and away from the traditional institutions of manor and community.

The core idea, though, of systematized experience had already been achieved: the dissemination of handbooks giving standardized instructions on how to farm. Early agricultural treatises, then, look both forwards and backwards. They express a mentality that embodies many of the features of pre-capitalist thought. At the same time, their place in a network of expanding knowledge is a key one in the genealogy of closure.

Writing the Landscape, Mapping the Land

Closure as described above goes hand in hand with the changing perceptions of space within the feudal/capitalist transition as described by Lefebvre (1991). Lefebvre links together the production of perspectival space through the 'geometricisation of knowledge', and the constitution of the rational human individual at the centre of the lines of perspective in Renaissance art. The transition in perception of space that Lefebvre, and following him Cosgrove (1985) and Gregory (1994), is describing here is very much an urban and polite transition in the way space is perceived. Lefebvre contrasts, for example, the symbolic space of the urban cathedral with the way perspective and façade are established in polite architecture.

One aspect of closure hinted at above is an imposition of 'polite' concepts and ideas onto the 'vernacular'. One artefact of this imposition is the large-scale topographical map. Maps, as Donald Wood (1993) has so lucidly demonstrated, are never purely objective statements of record: they serve certain interests, embody certain forms of power. In the early modern period, the interests served by maps were complex; like the agricultural treatise, the genealogy of the map is embedded in a complex web of economic, political and cultural relations (Harley 1988; 1992). Similarly, the significance of the map lies both in its form – what it says – and also in its mere presence – the explosion of surveying and mapmaking after 1500 (figure 4.3).

Maps before 1500 were rare. Most of the key technical innovations in surveying and mapmaking were made on the Continent and imported to Britain during the sixteenth century. In the course of the later sixteenth

Figure 4.3 Norden's map of Hertfordshire, published from 1593–8. In the text published with the map Norden addressed himself to 'gentlemen well affected to this travaille': he accompanied his map with an explanation of how to use the scale and the marginal figres and letters, discussion of place-names, lists of markets and fairs, towns, villages and great houses.

century, the map of the township, parish or locality became a common possession of the rural gentry, being listed with increasing frequency in household inventories along with landscape and portrait paintings: 'maps in general, scale-maps in particular, stopped being restricted to particular . . . purposes and started to become familiar objects of everyday life' (Harvey 1993: 48). I suggest that the significance of local maps in particular is that they again find a space in the widening gap between the landscape and what it means. The early modern map provided its owner with a key to understanding the land; it inscribed property ownership onto the landscape. As we have seen, such an inscription was provided by the subjective experience of the open fields in medieval landscapes.

It is interesting to note that just as husbandry manuals include discussions of the household, so early accounts of surveying practice include discussions of the manor. Rathborne in *The Surveyor*, published in 1616, includes in his practical account of surveying techniques a long account and definition of the institution of the manor, stressing the legitimating centrality of 'long continuance'. Norden in *The Surveior's Dialogue* of 1618 defines the manor in both physical, legal and moral terms: 'a manor in substance is of lands, wood, meddow, pasture, and arable; it is compounded of demeisns and services of long continuance' (cited in Kerridge 1969: 17).

Hints that the surveyor was seen by ordinary farmers as an enemy are also found in Norden. Norden's dialogue suggests that farmers saw the surveyor as an 'upstart not found out of late', a creature of the landlord whose aim was to find an excuse to extract more rent (Richeson 1966: 93). The use of maps for a variety of purposes within the local community continued to expand in the seventeenth century, though this was not a period of great technical innovation. General enclosure by agreement usually required an accurate survey of some kind to ensure the parity of all parties, and the maps commissioned as a result are often our best record of such transactions.

Along with new ways of mapping the landscape came new ways of writing about it. Topographic description, antiquarian writings, various forms of prose and poetry were all new genres of writing, like agricultural treatises, often deriving authority from reference to Classical writings, concerned with depicting landscape in new ways. Turner has explored the evolution of the concept of the land, noting that in the mid-sixteenth century, prose descriptions of landscape were jumbled and disorganized. In the early seventeenth-century, prose and poetry describe landscape in a new, more organized form. Turner notes parallels with the way in which landscape art developed at this time: anomalous and perverse elements of landscape were excluded, systems of scale and shadow introduced, a unity created. At the same time, landscape prose and poetry becomes more sensitive to relation of parts (Turner 1979: 10–35). The culmination of this trend is Denham's famous landscape poem *Cooper's Hill*, in which the view from the hill is structured by the text into a political allegory. The poet's movement of gaze across the Thames Valley to London turns a landscape into a complex political commentary on events of the English Revolution: 'The littleness of the City (in geometrical perspective) suggests its pettiness. The mist of aerial perspective corresponds to the malignant fog of Puritan business, and the romantic horror of the ruin-piece to political thuggery' (Turner 1979: 55).

Colonial Wilderness

As closure unfolded, so the view of the world beyond, the chaos and disorder beyond the hedge, sharpened. Charles Cotton was expressing the general attitude of literate culture when he wrote about a Derbyshire landscape beyond Chatsworth that is now considered one of England's most beautiful national parks: the ornate, ordered house and park are:

> Environ'd round with Natures Shames and Ills
> Black Heaths, wild Rocks, bleak Craggs, and naked Hills,
> And the whole Prospect so informe, and rude? . . .
> And such a face the new-born Nature took,
> When out of Chaos by the Fiat strook.
> (Cotton, in Hunt and Willis 1975: 95)

The seventeenth century saw the opening of two areas in which the farmer came face to face with what was perceived by the colonist as savage, howling, chaotic, unenclosed wilderness: New England and Ireland. The Puritan colonists in seventeenth-century New England constructed their own narrative of settlement on the landscape they confronted upon arrival. The colonists were, in their world-view, up against the natural state of land after the Fall, a land that was barren, desert, a wilderness. In fact New England's 'Desart Wilderness' was a narrative constructed from the 1630s onwards by various writers in order to stress the godly labours of Puritans, whose settlement thus became an act of imposing godly order onto a howling, hideous, heathen and dismal desert. Enclosure of fields was here part and parcel of converting the heathen: 'the Pilgrim Fathers intended to bring the heathen from their spiritual wilderness into the Christian civilisation of hard work and respectable clothing' (Bowden 1992: 6); it was a parallel process to taming the waste.

The plantation of Ulster and Munster was predicted to be just as difficult a process, the Irish being 'little better in their ways than the most remote Indians' (cited in Hill 1993: 135–6). In America the natives had, it was argued, no fences, and therefore no settled agriculture or civilized arts in general (Cronon 1983). In Ireland, the terms of justification were couched in the same terms. To the Elizabethans, the Irish were 'Tartarian';

that is, they were not settled and had no fences. (In fact, they did have boundaries termed 'balliboes': Andrews 1970: 179.)

It is in these colonial contexts, where the English settlers tended to perceive if not actively construct a *tabula rasa* whatever the reality, that we see the unfolding of closure in terms of whole areas of planned landscape. Robert Blair St George has traced how this was redeployed in terms of house and farmstead form in a variety of colonial contexts ranging from Ireland to New England (1990).

Maps again played a key defining role in this process: Andrews has commented that 'the planning of wholesale colonisation brought the state into a cartographic field . . . that had previously been reserved for private enterprise' (1970: 185). Irish resistance in the late sixteenth century was overcome by the disciplinary techniques of the English State as much as military repression: it was smothered in a morass of maps, accounts, and the other accoutrements of Tudor administration. Early Tudor maps of Ireland are sparse and stress the names of regional magnates, great lords. By the late sixteenth century a swathe of regional maps had been made up; in 1603 Bartlett published his *Generalle Description of Ireland*. Andrews's memorable comment needs no gloss: 'Bartlett, beheaded by the natives before reaching Donegal, died in the knowledge that he had reached the last frontier of regional cartography' (1970: 181).

Before the sixteenth century, medieval strategy in Ireland was as it had been in the Welsh Marches: to set down and extend a network of towns and castles along the main valleys and communication routes. This strategy changed in the sixteenth century. There was first a shift to a pattern of frontiers and forts before the introduction of civil colonies in the late sixteenth century. The Governor of Ireland proposed that the new plan-tation of Munster be walled in and provided with a geometric network of seven towns, seven bridges and seven castles, a strategy that leant on cartography. He also proudly announced that his shiring of Ulster in 1585 was based on uniform geometric principles. This of course was not actually the case.

As colonialism in Ireland moved into the wholesale plantation of com-munities in Ulster and Munster in the early seventeenth century, so closure unfolded with wider and more all-embracing schemes for replanning of the landscape (Robinson 1983; Canny 1986). After 1603 the state attempted to move away from reliance on the old lords, though again resistance hampered this process (O'Dowd 1988).

It is too simplistic to see closure in colonial contexts as a straightforward deployment of a new set of values. It is striking that as in thirteenth-century Wales, traditional medieval systems of manor, town and lordship were laid out. A traditional system of manorial control was set up in Ulster, while control over the Dutch settlers in New York was attempted by carving the area up into units of 'manors' with traditional rights, for example to hold courts leet and civil. It is striking nevertheless that the replanning of New York colony was done without introducing common fields or practices, and that the boundaries laid out were invariably straight. The planning of settlements in Ulster involved a variety of grid and linear plans. It was only partly successful; the native Irish continued to build traditional dwellings that outnumbered 'English' houses despite injunctions to the contrary, and the prevailing pattern of settlement continued to be dispersed rather than nucleated (Blades 1986: 266).

Conclusion

I have tried to explore some of the different dimensions of an archaeology of closure in this chapter. Two final qualifications must be made. First, regional differences militate against the drawing of an archaeology of closure in any but the most general terms. Specific contexts must be explored on their own terms before drawing out wider implications. Indeed, it is in these particular discussions that we get the most fascinating insights into closure: particular persons or communities acting out particular ideas that are in themselves creative renegotiations of wider concepts.

These local, particular differences were also in part conditioned by historical antecedents. The history of enclosure in the Midlands, for example, unfolded as it did in part because certain forms of open-field system had been created and sustained there since the earlier Middle Ages. The explanation of the presence of such forms in such areas is a matter for the early medieval historian. Conversely the creation of many field boundaries in wood-pasture areas is a matter for the Romanist. England was and is an old landscape, and this ancient nature intertwined with new forces in different ways in different localities. Thus, in the champion fields of the Midlands, closure hit weaker settlements selectively, resulting in depopulation; the bulk of settlements remained at least partially unenclosed till after 1750. Late eighteenth- and early nineteenth-century enclosure involved the erection of large farms in the outer areas and abandonment and dispersal of the main settlement. In areas of wood-pasture Suffolk, the broader outlines of settlement remained largely unchanged till the late seventeenth and eighteenth centuries, when settlements were actually swollen by the erection of numbers of labourers' cottages (Johnson 1993: 152).

Second, I want to repeat that I am not suggesting a 'new explanation' for enclosure; rather, I want to draw attention to its cultural parameters, and stress how enclosure must be placed back into the context of social and cultural life. If this is done a series of exciting and important insights can be developed, and an archaeology of closure can stand as a metaphor for a whole series of spatial changes and associated transformations in pre-industrial England. The succeeding chapters will in part expand this metaphor, and look at other, related spheres of landscape and community.

5

Ordering the World

This chapter is about the archaeology of documents. Medieval and post-medieval archaeologists often display a set of neuroses towards the use of documentary 'evidence'. Documents are often treated with excessive reverence, as a factual skeleton on which to pin 'speculation' about material culture; or alternatively documents are treated as the dusty preserve of a cripplingly narrow, limited discipline of traditional history, to be avoided if at all possible. In this chapter, I want to argue that archaeologists can look at documents in more interesting ways. I want to look at a series of cases – an old man writing about his parish, a yeoman ordering the probate records for his dead neighbour – where we can look at the structure of the document, rather than its use as a source of information about past events, to throw light on the changing mental structure of early modern England. They will build on and extend the observations on enclosure made in the previous two chapters. These examples will draw extensively on the work of social and cultural historians, though the archaeological perspective I want to use is partly new.

I shall argue in conclusion for an archaeology of pre-industrial landscape and culture that does not make an a priori distinction between physical and mental landscapes, that does not draw a disciplinary divide between these two fields but merely sees them as manifestations of different kinds of social practice – of people acting, making and writing things. Documents and artefacts may thus be viewed and related one to another in new kinds of ways.

Ordering a Parish

Myddle parish is whoaly in the hundred of Pimhill, in the county of Salop. Nevertheless part of the said parish is in the allotment of Myddle and

Loppington, and part of it is in the libertyes of Shrewsbury. That part of the parish which is in the allotment of Myddle and Loppington contains Myddle Lordship, and the town and township of Balderton, and is commonly called this side of the parish . . . That part of the parish which lies in the Libertyes of Shrewsbury, contains Hadnalls Ease, the town and township of Alderton and Shotton Farme, and is called the further side of the parish . . . It is not very needful to observe, that according to the computation of geographers, the middle of this parish is distant northwards from the world's Equator 52 deg. 53 min., and is in longitude from the meridian of the Isles Azores or Fortunate Islands 21 deg. 37 min. (Gough, in Hey 1981: 29).

The *History of Myddle* is a document dating to 1700 and immediately after. It was written by Richard Gough, a resident of Myddle parish; it was not intended for general publication, and appears to have been written for a local audience. The *History* was not mentioned in his will. It was only published over a century after his death, in 1834.

The document has two parts. The first, *Antiquities and Memoyres of the Parish of Myddle*, from which the above quotation is taken, is a fairly unexceptional example of an emergent genre of writing on the subject of local topography, society and antiquities. The second, *Observations concerning the Seates in Myddle and the familyes to which they belong*, is more unusual in its form. It consists of the histories of all the families in Myddle, and is ordered according to where they sat in the church pews.

Richard Gough's life serves in many ways as a microcosm of some of the themes mentioned in the last few chapters. Gough was born in 1635 as one of eight children, of whom four survived. His education included a knowledge of Latin and the Classical authors. Gough acted as servant for six years to Robin Corbett, one of the members of the ruling gentry families of Shropshire; subsequently he was employed in various clerical tasks for Corbett, one of which was 'to measure the lands and draw writings of the exchange' when Balderton open field was enclosed (Hey 1981: 281). His official tasks included serving on the Shropshire Grand Jury, at Quarter Sessions, as churchwarden, and as witness to wills and other probate records. When Gough died in 1723, he was described as a gentleman in the parish register recording his death. In his will, however, he described himself as a yeoman. He had visited London at least once, as had his neighbours, and he kept in touch with what was going on in the capital through 'the Gazet' and 'our News letters' (Hey 1981: 165 and 205).

The *History of Myddle* draws on a variety of sources, and stands at a critical point in the development of the topographic description of a piece of landscape as a discursive form. Gough used numerous citations of law books in his work, and his possession of a number of 'English and divinity books' is referred to in his will. The text is further peppered with citations from the writings of Classical authors, sometimes inaccurate, apparently quoted from memory without reference to a source. These citations are used in a summative way to point up the moral of a particular story.

Gough had read William Camden, whose *Brittania*, the famous sixteenth-century topographical and antiquarian description of Britain, had recently come out in a new edition; he refers to Camden as 'that famous Antiquary' (Hey 1981: 266); so the idea of writing about the past and relating that past to extant landscape was not new. The discussion of prehistory as legitimation of a national past, in England as in other European countries, was a standard genre at least one and a half centuries old (Ferguson 1993). A relatively new development was the writing of more detailed local topographical descriptions, accounts of particular localities such as counties combining a description of local families with landscape and antiquarian features. Gough does not however refer to more recent writers of county and local histories such as Dugdale and Pratt, of which several had recently been published; Reyce's 1618 *Breviary of Suffolk* was not generally known at this period (Hervey 1902). Gough also does not intend to publish his account; and also includes an apparently unrelated final section of religious meditations. Gough appears to have been an orthodox Anglican of 'moderate' views.

Gough draws boundaries around and between the members of the community he knew in a distinctive way. Perhaps surprisingly, his descriptions of people's characters and village relations make little mention of degrees of social rank and distinction in the normative way that we might have expected after the survey of social ranks given in chapter 3. Such an overt delineation by rank was followed by other writers; Reyce for example, almost a century earlier, who in his observations on Suffolk gives comments on an ascending social scale of Poore, Husbandmen, Yeomanry, Townes-Man, Gentleman, and Knights (Hervey 1902: 56–61).

Gough's perception of gender does appear to centre on the familar stereotypes of drunken husbands and often unruly wives. Elizabeth Bickley 'was accounted a lewd woman, and had several daughters who had no better a repute'; Thomas Hayward 'had little quietnesse att home which caused him to frequent publick houses merely for his naturall sustenance, and there meeting with company and being generally well beloved hee stayed often too long . . . This Thomas Hayward sold and consumed all his

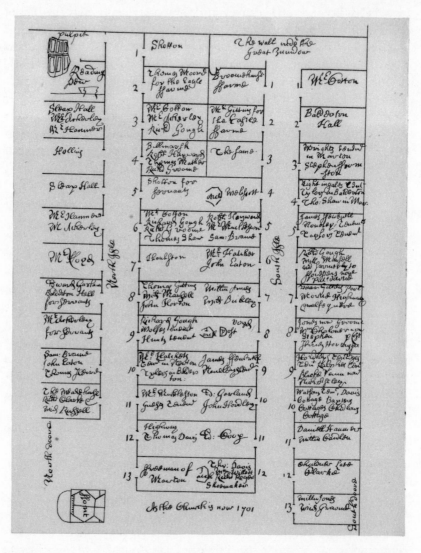

Figure 5.1 Richard Gough's map of the pews in the parish church at Myddle, Shropshire, 'as the Church is now 1701'. Gough has omitted the chancel from his plan, which is above the pulpit on this plan. Gough also gave a plan entitled 'As the Church was anciently', showing a different arrangement of pews but without owners and an elaborate 'partition between the chancell Church'. Taken from R. Gough, *History of Myddle* (1875), Bodleian Library.

estate and was afterwards mainetained on charyty by his eldest son' (Hey 1981: 180 and 195).

Instead of describing degrees of people directly, Gough drew his social and cultural boundaries, ordered the parish of Myddle socially and topographically, by reference to seating position in church. Gough made a plan drawing of the pews in the parish church of St Peter, writing in the names of different occupants' and then discussed each pew in turn (figure 5.1). The *History* also delineates the social and cultural order more subtly by implicit reference to position within the physical and cultural landscape.

Ordering the Church

A Peiw is a certain place in church incompassed with wainscott, or some other thing, for several persons to sitt in togeather . . . And a peiw may belong whoaly to one family or it may belong to two or three famileiys or more. The disposall of Seates in the body of the Church des beelong to the ordinary, and noe man can claime a right to a seate without prescription or some other good reason . . . A peiw or seat does not belong to a person or to land, but to an house . . . A seat, or the priority in a seat, may be claimed by prescription, at common Law . . . If a man sell a dwelling-house with the appurtenances, the seate in church passes by the word appurtenances (Gough, in Hey 1981: 77).

Gough gives for his readers two plans, the church as Myddle 'as it was anciently' and as it was in 1701 (figure 5.1). These plans, and the layout of the church they represent, can be seen as one means of formal codification of the social structure of Myddle parish.

This structure was one of hierarchical social ranking based on seating priority. The chief families of the parish sat at the front; the lesser in varying degrees to the rear. The last pew 'is a small seat att the South dore of Myddle Church. It was made by Evan Jones . . . of some waste planks and boards that were a spare att the uniformeing of the peiws . . . hee was servant to Mr. Gittins of Myddle' (Hey 1981: 247–8). In some churches, though apparently not at Myddle, seating was gendered, men and women being segregated on different sides of the church (Yates 1991: 37).

The appearance of formal order conceals an ambiguity in Gough's text around the formal basis of seating priority within the church pews. The introduction to his discussion is cited above, where Gough indicates that particular pews are attached to particular 'houses' or farmsteads. Despite this simple assertion, at later points in the text assignation of pews is also assigned on the basis of other factors: to the rank or status of a family, to level of rent, or to social order in a general sense.

Organization and layout of pews was a matter of dispute between the (usually) male heads of families, resolved by parish courts and officials and often governed by apparent consensus. Thus for example one pew near the pulpit was open to general use: Gough's 'father, who was thick of hearing, did sit in them'. A typical case of dispute was that between 'John Downton, of Alderton, and William Formeston, about the right of kneeling in the sixth pew on the south side of the north isle, and John Downton putt a locke on the pew doore, butt William Formeston . . . giveing the pew dorre a suddaine plucke, broake off the locke'. A parish meeting was held to settle this along with other matters, for 'it was held a thing unseemly and undecent that a company of young boyes, and of persons that paid noe [church-rates], shoyult sitt . . . above those of the best of the parish' (Hey 1981: 117). Gough's account therefore starts with formal legal definitions, but goes on in practice to merge the criteria of ability to pay church-rates, social standing, and historic priority of certain houses.

The ambiguities and tensions in Gough's account thus make sense within a larger picture of the way space was viewed within the parish church, a shift that was actively renegotiated in the course of the seventeenth-century. Upton (1986) and Isaac (1983) have pointed the way forward in seeing the church as a stage, an arena for the playing-out and renegotiation of tightly structured relations, in the context of eighteenth-century Virginian society. Many of their comments find resonance in cultural historians' descriptions of community and parish in seventeenth-century England (Wrightson 1982: 39–65; Underdown 1985). Gough's perception of change fits in with an account of the restructuring of architectural authority in the church.

The fabric of Myddle church, like most churches in rural parishes in England, was at least several centuries old by 1700. The church had been founded before the Norman Conquest, though no trace above ground now survives from this period. The medieval nave and chancel were replaced in the nineteenth century; the tower was rebuilt in 1634 after the collapse of the steeple. Like many such seventeenth-century provincial buildings, the rebuilding of the tower was in traditional Gothic style rather than in Classical. The community of Myddle thus assembled on Sundays within a space that was several centuries old.

Though the church had existed for centuries, it had been changed

radically in terms both of its layout and in terms of the cultural meanings
it carried. Gough comments on parish churches in general, repeating the
'tradition, that there was no peiws in Churches before the Reformation'
before qualifying it. His perception here is interesting since in fact pews
had been common in parish churches in many regions of England since the
later Middle Ages. He suggests that 'at first there was onely three rows of
Seates in Myddle Church'. The church was then furnished in part with
wainscotted pews, 'and after, all the rest was furnished with formes' (Hey
1981: 77 and 78). At the same time a new pulpit, communion table, and
communion rails were laid out.

Such changes in church seating were not untypical of changes in
ordinary sixteenth- and seventeenth-century parish churches across
England. In churches which had seats in late medieval private chapels,
the seats were often rearranged. Early seats were often in the form of
open benches; many churches had replaced these with more private, segregated box pews by the seventeenth century. These changes had very
complex meanings, and contemporaries related them to landscape and
social change as a whole. To take one example among many, Edward
Burrough, a Quaker, saw church pews as similar to enclosed fields, with
'lined stalls for the rich, with a lock and key to keep the poor out' (Reay
1985b: 37).

Gough's discussion straddles many of these meanings. It tends to merge
in practice the different criteria of ability to pay church-rates, social
standing, and historic priority of certain houses. It has been suggested that
this period saw a shift from criteria of social standing towards that of
wealth through the renting of pews; this shift is far from clear from
Gough's picture. It may well have been a shift that occurred in most parish
churches subsequent to 1701. The eighteenth century certainly saw more
privacy and segregation in the layout of the church, with more 'parlour
pews' with chairs, tables, fireplace, often entered through a private door
(Yates 1991: 37–40).

What did these changes in the layout and internal furnishings of the
church, as related by Gough and understood by us in the context of
developments in church architecture and furniture as a whole, mean? How
did they fit in to the pattern of social and cultural order in Myddle as a
whole? Anthropologists of ritual such as Victor Turner have often viewed
changes in the ritual sphere in part as a 'periodic restatement of the terms
in which men [sic] of a particular culture must interact if there is to be any
kind of a coherent social life' (1968: 6). The layout, appearance, decoration
and symbolism of a church can therefore be viewed as a statement about

community that is complex in form and interpretation. It can be seen as a commentary on perceptions of cultural order, on the terms of the everyday, the profane and the material. Such a commentary might be a subtle one, and might involve ambiguity and a possible diversity of readings by different observers. Gough's view of the space within the church as laid out above is one example of a diversity of early modern views about the content of religion, and its relationship with secular life. These could be moulded and remoulded at least partly through architectural references.

Such a social resonance to Church doctrine and its physical expression in the church was all the more important in a community where religious observance was congruent with social order. The Church of England was 'established'; the parish community paid for the church through tithes and church rents. Since the Reformation, the monarch and the head of the Church of England were (and remain) the same person. Ordinary parishioners, in kneeling towards the altar, could not fail to make an association between it and the royal coat of arms commonly painted over the chancel arch. Attendance of all members of the parish at church on Sundays was at least formally compulsory, non-attendance being punishable by fines. It was not till after the mid seventeenth century that Dissenting congregations reached any number or enjoyed limited toleration. Offences against public morality, including blasphemy and disrespect to priest and God, were punishable in the church courts. The parish church was used as a weapon of political authority, royal proclamations being read from the pulpit. 'People are governed by the pulpit more than the sword in times of peace', Charles I told his son (cited in Hill 1964: 38). The Church was thus immediately locked into political and cultural struggles.

Space in late medieval churches was again, like the domestic and agrarian landscape, reflective of the medieval community. Space within churches was divided into nave and chancel (figure 5.2), the upkeep of the nave being the responsibility of the parish, the chancel that of the priest. This division was symbolically reinforced in a number of ways. Late medieval rood screens ran across this division, obscuring the congregation's view of the Mass and increasing its mystery. Pews were introduced in the nave. Liturgy prescribed the priest's movement between the altar and congregation, the position and orientation of the priest's body becoming a complex symbolic field (Graves 1989).

There were profound changes in later medieval liturgies, and much rebuilding and refurnishing of parish churches, reflecting many of the newly wealthy in, for example, the cloth-producing communities. The later fifteenth and early sixteenth centuries saw churches in cloth-produc-

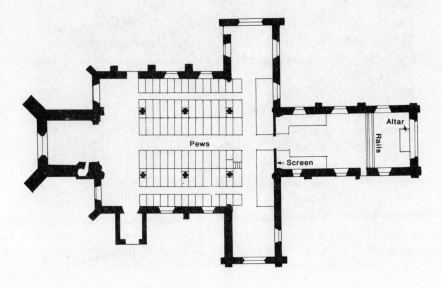

Figure 5.2   A parish church: Sedgefield in County Durham, showing position of rood
screen, pews and altar rails (after Addleshaw and Etchells 1948).

ing centres like Lavenham being rebuilt on a lavish scale, often too large for
the congregations that used them. Pulpits were also introduced in increasing numbers, reflecting the growing popularity of sermons among the
middling sort, and with them seating for the congregation.

The Edwardian Reformation of the 1540s and 1550s and the subsequent settlement under Elizabeth marked a profound shift in the way
churches were laid out and furnished. Whether these changes were driven
by political priorities from the top or in part by genuine popular pressure,
they had deep consequences for the way people worshipped and saw their
relationship with God and 'Man'. The late medieval church communicated
to a largely illiterate congregation through depictions; many had graphic
images of Hell and Purgatory on the walls, and depictions of saints and
other images on screens and in the stained glass of windows.

Many of these images had been smashed or obliterated by the agents of
the Reformation. This wave of iconoclasm that swept the parish churches
may have been fuelled by the desire for loot, but in the long term it may
have acted to transform the religious experience of ordinary people. Images
of the saints were prohibited, and depictions of Hell whitewashed over,

Figure 5.3 The royal coat of arms above the chancel arch at Brancepeth Church, County Durham. Sedgefield and Brancepeth were two churches refitted in the seventeenth century that were not heavily altered by the Victorians.

removing one source of information in a largely illiterate age. Instead churches were whitewashed, and walls were often covered with texts such as the Ten Commandments. Above the chancel arch the medieval images of Hell and Purgatory were replaced with the Royal coat of arms (figure 5.3). Below the arch, the pulpit represented a new stress on the spoken word, while the rood screen was removed and the altar often brought into the nave. Ordinary people were no longer to be terrified by superstitious pictures and encouraged to supplicate to saints; now they were to more actively understand the service, to be more closely instructed and monitored in religious observance. This instruction came from the State, which specified in 1566 that 'rood-screens to remain but all above the beam, the loft and the figure of Our Christ with Our Lady and St John, to be removed and replaced by the Royal Arms. The communion-table was to be placed against the east wall of the chancel . . . and the Ten Commandments were to be set up over the table' (Yates 1991: 31; Phillips 1973).

Closer instruction and monitoring of religious observance went hand in hand with other forms of discipline within the church. Regular visitations to parish churches from agents of diocesan courts were organized to ensure that instructions had been carried out; these instructions covered not just images and ceremonies, but disorderly behaviour within the church, disputes over pews, and parish matters such as the keeping of order in alehouses, accusations of witchcraft and so on (Purvis 1948).

The religious and political meanings of these changes are too complex to be explored fully here. What is clear, however, is that the post-Reformation parish church was a battleground of conflicting ideologies which offers to archaeologists a fascinating picture of people renegotiating space and its meanings. At the overt level, Puritanism and Arminianism prescribed very different relations between altar, priest and congregation; both these political parties within the Church were linked to conflicting views of the world, views that were much more than purely religious dogma; and these views were explicitly played out through the spatial organization of thousands of parish churches up and down the land. Impetus for change often came from the State, attempting to impose its will on localities through a network of centrally appointed diocesan courts and committees, inspecting and reforming local practices. But reform could be popular as well as driven by the State. One of the most common charges against clergy during the purges of the English Revolution of the 1640s was that they had complied 'too readily' with the restoration of rails and other divisions between altar and congregation. Thus for example the parishioners of Stratford St Mary in Suffolk complained of their rector's opposition to Parliament in the English Revolution, noting in the same breath that 'the commmunion table was sett alter wise within the railes, which did occasion many of the parish to withdrawe themselves & not receive the Sacrament'; their fellow parishioners in nearby Blakenham complained also of their rector's 'zeale for the bringing in of Innovations' and that 'contrary to his parishioners' knowledge & consent, sett men to work to make & sett upp rayles, rayse the ground in the Chancell three steps high, paint the Church, [and] bought a hood & surplice' (Holmes 1970: 37 and 40). Differing altar arrangements thus corresponded to differing political and religious positions before and during the English Revolution and were explicitly recognized as such by the participants. Such arrangements however did refer to deeper conflicts in changing power relations in parish communities even if these surfaced only implicitly (Underdown 1985: 78).

It is interesting to note in this context the changing architecture of Dissenting chapels after the middle of the seventeenth century. These became more austere and secular in appearance (Williamson and Bellamy 1986: 188; Snell 1986), while the parish church, having lost many of the elements of conflict pulling it apart in the earlier seventeenth century, became a less controversial arena for the laying-out of unequal social relations.

One powerful implication of this discussion of ritual space is that ordinary people were aware of many of the changes going on around them. The space and fabric of Myddle Church, and the ambiguities and tensions in Gough's account of it, are a complex and sophisticated statement on religion, society and politics in the early modern period.

Myddle Parish

Like the church, the locality that Gough wrote about embodied many of the changes already discussed. The history of Myddle parish in the two centuries before Gough was writing has been admirably surveyed by David Hey (1974) in a classic local study of its kind, drawing together Gough's account and relating it to parish and other local records. In addition, some of the houses described by Gough have been located and surveyed, yielding interesting conclusions on the nature and permanence of ordinary housing in one seventeenth-century parish (Moran 1989).

We are thus able to ask: how does Gough use the plan of the church as a template for the ordering of the parish? This part of Shropshire was 160 miles from London. It was a wood-pasture landscape, mostly of hamlets and isolated dwellings: Gough himself lived a mile from the church. As indicated above, Gough indicates Myddle's position on the globe, though its position within England as a whole close to the Welsh border and relative to London is not mentioned. The bounds of the parish are listed by brooks in the fashion of early charters.

The layout of the parish is discussed with reference to a variety of practices. The popular custom of beating the bounds is not mentioned in the primary definition of the parish, though it is mentioned in a specific case of dispute over Bilmarsh Green, which was 'much controverted . . . all that I can say is, that when the Inhabitants of Myddle parish doe walk their boundaryes, they take theire small common whoally within their bounds; and when the parishioners of Broughton doe walk theire boundaries, they take it, and a little croft that lyes between it and the barne at Billmarsh within their bounds' (Hey 1981: 63–4). The use of 'they' implies that Gough probably did not accompany other parishioners on this perambulation, and may not have identified with the custom.

The social structure of Myddle was grouped around 12 gentry farms, the fortunes of whose occupants form the core of Gough's account, their narratives being told in detail; naturally, those seated furthest forward in the church were given priority in the text. There were also almost 50 middling 'tenements' of yeomen or husbandmen.

Myddle was mostly enclosed by 1700. As in most wood-pasture communities, this was mostly piecemeal activity, though disputes did occur. One instance from Myddle has already been cited in chapter 3. The servant Evan Jones engaged in a typical piece of encroachment, apparently without opposition: he 'built a lytle hut upon Myddle Wood near the Clay lake, att the higher end of the towne and incloased a piece out of the Common. This lytle hut was afterwards burnt, and haveing a collection made in the parish and neighbourhood hee built a pretty good house' (Hey 1981: 247–8).

Gough frames his account around a community that was coming under increasing stress. Larger numbers of vagrants and landless labourers were entering the parish. Against this Gough's landscape is one of formal legal precedent backed by extensive research; he comments that 'I have seen the antient deeds of most freeholders in this Lordship' (Hey 1981: 48). Oral tradition is repeatedly cited as legitimate evidence, however, with little sign of distrust.

Gough's landscape is an old one, with critical comments on the views of Camden, a detailed description of the ruins of the now destroyed castle, and extensive and to our eyes protracted discussion on legal precedent. It is also a landscape in which social order is articulated and embedded within the church, whose order is related outwards to the landscape as a whole. At the same time, as a text written by a socially middling, literate man, with only incidental reference to popular customs and a desire to formally codify many of the elements of the landscape, the *History of Myddle* stands at the centre of a series of threads in the history of landscape change in early modern England.

Ordering the House

Figure 5.4 is a photograph of an example of one of the most common classes of historical document used by archaeologists, the probate inventory. It is easy to see how the inventory can act as a rich source of information on household objects, the domestic interior, household and farming activities, and so on. Many studies have used inventories in precisely this manner, and much of the subject matter of chapters 7 and 8

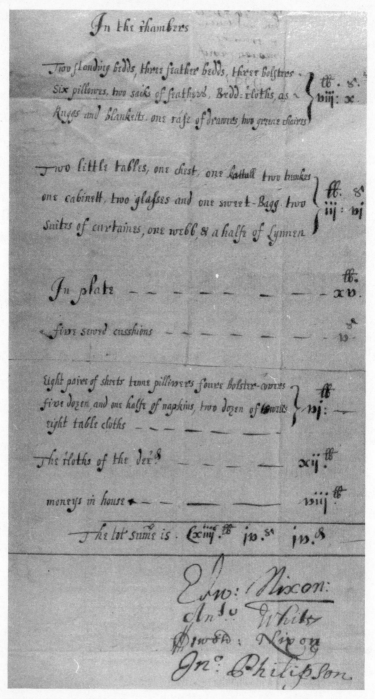

Figure 5.4   The second page of the inventory of John Simpson of Newcastle upon Tyne 1666. Durham University Library, Archives and Special Collections. Durham Probate Records. Inventories such as these were drawn up at a householder's death.

is derived from this source. The purpose of this section is to consider inventories not as a source but as an artefact; to understand the way the inventory divides, disperses, reorders the early modern world.

What do inventories constitute as a form of discourse, a way of speaking about the world? Inventories are lists of things. Documents of this kind dealing with domestic possessions have a long genealogy stretching back to the accounts and inventories of royal and noble households in the middle ages. But why draw up a document of household goods for socially middling groups in this manner? Traditional historians are full of proximal reasons that do not really get to the heart of the matter, such as: consistory courts needed to have an inventory to 'prove' or legally affirm a will. But why did they need this?, and why was this need so apparent from the middle of the sixteenth century onwards?

One way to see the inventory and associated probate records, wills and probate accounts, are as artefacts of a new form of administration and, therefore, of power. Ultimately it is necessary to remember that inventories were part of an explosion of administrative and financial documents of all kinds from the middle of the sixteenth century onwards. They were made possible, then, through the same mechanisms that enforced the changes that the Reformation brought to the parish church: the rise of the Tudor state, with its powerful bureaucratic machinery extending through secular and religious channels out and down to the regions. The form of power that they embodied was one tied to new codes of behaviour for non-elite groups, new religious ideas, a new sense of individual, household and community discipline.

This new sense of discipline was partly one that dovetailed with new forces of cultural and political centralization. The drawing up and court approval of inventories were practices that had been ordained by legislation at a national level. They were enforced through county, church and other local courts, by officers drawn from the ranks of the local gentry, clergy, and increasingly also the 'middling sort', who thus in many ways became the officers of their own discipline. Distinctive regional customs and practices in drawing up inventories nevertheless survived in many areas, such as that of the Diocese of York (Watson 1989).

The practice of listing things, we have noted, goes back to the Middle Ages, but this form of close monitoring of possessions and the way they are deployed in space is very new at this social level. In some ways, then, the internal composition of the inventory reflects the rise of the middling classes in terms of material affluence during the later sixteenth and seventeenth-centuries.

It also reflects the rise and incorporation of the middling sort into the political body, or more accurately that body of 'men' or householders whom contemporaries considered constitutive of 'government'. Socially middling male householders were exhorted and wheedled by moralists and political commentators to new forms of behaviour and support for the existing social structure. Advice books frequently written by social superiors gave instruction on husbandry, discipline in the household, marital relations, even sexual behaviour. At the same time the governmental structure, through inventories, was ordering socially middling households in new ways. It sorted, listed and classified its material possessions, usually room by room; it codified the deceased's wealth and gave a formal, authoritative stamp to the deceased's will. Just as church courts appointed local agents to do their will in rooting out local superstitions and imposing a uniform national pattern, so they appointed men of good credit to take the inventory and to countersign the document.

The inventory thus reflects a new will to discipline at a household level on the part of the administrative machinery of the time. It also reflects a new attitude to space. The inventory is one way among several that goods are separated, commodified, placed in discrete settings, given a fixed cash valuation; it is possible to interpret this as a shift away from medieval ideas of the social embeddedness of property and property relations to more privatized, capitalistic ones. More fundamentally, movable goods are seen as important. The inventory records movable property but not real estate; this leads to all sorts of problems in determining individuals' wealth from their inventories (cf. Spufford 1990: 150–60). Movable goods define what a room is, what its function is, in a way that is very different from the fixed architectural features of the medieval hall. So the inventory represents a new kind of monitoring at middling social levels: monitoring of space and of goods within that space.

Who are the actors in an inventory, who is acted upon? The names of the appraisers are given, men of good credit and standing in the community. So is that of the deceased, the householder, usually male. Those who are silent, who are not present, are the widow, the servants and children, though some historians have seen their presence in goods that for one reason or another seem to have mysteriously disappeared from the house between the death and the taking of the inventory. (The widow in particular is usually mentioned in the associated will and probate account, but usually only as object, recipient of goods and bequests, rather than subject.) So the inventory encodes many of the values, the formal mentality, of the age: that of patriarchy. It does so through ambiguity, through reduction of those not covered by the term 'Man' into silence.

Property and inheritance law in pre-industrial England is a very complex topic; its interrelation with gender relations has been explored by Amy Erickson. Common law 'doctrines of coverture in marriage and primogeniture in inheritance' (1993: 5) concealed a more complex demographic reality in which only 60 per cent of marriages produced a son and in which a variety of legal practices could be mobilized to gain and protect a woman's property rights at different stages in her life cycle.

Women did occasionally leave wills, and these wills have been interpreted by some in terms of women's agency (Amussen 1988). An exceptional artefact that shows the interaction of women's agency and the patriarchal structure is that of Margaret Lane, a noblewoman who drew up her own will in 1562. The male secretary whose responsibility it was to transcribe such wills into official records usually decorated the transcriptions with heraldic marginalia stressing the antiquity and nobility of the family concerned. Here, however, he chose to comment on Lane's behaviour by drawing a series of unnatural and deformed babies and animals as a commentary on such an offence against the natural order of things (Prior 1990).

So the inventory, as part of the structure of probate records in general, is patriarchal: women are rendered silent, made into objects. At the same time this is what the architecture of the sixteenth-century house does. The central hall is both public space and an arena for the playing-out of unequal social relationships. Women, servants, children are rendered 'silent' by the architecture. Medieval technical systems and patterns of space reflected values of social relations: the architecture lost these values as the seventeenth century progressed.

What I have tried to do is to show how, internally, both archaeology and documentary evidence can be used as a form of discourse, and how questions about how that form is changing in material and mental terms can help produce deeper understandings of the archaeology of capitalism. Foucault used a distinctive metaphor for this (1972: 7): he suggested that archaeologists turn monuments into documents. In other words, we take material things and translate them into writings about the past. Historians on the other hand should make monuments out of documents. That is, they should attend to the physicality of their sources, they ask how such massive piles of paper as we find in record offices came to be produced. A contextual linking of monuments and documents can yield profound observations on the changing nature of space, the emergence of new forms of landscape, the emergence of processes of commodification of the land and of objects, the rise of particular forms of discipline. Archaeology should thus take up what Foucault sees as history's primary task:

> not the interpretation of the document, not the attempt to decide whether it is telling the truth or what is its expressive value, but to work on it from within and so develop it; history now organises the document, divides it up, distributes it, orders it, arranges it in levels, establishes series, distinguishes between what is relevant and what is not, discovers elements, defines unities, describes relations (Foucault 1972: 6–7).

Ordering Space: Maps

Such a model of argument can be used for a whole series of classes of documents that deal with administrative, ecclesiastical and financial matters. To take another example, we can consider the archaeology of maps. As we have seen maps are a key source in the writing of the history of enclosure and agrarian change; as a source they are usually used, again, by referring to external events. A common technique is to line up a series of maps, charting the changes from one 'time-slice' to another; the first map in such a sequence can be examined for traces of earlier landscape. Again, such an approach is a fruitful one, but needs to be complemented by a questioning of the internal discourse of maps. Like inventories, maps are monuments, artefacts of the very change they act as 'sources' for. Why are there so few medieval maps at the parish or township level? Why the explosion, again from the sixteenth century onwards? Again, proximal reasons may be sought in the rise of surveying as a profession and the development of new techniques of land survey; but this is merely to restate the question in different terms.

Maps and the attendant rise in surveying techniques that they embody, I would argue, again tell us about changing discursive forms. The very fact that a map can be seen as encoding objective knowledge about a landscape is a transformation away from medieval mentalities. In the medieval view of the world, everyday social practices are embedded in the countryside; the open fields are both a way of organizing economic activity and at the same time an expression of the values of the community. With such an embeddedness of social values within the landscape, the idea of creating an objective record of how the physical landscape is constituted independently of the social landscape. So the origins of maps lie in the changing nature of power over the land.

From the sixteenth century onwards we see an increase in numbers of maps, at a range of levels. Those drawn up for larger landowners would often be accompanied by heraldic marginalia, thus juxtaposing symbols of the real or fictive ancestry of the family with their power over the land. At a wider level, the sixteenth and seventeenth centuries saw the production of maps of the nation-states and of the Old and New Worlds.

Maps do not simply depend on the development of new techniques of surveying, though these in themselves embody many of the changes under discussion. Such maps require a concept of perspective and proportion. Such concepts were derived in proximal terms from the influence of the Italian Renaissance on northern Europe, and can be seen in the different spheres of art and architecture as well as in mapping. Again, we must ask why it was that increasing numbers of upper and middling people wanted these maps at this time. In this sense the demand for maps derived ultimately from the shift in the understanding of space, from space as subjectively experienced as a locale of social relations to space as objectively measured as a form of commodity. This was true in several senses. Those drawn up for taxation purposes, such as tithe maps, or for enclosure proposals had an obvious and direct relationship to changing power over the land. But at the same time it marked a new way of annotating the relationship between land and finance, away from the feudal terminology of bovates and furlongs to that of land as a measurable commodity existing in Cartesian space. Maps embody this shift at a range of spatial levels, from the depiction of small communities to the ordering of colonial conquest. They render unnecessary and are opposed to subjective folk experience of the landscape, through for example stories and myths (Simpson 1986), or popular terminology as revealed in place-names (Thomas 1983).

Reordering space went hand in hand with reordering time. The rise in the genre of landscape pictures, for example, can be linked to the surge in antiquarian writing in the eighteenth century (Wilks 1980: 60). Enclosure carved the landscape up physically; maps carved up space mentally; time was also being ordered, systematized, divided in new ways. All these processes were closely related and embedded in new conceptions of the nation-state (Bender 1994a: 260–2) and are linked to new conceptions of time in the work of Camden, Llhuyd and others in the British topographical tradition. So time was being segmented in new ways and linked to 'rational' studies of artefacts whose position and forms were precisely mapped in the landscape.

It is clear that the origins of British archaeology itself lie within this process. Early antiquarians linked topographical observation, new surveying and mapping techniques, and new senses of local and national identity among the literate gentry. Again, the writings of early modern antiquarian scholars had philosophical aims of ordering the world itself: Browne's *Hydrotaphia* published in 1658 linked the discovery of ancient burial urns in Norfolk with a meditation on death, contrasting the solidity of the urns with the difficulty of assigning even a date to them let alone a set of beliefs (Robbins 1972).

Ordering People

Fields were enclosed, maps were drawn up, texts written; new forms of financial and administrative documents were created. There is an explosion of documentation from the mid-sixteenth century onwards. Many of these forms had medieval antecedents, most famously Domesday Book but also in the Poll Tax and Lay Subsidy Returns, but were new in scale, detail and implications for administrative organisation. Traditional historians have seen the impetus for this in the administrative policy of Henry VIII and his ministers; one can see more broadly the increasing power of a bureaucratic State and its perceived need to pry into the 'dark corners of the land'. Also, there is the increased importance of physical property as commodity and hence the need to list and tax it in ever more detailed manners.

More fundamentally there is an associated imposition by authority at a series of levels – State, Church, county courts, down to household heads – of spatial and temporal discipline. The outward forms of that discipline have a long genealogy going back to the Roman period, but its particular form in early modern states and communities is clearly linked to the structural needs of nascent capitalism. It is true that many of these disciplinary techniques were introduced as part of a series of short-term responses to crises such as food riots, but its long-term implications and retention demand a deeper explanation (Sharp 1980: 43).

As the stress on discipline was sharpened and its forms multiplied in the later sixteenth and early seventeenth centuries, so did perception and fear of the object of that discipline. There were monsters lurking at the edge of the early modern world of order; monsters whose nature and terrifying form reflect back on the changing nature of the early modern social order: disorderly women, servants, the unruly mob, the growing numbers of vagrants, the labouring or idle poor (Hill 1965).

Such fear was partly of a social kind: 'masterless men'. Beier has discussed how the period 1560–1640 sees a perceived rise of vagrants of various kinds, in particular young men, migrant labourers and beggars who had often been made landless through enclosure and who slipped through the net of the new poor law legislation. The margins also included numbers of gypsies, as well as Irish escaping famine and English plantations at home (Beier 1985: 62–5).

This perception of spatial disorder on the margins of society contributed to and was in turn sharpened by a new system of spatial and social discipline. Again the genealogy of disciplinary practice can be traced back to the later Middle Ages. The examination procedure is first found in a statute of 1383; the practice was extended and 'received its most detailed statutory statements in 1554–5 in the wake of numerous rebellions and consipracies'. Examinations were 'designed to discover [conspiracies against the State] through detailed questioning of suspects about their movements, confederates and haunts'. There were suggestions by seventeenth-century writers and legislators for the creation of houses of labour. Transient vagrants were expected to have valid papers and required to wear 'some notable badge or token'. Regular roundups were organized. When caught, beggars were whipped and often branded to identify repeat offenders. Some were impressed into the Navy or transported to the colonies (Beier 1985: 12–13 and 153–64).

One artefact of this later sixteenth- and early seventeenth-century concern was the bridewell. Its purpose was to reform vagrants through work. Bridewells were segregated by sex and regulated, with regular working hours, diet and dress. At Norwich the prisoners worked from 5.00 a.m. in summer, and from 6.00 to 7.00 or 7.30 p.m. in winter, with half an hour to eat and fifteen minutes to pray. The structure, though much modified, still stands. Bridewells failed through lack of resources, given that 'the number of such vagrant poor . . . will be overlarge for one common receipt, or house of correction, and for the masters, governors of the said houses, to oversee and correct'; they were increasingly used rather as prisons for punishing offenders (Beier 1985, 165–6). Bridewells do not have the physical appearance of vast panoptica as a reading of Foucault might predict: but it has recently been argued that the organization of space in many modern buildings such as asylums has not been governed by panoptic principles also (Philo 1989).

So the growth in documentation that we see is not just a new source of information about the past; it is also an artefact of closure. One presumably unintended consequence of this aspect of closure is that it produced in the late sixteenth and seventeenth centuries such an explosion of documentary material pertaining to the middling and lower orders of society, material that has enabled a different kind of historical anthropology to be written for these periods.

Conclusion: Theorizing Historical Archaeology

The territory of the document-as-artefact is critical to archaeology in the early modern period. It is crucial to understand the rules of discourse governing the production of documents, and to relate those rules of discourse to the material world, if we are to really get to grips with the archaeology of capitalism.

This is a point made for a later period by Thomas Markus in his recent book *Buildings and Power* (1993). Markus deals with a range of modern building types – factories, hospitals, asylums, poorhouses, lecture theatres. He relates the systems of freedom and control that these types embody to the modern ordering of knowledge and the modern system of bodily discipline and moral and mental reformation that industrial society requires.

The reordering of spaces that Markus delineates has its origins in the early modern period. New ways of ordering people, spaces and knowledge were hammered out in the sixteenth and seventeenth centuries; only a few of these lines have been traced above. But these lines are at once both physical and mental, at once the province of both archaeology and history. Indeed it is their interaction and dispersal over both fields that gives new systems of ordering and discipline their power, invests new systems with simultaneous bodily, social and mental control. The archaeology of capitalism thus extends into the structure of the document and demands that it be treated as an artefact.

6

Archaeologies of Authority

Thou art not, Penshurst, built to envious show,
Of touch, or marble; nor canst boast a row
Of polish'd pillars, or a roof of gold:
Thou hast no lantern, whereof tales are told;
Or stair, or courts; but stand'st an ancient pile,
And these grudg'd at, art reverenced the while . . .

(Ben Jonson, 'To Penshurst')

Like fields, the country houses and estates of England are ambiguous symbols, symbolic at once of 'Englishness', heritage, a happier and more ordered past. Like fields, however, their apparent timelessness is belied by the reality of their changing history, the many transformations and ruptures they have undergone. Country houses have had a central position in the structuring of the genealogy of rural capitalism. They have been paid for out of peasants' rents or the revenues of colonial exploitation; an understanding of their form is integral to an understanding of their role as centred on elite authority and power. This chapter will explore the changing physical and mental form of the great house through its archaeology, and the way that form carried different cultural meanings.

Jonson's early seventeenth-century poem 'To Penshurst', whose first six lines are cited above, is one such attempt to explore the cultural meanings of a great house and by implication its owner, Jonson's patron. 'To Penshurst' is a complex poem that deserves to be read carefully and in full by any archaeologist interested in the way buildings are invested with status. The way the poem and its readings do this is too multifaceted to elucidate in full here; Kelsall's masterly discussion serves this purpose in any case (1993: 22–33). The poem is a panegyric based partly on Classical literary models, but the house itself is medieval in origin. Penshurst is dominated by its great hall, at the centre of an organic accretion of medieval and sixteenth-century buildings surmounted by ornamental battlements. The house is at the centre of a working estate, with church close by; the ordering and symbolism of both the architecture and Jonson's poem present the country estate as a 'peaceful organic community' (Kelsall 1993: 33).

Jonson acclaims Penshurst as a place of hospitality, where great lord and humble tenant are united within the great hall. As such 'To Penshurst' has been interpreted by Marxists as a piece of ideology, of misrepresentation; its pre-eminence, and thus that of its owners, is such a natural given that even the fish and fowl of the area willingly give up their lives for consumption in the estate. The family who own Penshurst, and who remain anonymous in the poem, are presented as an old, established dynasty; but in fact the family, the Sydneys, had only acquired the property in 1552. This is certainly the case; the grounds, for example, are divided into 'lower land', 'middle grounds' and the haunts of gods, reflecting and naturalizing the social and spatial divisions in the hall. There is more to the poem than this, however. The poem is also an attack on other members of the ruling elite. Jonson specifically attacks 'envious show' on the part of other great landowners, linking such show with rural oppression. He comments that 'though thy walls be of the country stone, / They're rear'd with no mans ruin, no mans groan', an implicit criticism of the 'proud, ambitious heaps' of other owners.

One of the most striking aspects of the poem is the way it is turned inwards; we shall see below that traditional houses were also built to an inward-looking plan, centred around the internal courtyard. The centre of hospitality is the hall with its hearth and table, 'Where the same beer, and bread, and self-same wine / That is his lordship's, shall be also mine'. In the case of the poem this involves exclusion of less traditional architectural elements as the long gallery, which as a social inferior to the master and mistress of the house Jonson may not have had contact with. The poem also fails to mention the absences of its master, who was required to attend the court in London where political crisis was deepening with increasing frequency.

Poem and house thus stand at a central, critical point in the genealogy of elite architectural authority, looking both forwards and backwards. In the rest of this chapter I want to look at the archaeology of the elite through a consideration of the design and layout of elite residences, putting these in their landscape and cultural context. I shall consider how their layout and symbolism relates to the system of social and cultural power they embody, and how an archaeological perspective might help to relate their physical form to their function as loci of power.

I shall start by exploring some of the ways the medieval house and castle actually worked as a symbol and expression of authority, and how the practices represented by the castle and other medieval high-status architecture went on to be redeployed in sixteenth- and seventeenth-century buildings. I shall be arguing that a very different distribution of practices and meanings was created in this process, a distribution that encoded several of the principles of closure we have already seen. These new practices and meanings created a new kind of elite.

At the same time, I want to look at symbols of authority in their immediate context – the changing way they related to the landscapes around them, the way those landscapes were differently viewed and reordered, and the way that change can tell us about the changing social relationships between elite and mass, landlord and tenant, lord and governed.

The Idea of Hospitality

Traditional houses such as Penshurst (at least in Jonson's conception) and their feudal antecedents were mobilized around the idea of hospitality, a concept recently explored in depth by Felicity Heal (1990). The great hall, in this idea, was the centre of the physical house, the social idea of the household and the moral idea of the community. As with other ideas embedded in custom and tradition, hospitality received its most formal codification when it was under threat. In the sixteenth and seventeenth centuries, hospitality became a formal and explicit code, deriving its values in part from Classical writers. Before these changes at the end of the Middle Ages, however, the hall can be seen as a staged social arena in which the idea of hospitality was played out.

By the fifteenth century, there was a plethora of elaborate ordinances governing social rank in the great house, relating it to seating at table. Hospitality was not simply voluntary; it was also enforced through social pressure, for example through charivari (Heal 1990: 12–13). By this time, however, the ideal was already at variance with everyday practice in many households. Many 'great men' had already withdrawn from the commensality of the hall, and ate privately. In any case, the commensality and community of the great hall were at least partly symbolism rather than everyday practice. Those eating in the hall were often only tenants and neighbours; the poor were served outside, either from scraps collected in the hall and served at the gate or at a serving-hatch in the service end of the house. It is unclear how far such gatherings were for 'men' in the specific sense of the term in any case (Girouard 1978: 28).

It was also an ideal mobilized at specific points in the year rather than necessarily being tied in to everyday practice. Christian and agricultural festivals were times for feasting, as were as funeral wakes. Parallel ceremonies and gift-giving were held between women at the birth of a child (Heal 1990: 80–2). In any case, the medieval household tended to be peripatetic, moving between a series of residences in different locations across the lord's scattered estates.

Such ceremonial hospitality had a political purpose. It was used to reinforce and mobilize the power of great feudal lords through the ties of reciprocity and allegiance. The ceremony of the meal was a playing-out of feudal ties between master and 'man'; visitors would admire the numbers of retainers bustling between hall and kitchens, the vastness of the hall, the stage of the dais, and make inferences about the political power of the owner of the house. The values of hospitality from lord to social inferior were also values of deference to the lord. It is time to look at how these values were expressed and renegotiated architecturally.

The Castle as Symbol, Code and Grammar

The medieval symbol of elite authority par excellence was the castle. Standing above its estate, the keep 'nailing the valley', its sheer presence, weight and architectural density proclaimed its nature as the keystone of the power of the feudal lord. Such a past has again been redeployed at critical moments of redefinition of Englishness. This happened most evocatively with Victorian redefinitions of chivalry and chivalric conduct to suit the ambitions of an Imperial age (Girouard 1981); such images inevitably colour our own perceptions of castles and what they meant to medieval and early modern contemporaries. It may therefore be worth restating some of the central functions of such structures.

Castles were fortified residences of lords. Unfortified houses and palaces were common in the later Middle Ages, and castles were one specialized version of such residences. There was indeed no clear dividing line between 'the castle' and 'the unfortified house', many fortifications being decorative and symbolic in nature (figure 6.3). Many castles were royal, having been built by or fallen into the hands of the king, but most were feudal or privately owned. Lords had the right to keep men-at-arms, and before the fourteenth century many forms of tenure had 'castle-guard' or duties of armed service attached to them. The castle thus had embedded within its physical and mental fabric several ideas.

Castles were firstly military strongpoints. They served as places to gather troops in time of war, and medieval history is littered with accounts of sieges. The *Anglo-Saxon Chronicle* accounted the success of the Normans to their use of castles to subjugate the population. Nevertheless, most castles outside the marches of Wales and Scotland were besieged infrequently – perhaps two or three times in 400 years.

Castles were also symbols of feudal authority. Their placement on summits of hills and at critical points in the landscape had symbolic as well as military purpose. Their position was often superimposed on earlier landscapes. Castles were physical settings for the social life of medieval lordship. Justice was meted out in their halls; the provision of a dungeon was as much to collect prisoners for trial as for later punishment.

We can see, then, that like other medieval features of the landscape, castles were embedded within social practices. The castle functioned as a nexus of consumption, where the large household would consume the agricultural surplus of the surrounding countryside before moving on. Again, therefore, we see the question 'is this aspect of medieval practice military, economic, social or cultural in nature?', raised in previous chapters with reference to agrarian practices, to be a meaningless one. All aspects were embedded one in another. They were not separable as discursive objects.

How was this embedded cluster of functions and meanings mapped out spatially? There is no such thing as a typical castle, though most included the elements of an impressive gatehouse, chapel, and prison. There would be at least one great hall, and frequently two; one for everyday use, and one for use as a place of justice or for major ceremonial occasions. In later medieval castles and palaces there were often separate halls for different social groups within the structure.

Let us take the plan of Kenilworth as it existed in the fourteenth century as an example (figures 6.1 and 6.2). Kenilworth was one of the largest and most famous castles in the country; it had its origins in the early twelfth century. The ovoid form of the Inner Court, though largely of later date, follows the line of the earlier defences. On one side of this bailey, the huge later twelfth-century keep sat on the site of the earthen motte of the earlier castle. Kenilworth was thus already an 'ancient pile', the locus of histories

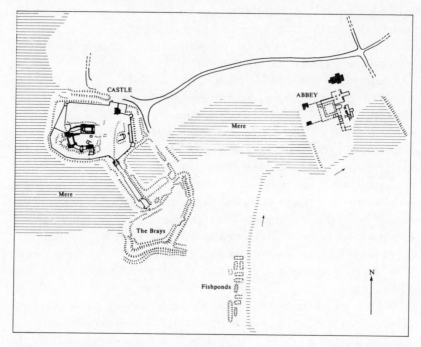

Figure 6.1 The landscape context of Kenilworth Castle, Warwickshire, showing the earthworks retaining the mere (after M.W. Thompson 1991: 6). The southern entrance to the castle is through the Brays and across the causeway. To the west of the mere was the Pleasaunce, a moated, enclosed pleasure garden created in the fifteenth century. When Queen Elizabeth visited in 1575 she was greeted at the Brays Gate in verse before being offered the keys to the castle at the inner gate. As she traversed the causeway, the lady of the lake and two nymphs appeared on an island in the Mere. A poet then welcomed her at the Inner Gate (M.W. Thompson 1991: 30).

and meanings by the later middle ages, in particular of the famous thirteenth-century siege of Simon de Montfort's followers.

The inner bailey was remodelled in the late fourteenth century by John of Gaunt into a huge and luxuriously appointed palace. The Great Hall in particular is a huge example of its type. It is at the centre of a series of nested spaces, surrounded by a huge artificial lake that is kept in place in turn by a series of embankments.

One explanation of such nested spaces is in terms of the provision of successive lines of defence. I do not want to dispute this explanation here, but I do want to illustrate how defensive needs were embedded in the social coding of space. This is best illustrated by considering the subjective

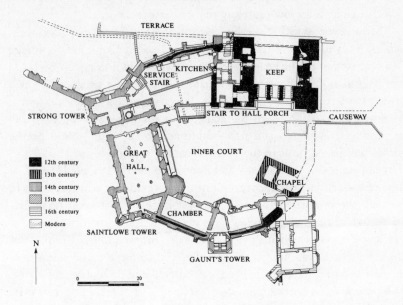

Figure 6.2 The inner ward at Kenilworth (after M.W. Thompson 1991: 9). The sixteenth-century block at the south-eastern corner was added by the Earl of Leicester in the 1570s, with suites of rooms for visitors such as the Queen.

experience of entering Kenilworth rather than by consideration of the plan. The medieval visitor to Kenilworth would pass through a series of spaces. Access to each successive space would be more closely monitored and controlled than the last; the visitor's ability to penetrate each space would be partly determined by his or her social status. The entrance to each space would be marked by symbolic elaboration: often a large gatehouse with several gates, surmounted by heraldic or other kinds of decoration bearing very definite social and symbolic messages.

To pass through Kenilworth Castle from the outside to the most private, intimate, highest status areas is to travel a tortuous route through a series of spaces, each carefully bounded. First, between the twin bastions protecting the outer gateway to the interior of a crescent-shaped space bounded by an earthen bank called The Brays; this had the military function of protecting the dam and sluice that retained the system of pools, lakes and meres around the castle. From this space the visitor would have a view of the main part of the castle across the artificial lake. The visitor would then turn at an angle to the outer gate, and pass across a bridge and gate and along a narrow causeway that ran across the mere.

The causeway ended at the impressive gatehouse of Mortimer's Tower, flanked by twin towers. This gate gave access to the Outer Court, a large area that contained the chapel and other ancillary buildings for the castle such as stables. To gain access to the Inner Court, the visitor would again make a sharp turn, this time to the left, and cross another narrow causeway. As visitors gained access to the court, they would be confronted by an impressive array of old and new buildings. To the right would be the ancient keep, first built in the twelfth century; straight ahead the stair to John of Gaunt's Great Hall, tall and impressive; on the left would be a fine suite of residential apartments. Mounting the grand set of stone stairs to the hall, the visitor would notice the vast kitchens with their huge fire-places and facilities to the right before making yet another turn to enter at the 'lower' end of the hall to view one of the loftiest and most impressive domestic spaces ever built in the Middle Ages; with the raised platform of the dais and high table at its head, carpentered and decorated roof above, lit by a row of elegant windows with stained glass. One distinctive oriel window lit the raised area at the other, upper end of the hall, an area that would also be marked out by physical height and other architectural indicators. This was where the lord would sit at mealtimes; the visitor might well sit at the lower end of the hall. Behind this dais was a private suite of rooms and audience chambers for the lord to which access would be still more restricted.

The layout of Kenilworth Castle worked, then, to impress an idea of many different spaces, each signifying successive social gradations, on the visitor and observer. It did so by manipulating the subjective experiences of moving through its spaces through a series of impressive gates, well guarded by retainers in livery bearing the devices of the lord, through the need for angled turns at critical moments, through movement past already old and ancient buildings like the keep. Militarily knowledgeable observers – in other words, men belonging to the knightly class – would also observe and comment upon the skill of the layout and form of the defences: the spacing of towers, the provision of flanking fire along the curtain wall, the number and strength of portcullises and gates. They would thus indirectly make a comment on the military and knightly prowess of the builder and owner of Kenilworth.

Kenilworth was one of the largest and most important castles of its day, but smaller medieval castles would often also have a series of courts, each nested within the next. At many castles only the inner bailey remains, the outer bailey having housed a village or been encroached upon by urban tenements. There is therefore no such thing as a typical castle, but there are elements of a common grammar in the spatial arrangements of most. To clarify, once one is aware of the main elements of medieval castle design, one can 'read' the layouts of most such buildings quite readily. Like fields, this ability to 'read' the layout of castle or house is true both of the contemporary historian and the medieval person.

Thus, the layout of the fourteenth-century hall and kitchens at Kenilworth was on a huge scale, but its pattern was one that had been and was to be repeated endlessly in castles of all shapes and sizes. This repetition of architectural arrangement is found both in terms of other castles and elite residences, and in terms of buildings all the way down the social scale. Two elements can serve as examples. The entrance was always an area of elaboration where defensive arrangements reinforced the symbolic importance of the threshold. This would be achieved through the use of a pair of flanking towers or by placing the gate within the tower itself; by the end of the middle ages, the gate tower, by this time almost purely symbolic rather than defensive in nature, was more or less standard in buildings of all measure of defensive pretension (figure 6.3).

The layout of the domestic block or blocks within the castle was similarly subject to a more or less standard arrangement. The hall would have upper and lower ends, a raised dais at the upper end, a bay window lighting the dais, private apartments behind the upper end, a buttery and pantry at the lower end, between them a passage leading to the kitchen, and a cross passage or screens passage between hall and service block. Such a pattern can be found with almost all types of residence outside the monastery and for different groups of the elite, from the lesser gentry to royalty, in the later middle ages.

Often there were two or even more such halls, but in such cases the spatial pattern is then repeated. Thus at the fifteenth-century castle at Warkworth (figure 6.4), one of the residences of the great Percy family of the northern marches, there were two halls. One large hall was in the outer bailey; it was originally of twelfth-century date but was substantially remodelled in the fifteenth century, with two internal towers marking separate doors to upper and lower ends. The second hall is smaller, above the cellars of the highly unusual fifteenth-century keep. The keep is laid out on top of an earlier earthen motte, a common enough pattern; but the keep follows a highly unusual overall design that it is difficult to find parallels for. Despite its unusual arrangement at first sight, familiarity with more conventional late medieval layouts enables one to 'read'

Figure 6.3 The gate tower at Oxburgh Hall, Norfolk, built in the late fifteenth-century. After Pugin *Examples of Gothic Architecture* (1838). Courtesy of the University of Durham.

Warkworth keep. Once one locates the hall it follows the by now familiar pattern of being over the cellar, entered at the lower end, and with a buttery, pantry and kitchen beyond the lower end, and private accommodation accessible from the upper end of the hall. Warkworth thus illustrates the proliferation of halls in many castles, and also the way a common code may underlie apparently very different design elements.

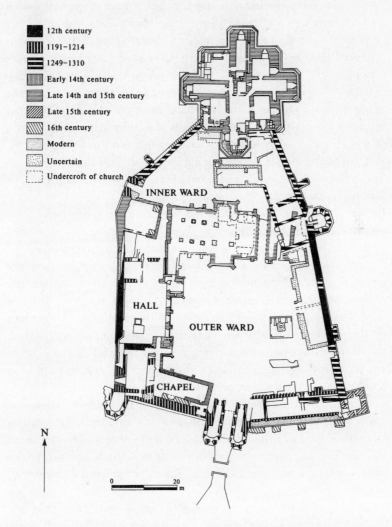

Figure 6.4 Warkworth Castle, Northumberland (after Honeyman and Hunter Blair 1990: 19–20). The form of the fifteenth-century castle follows that of the twelfth century. The keep is of unusual form: it houses a hall, service and chapel in the floors above the cellars. A second hall is in the bailey, with porch and door at the lower end, buttery, pantry and kitchen beyond, and solar and chapel at the upper end. The church was probably never finished.

The power of the code that underlay the constitution of the hall was its repeated use in a much simpler form further down the social scale. We shall explore the use of smaller, less impressive versions of such halls in the next chapter, and similar spatial layouts were used in ordinary peasant dwellings. Austin and Thomas (1989), for example, have explored how such values resting on the deployment of upper and lower space within the hall made medieval peasant houses microcosms of the world-view of their inhabitants. On walking into the great halls of Kenilworth or Warkworth, people of all social degrees would have understood something of the meanings of the grammar of space being deployed. This does not necessarily mean that such meanings would have been overtly articulated, or that they actively subscribed to those meanings.

The overall plan of a castle courtyard often shows little overt concern for symmetry. The way in twists and turns; views are critical at various points, but there is no central overall point of orientation from which to view the logic of the whole structure. Thus at Warkworth the main gate is at the other end of the castle from the high street of the town, though the inhabitants did have a huge piece of heraldry, a carved image of the Percy lion, looking down upon their every move. Within the castle, the modern eye would expect an undisturbed vista from main gate to keep, but an unfinished chapel was placed squarely across this line of view. Late medieval castles such as Bodiam show a great deal of symmetry, but this is in terms of external appearance rather than internal arrangement.

One of the neglected aspects of castle design is the study of the way in which the castle was integrated into the landscape around it. Early castles would be laid out in conjunction with planned villages or towns, as at Warkworth. The late fourteenth-century castle at Bodiam was surrounded by gardens that have only just been recognized and surveyed (Taylor et al. 1990).

Castles derived power from the past. Warkworth keep sits on top of a motte that is centuries earlier, and the overall plan of the castle follows in part the lines of the motte-and-bailey earthwork castle. I suggest that this reuse of earlier features is more than simply blind inertia, conservatism or continuity on the part of later medieval builders. By the later fourteenth century new castles such as Bodiam, Herstmonceux, Bolton and Wressle were being laid out on rectilinear plans with elements of symmetry in their external appearance. Such complete rebuildings as Kenilworth and Warkworth could have followed this pattern with little extra effort.

Castles were stage settings: they, or elements of their architecture, have been compared to theatre. At the castle of Knaresborough in Yorkshire,

Edward II built a new tower for his 'favourite', Piers Gaveston; Phil Dixon
has interpreted the architecture of this tower as an elaborate setting to
show Gaveston off as the King's man in the North, with its fashionable
polygonal form, complex arrangements for entry, and a raised dais for the
master lit by a flood of light from a specially placed window (Dixon 1988:
121–40).

In particular, the castles and great houses of the later Middle Ages
derive power from heraldry. Heraldry was a way of signifying through
images the antiquity and honour of a knightly family, often stressing their
fighting prowess. The use of heraldic devices was a practice that expanded
in complexity and regulation in the fourteenth and fifteenth centuries.
Placed prominently on the livery of retainers, on architecture and other
fittings, heraldry was a complex symbol, indicating affiliation or loyalty to
a lord or patron, as well as the antiquity and illustrious ancestry of that lord
or patron. Heraldic devices used military metaphors (shields and helmets
upon which devices and symbols were placed) and metonymic symbolism
(rebuses, animals).

Castle to Palace

If castles are not the simple, grim fortresses they are sometimes portrayed
as, neither is the development of unfortified palaces and mansions as
straightforward a process of emergent comfort and convenience as it might
at first appear. The first point is that the unfortified house or palace had a
long history stretching back to before the Middle Ages. Crenellation on
buildings such as monastic gates and other clearly unfortified buildings
was used for symbolic purposes (Coulson 1982). In any case, it is a moot
point whether any of the later medieval castles discussed above, or adap-
tations to older castles such as Warkworth and Kenilworth, were ever
seriously defensive in intent. 'Licences to crenellate' giving permission to
fortify one's house were frequently given to such structures and sometimes
cite military need, but it has recently been argued that such a licence was
a status symbol itself rather than of intrinsic importance (Coulson 1993).

The early sixteenth-century palace has often been described as 'conservative' in design. It certainly used elements that had been a familiar feature
of the medieval architectural landscape. The decorative style was late
Gothic (figure 6.5), and the arrangement around a courtyard plan – often
now a double courtyard, with parallel arrangements for the household at
two social levels – was a familiar one from the late fourteenth century

Figure 6.5   Thornbury Castle, Gloucestershire, left unfinished in 1521 after the execution of the Duke of Buckingham. The crenellations are ornamental; the whole is in late Perpendicular Gothic style. Taken from J.H. Parker, *Some Account of Domestic Architecture in England from Richard II to Henry VIII* (1859). Courtesy of the University of Durham.

onwards. Nevertheless I suggest that these features must be seen in terms of deliberate social strategies rather than merely in terms of an untheorized 'conservatism'.

These new houses were the centres for new scales of conspicuous consumption. At Acton Court, Avon, most imported pottery came onto the site specifically for the royal visit of 1535 and was broken or discarded soon after rather than being kept for decades. This pottery included Rhineland stoneware, Iberian tin-glazed wares, as well as tableware from the Low Countries and Italy (Vince and Bell 1992).

A classic instance of very new influences coming in under the cloak of old practices is that of Ightham Mote in Kent. Ightham is a late medieval building, built to the traditional courtyard plan and is surrounded by a moat.

Ightham Mote was remodelled between 1509 and 1528 by Sir Richard Clement. Alterations involved the refronting of much of the older house, and the imposition of a new decorative scheme. This scheme included prominent use of the heraldic badges of Henry VIII and his then wife, Catherine of Aragon; these badges appear on the bargeboards running along the gables facing into the courtyards, as well as in the newly reglazed hall windows and rebuilt hall chapel.

It has been suggested by David Starkey that the ceiling of the newly built chapel is composed of reused timbers from temporary structures erected at that great Tudor celebration of chivalry, the meeting between the kings of England and France at the so-called Field of the Cloth of Gold in 1511. Whatever the case, these symbols certainly referred back to traditional social forms and values. In a direct sense the use of badges was a common late medieval practice: it was 'an heraldic labelling device, by which any object . . . could be marked out as the lord's own' (Starkey 1982: 155). The royal badges decorating Ightham Mote therefore had double signification: they signified the owner's affiliation to his (in this case royal) lord, and they also indicated royal favour and support for that owner. Indirectly, the use of such motifs referred back to a feudal set of values mobilized in the earlier sixteenth century for political purposes. In this particular case, the Tudor kings had outlawed private lords' use of badges and the systems of livery that went with them. Royalty had thus moved towards achieving a monopoly of political power and authority that went with the symbolic practice.

The career of Sir Richard Clement illuminates and provides further detail on these points. Clement was not a member of an established elite family; he worked his way up the social scale through service in the royal household, and then married Anne Whittlebury, a widow with both lands and money. Clement established himself within the county community by buying Ightham Mote in 1521; his success in portraying himself as an established landowner can be seen in his acceptance into Kent society. He was knighted in 1529 and made a Justice of the Peace in 1531 (Starkey 1982: 159). His success was made complete after the death of his first wife in 1528, whereupon he married Anne Barley. His second wife's family connections with the higher circles of Court made Clement a very powerful man.

The insecure and shifting nature of this power is, however, very clear. Clement was not of aristocratic stock, nor did he possess a large estate in his own right. His career success depended largely on royal favour, and his lands and money on marrying into the aristocracy. Further, Sir Richard Clement's strategy had teetered on the brink of failure. Before his purchase of Ightham Mote he had tried unsuccessfully to establish himself in Northamptonshire society. In 1534 he appeared as defendant in a Star Chamber suit after assembling some 200 armed men to help settle a land dispute by violent means. The outcome of the Star Chamber trial is not known, though Clement's court connections probably swayed the decision in his favour.

Often irregular in plan, covered in heraldry, the late medieval and early sixteenth-century house signified a series of meanings clustered around the themes of hospitality, deference, and community. At the same time, however, as such architectural and social traditions were most insistently stressed, new architectural and social forms were developing, new forms that can ultimately be related to the values and techniques of nascent capitalism.

Mock-Beggar's Hall

These new forms are in part those attacked by Ben Jonson, and satirized and condemned by many other contemporary writers. Felicity Heal has discussed the literary trope of Mock-Beggar's Hall. In this trope, a weary peasant or traveller arrives at a splendid new country house. Expecting to receive traditional hospitality to match this splendour, he is disappointed to find the gates barred and the family away; usually having gone to London. The trope of Mock-Beggar's Hall stands as one element of a contemporary commentary on a society in crisis, where increasing condemnation of what was perceived as lack of hospitality reached a peak between

1580 and 1630 (Heal 1984). Such writing refers to a transformation in the nature of the landed elite in the sixteenth century, and in the way that transformation was mediated and expressed in the meanings of polite architecture.

This long-term social transformation had several elements. In the first place, the large, peripatetic medieval household was getting smaller. Where previously sons and daughters had been sent to other households for service and education, often to a household a social grade higher than that of their family (McCracken 1983), now elite sons and daughters were kept at home and taught by private tutors. With the decline of the great household came the decline of the peripatetic nature of its existence. The household moved less frequently and between fewer centres; and more of the year was spent in London.

If the elite moved around less, it was also increasingly socially fluid in

Figure 6.6 Titchfield Abbey, Hampshire. This was acquired by Thomas Wriothesley, future Earl of Southampton, at the Dissolution; he destroyed the eastern part of the church, the foundations of which are clearly visible. The nave and cloister ranges were adapted for use as a courtyard house, of which only the gatehouse and front range remain. The turreted and battlemented gatehouse is typical for its mid sixteenth-century date; it has been placed on top of the nave of the abbey church (Knowles 1974: 270). Cambridge University Collection of Air Photographs: copyright reserved.

nature. Many older families had died out by the middle of the sixteenth century; many 'new men' like Sir Richard Clement had risen through Court office and favour to positions of great power. The early modern perception of England was that it possessed an 'open elite', in which families could, even if over several generations, move up the social scale. Stone and Stone (1984) have questioned the truth of this perception but it is nevertheless the case that it was a view widely held by contemporaries.

This social mobility helped stimulate the land market; further stimulation was provided by the dissolution of the monasteries (Payling 1992). Monastic land fell into the hands of great landowners, many of whom rebuilt or adapted the monastic buildings as centres of new country estates (figure 6.6). Hengrave Hall was built at least in part from stone plundered from the dissolved Abbey of Bury St Edmunds a few miles away (Airs 1975: 18), and many sixteenth-century houses of lesser social standing nearby also contain monastic stone (Johnson 1993: 81).

There were new social divides opening up. It became increasingly necessary to spend time at Court in London to participate in the political life of the nation, or at least to protect one's interests and obtain royal office. Consequently, local communities often found themselves without great patrons. Many areas were increasingly dominated and given political leadership by an oligarchy of gentry families rather than a few great landowners. In Suffolk for example most great families had been dispossessed or had moved away by 1600, and the political life of the 'county community' was increasingly run by the gentry alone (Macculloch 1986).

These and other changes have led Lawrence Stone to talk of the period 1558–1641 as 'the crisis of the aristocracy' (1965). Such a view is controversial; but it does isolate the period from the middle of the sixteenth century onwards as a critical moment in the self-fashioning of the ruling classes. This was also a critical moment in the fashioning of new forms of 'polite' architecture. If we want to understand the changes that overcame great houses in the early modern period, we have to grasp the way in which these changes in form and style related to these and other changes in the landed elite.

In the first place, one key to understanding the architecture of the early modern great house was knowledge, and Classical knowledge at that. It is this new concern with knowledge, with sensibility rather than the sword as the defining characteristic of the apex of society, that helps us understand changing forms rather than reference to the 'influence of the Renaissance'.

The Italian Renaissance did not have a straightforward or unproblematic 'influence' on English polite architecture, to use the diffusionist terminology of traditional scholars. Patrons in England and Wales continued to build in late Gothic styles up to and in some cases beyond the middle of the sixteenth century (figure 6.5). After this date, the use of Renaissance or Classical rules and models was selective and creative rather than wholesale (figures 6.7 and 6.8).

The Gothic style continued in use in a variety of contexts, for example at Puritan colleges at Cambridge and in regional Anglican churches such as Myddle (chapter 5); or later still, in churches and domestic buildings refitted in the later seventeenth century by Bishop Cosin in County Durham. In secular architecture, there was a resurgence of Gothic motifs after the 1570s due to new ideas of chivalry, for example in the houses of Robert Smythson (Girouard 1983). The Elizabethan manipulation of chivalry is seen in the 'imaginative refeudalisation of late Tudor society' (Strong 1977: 129), though this was shot through with the Elizabethan love of riddles. The North Gate at Kenilworth was rebuilt with turrets and battlements by the Earl of Leicester in the later sixteenth century (figure 6.2). Like the Victorian reuse of Gothic, this nostalgia for medieval forms must be understood in its own terms rather than as conservatism.

Much of the early utilization of Renaissance ideas went hand in hand with the 'New Learning', the use of Classical precedent and models in other areas such as the agricultural treatise and new genres in poetry. The New Learning also developed in conjunction with the growing practice of foreign travel for pleasure and education. Standing in the gardens of the Villa d'Este near Rome, with its terraces, fountains, geometrical layout and Classical statuary, John Raymond announced perhaps rather ambitiously that 'this shall be my pattern for a Countrey seat'. At Kenilworth, the earlier sixteenth-century Tudor garden was remodelled with Italian-derived terracing, fountains and obelisks. These gardens were used as a theatre by the Earl of Leicester to present a masque to Queen Elizabeth in which the latter was presented as Diana the huntress (Hunt 1986: 103–5).

Italian patterns were used more frequently in the earlier seventeenth century and were linked to a search by elite writers for a Classical past in prehistoric Britain itself. The work of Inigo Jones shows the links between foreign travel, architecture, theatre and antiquarianism. Jones had been taken on an Italian tour in 1613 by his patrons, the Howards (Cain 1992: 110). His Italian experience gave him knowledge of the full Classical system of perspective, symmetry and the Vitruvian orders of Classical architecture. Jones's designs for backdrops for theatrical masques showed garden scenes full of complex allusions to Classical symbols; they were organised along lines of perspective that could be best viewed from the

Figure 6.7   A roundel with bust of the Roman emperor Nero on the front gate of Hampton Court Palace, on the Thames near London. One of the first examples of the use of Classical features, here deployed on a late Gothic royal palace.

Royal seat. Finally, Jones was one of those attempting to construct a Classical past for 'Britain' as a nation, claiming amid much controversy and opposition that Stonehenge was Roman in origin (Strong 1979: 159).

Francis Bacon's famous essay 'Of Building', first published in 1625, was

Figure 6.8 Kirby Hall, Northamptonshire, a house built in the 1570s for Sir Humphrey Stafford on a traditional courtyard plan but with Classical decoration and new features such as a long gallery and loggia. The south range illustrated here houses a traditional hall with porch and screens passage at its lower end (left), and large window at the upper end to the right, with private rooms beyond. Ionic columns and other Classical details, however, have been placed on this form; the decoration of the porch is especially striking and is partly derived from French models. Vases surmounted by heraldic beasts are placed above the columns on the parapet.

peppered with Classical allusions and references: in it, Bacon described his ideal house as symmetrical, with opposed wings for household and ceremonial use. At the centre of the house, however, Bacon placed a court in the traditional manner which he specifically recommends to be left unpaved (Hughes 1980: 11–15). Bacon may have been drawing here on the layout of his own house of Gorhambury in Hertfordshire, which an earlier sixteenth-century owner had adorned with Classical pilasters plus gardens with Roman busts and a labyrinth of Venus (Prince 1982: 35).

Such deployment of specific forms of knowledge through architecture and gardens was done in a receptive context. It was expected, for example, in other discursive forms such as art. The sixteenth century was a time when art and associated material culture was expected to carry both overt and implicit meanings: thus for example a painting could have a whole series of riddle-like overt and hidden meanings to do with the politics of the time, to the extent that an entire modern scholarly book can be written about the iconography of one sixteenth-century painted scene (Aston 1994). The need for art to carry complex allusions was seen at its most acute in the creation and re-creation of images of Tudor kingship (Anglo 1992; figure 6.7), especially with Queen Elizabeth: the iconography of her portraits tries to negotiate the fact that she is a woman at the head of a prevailing patriarchal structure (Strong 1977; Belsey and Belsey 1990).

If polite architecture and art carried complex meanings, so did the bearers of polite culture. It was also a context in which the meanings of being a member of the elite were being renegotiated. The image of the gentleman in sixteenth- and seventeenth-century England was not simply one of denoted status: the gentleman could be seen by his 'port' and 'countenance', both ideas 'symptomatic of closer concern with the regulation of the body' (Bryson 1990: 153). In this closer regulation of the self within polite society the skill of rhetoric was more highly valued than the feudal skills of martial valour. If the self was being more closely disciplined by the end of the sixteenth century, this had clear implications for the housing of the self.

Viewing the House

The way in which these new systems of knowledge were imparted was through the gaze. The production of 'space dominated by the eye and the gaze' (Gregory 1994: 392) was one artefact of the closure of architectural space, in which the rational human subject is placed at the centre of space, the eye is detached from the body and a commodified view of architecture and landscape created. It was through the gaze that 'like dress, the outward appearance of architecture became part of the act of self-fashioning one's public image' in the sixteenth century (Howard 1990: 199).

Views became increasingly important in a variety of ways. First, the medieval courtyard plan was abandoned by degrees. The medieval house presented a defensive face to the outside world, particularly so in the case of castles; even the Hampton Court Palace, built by Cardinal Wolsey and extended by Henry VIII, was a series of inward-looking courts, presenting a jumble of roofs and chimneys rather than a symmetrical front. It was only when one penetrated the court inside, whether regular or irregular, that the pattern and layout of the house became clear.

Second, the setting of the house became increasingly important. The gaze required that the houses be viewed along definite lines of perspective, from afar. Late medieval houses were often surrounded by smaller, lower, outer courts serving ancillary functions such as stables and orchards. With the need for a clear view of the house, the setting within parks and gardens whose design allowed for straight lines centred on the house itself became increasingly important.

If others could see the house as a geometric unity from the outside, so the ordered and coherent view of the landscape from the house was equally stressed. The increased use of window glass may have been as much to do with the rise of the importance of having a view over the estate and outside world as with higher standards of personal comfort. There was a huge rise in demand for window glass in the sixteenth and seventeenth centuries, both because of rise in the rate of new building and also the use of larger and more numerous windows. In the earlier sixteenth century, some houses appear to have only partially been glazed; later, there was a fashion for large expanses of glass, most famously at Hardwick Hall (Godfrey 1975: 205–7).

This glass illuminated new architectural features within the house such as the long gallery often running the whole length of the building, from which one could range one's view across the landscape (Coope 1984: figure 6.9). Windows in these galleries were often juxtaposed with portrait paintings of the ancestors of the owners.

The gaze dictated that what previously had been implicit and unspoken became overt and articulated. The Duke of Buckingham may have been beheaded in the earlier sixteenth century in part for building too grandly, but the rules which separated buildings of different degrees were far from being an overt system. By the end of the sixteenth century, England had seen the appearance of recognized architects, the publication of Vitruvius and other Classical authors on architecture, the publication of advice on how to build a suitable country seat, and increasing numbers of both artistic and poetic depictions of buildings from a variety of perspectives. It is hardly too fanciful to see all these developments as formally connected, as part of a new set of discourses framed around the deployment of the gaze.

The gaze required that rules of perspective be brought to bear on the elite landscape. We have already seen in chapter 5 how enclosure reflected similar trends in vernacular landscapes: the use of the map, the application of 'rational' knowledge to farming practices, the role of the farmer in bringing order to a disorderly Nature. The rise of an outward view of the elite house militated against Jonson's inward-looking concepts in which social values were merged at an implicit level within the architecture. Jonson's poem can be contrasted with that of Andrew Marvell, 'Upon

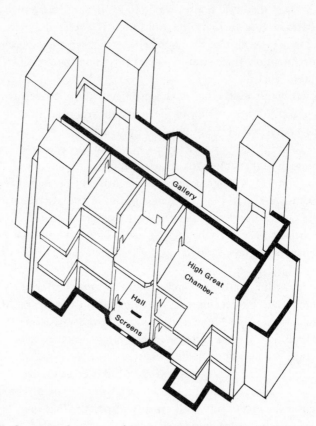

Figure 6.9 Symmetrical cutaway of Hardwick Hall, Derbyshire, built 1590–7 (after Girouard 1978). Hardwick is a three-storey block two rooms deep; though it retains elements of a traditional plan with screens passage, the great hall has become a vestibule with Classical detail; it runs across the house rather than along it, the social axis of the hall thus being lost. The upper floor is a long gallery. The overall plan is a symbolic 'device', being two linked Greek crosses, each with a tower at the end of three of its arms. Hardwick is notable for its use of huge windows, celebrated in the traditional proverb, 'Hardwick Hall, more glass than wall'. The initials 'E.R.' on the parapet visible externally are for its builder Bess of Hardwick. Bess remodelled the Old Hall in the 1580s before abandoning it; it was kept on to accommodate visitors. The ruins of the Old Hall survive to one side and still dominate the view. It was this kind of house that Jonson was attacking in 'To Penshurst'.

Appleton House', in which architecture overtly had a moral purpose: geometry is here applied to human life. Marvell's Appleton achieves this despite its pre-Classical appearance. The estate is an ordered whole – 'one perfect peece'. It has been suggested that the whole poem is a piece of

Vitruvian architecture. Again, Denham's famous poem 'Cooper's Hill' uses the view from the hill to convey a political message very specifically through the movement of the gaze. The poet's eye moves upwards to view Royalist country seats as centres of order and authority, and downwards into the mire of London, its Parliament, church-breakers and the mob (Turner 1979: 50–5 and 78–83).

The internal layout of the house was increasingly governed by new techniques of segregation. As we have seen the medieval house had already involved segregation between masters and servants for a long time, but such systems became increasingly complex and governed by different social values. Whereas the sight of many servants and retainers bustling about in the hall had been used to convey a sense of social status, by the mid-seventeenth century architectural writers such as Pratt and North were advising the relegation of service activities to the basement, linked to the 'main' rooms by a separate set of stairs. Thus staff, 'idle fellows who will be spunging in the kitchen', would not be seen: instead, 'no dirty servants may be seen passing to and fro by those who are above, no noises heard, nor ill scents smelt' (cited in Platt 1994: 41).

As with the houses of the middling sort discussed in the next chapter, these new techniques of internal segregation were more than simply a reflection of a 'rise of privacy' that needs no further theorization. Where numbers of bodies articulated status and power in the medieval household, numbers and different kinds of furnishings carried these meanings by the end of the seventeenth century. Where social status was indicated by the architectural denotation and asymmetry of different ends of the great hall in the later middle ages, different classes had now completed the withdrawal into separate rooms of different status, each smaller and now symmetrically arranged. Where experience of space within the castle was corporeal and physical, depending on bodily movement from one space to another, the gaze was detached from the body, the view taking in a pleasing prospect of the house from a suitable vantage point in one detached sweep. This shift in the way household space was organized carries implications for the idea of commodification discussed in chapter 8.

The post-medieval country house thus turned the castle inside out. Where the castle controlled access to internal spaces that were critical to the exercise of power, the power of the country house radiated outwards, across the ever-larger estate. Where the castle looked inwards to the courtyard and its social meanings, the country house turned its gaze out onto the landscape as a whole. Where the subjective experience of the architecture of the castle depended on individuals of different social statuses being able to read a common coding of space, the country house depended on that coding being the exclusive property of the upper social classes. Where the castle keep gave the impression of nailing the valley, the country house, through its uninterrupted views stretching across parks and gardens, and its judicious, symbolically complex use of portrayal in landscape art, gave the impression of constituting the entire landscape.

These new principles of architecture were formalized into one system in the Venetian landscape of the later sixteenth century. There, Cosgrove has explored how the architect and landscape designer Palladio drew together Classical ideas in a context where systematic drainage of the marshes around Venice was allowing the creation of rural estates with villas at their centre (1993). Cosgrove links this new system with the mass reorganization of the landscape and in turn to the nascent mercantile capitalism of the Venetian state, for which the geometry underlying the values and techniques of mapmaking in particular were all-important. Palladianism

Figure 6.10 Whitehall Banqueting House, London. This was an early seventeenth-century addition to the older royal palace of Whitehall, now largely destroyed. Designed by Inigo Jones, it was one of the first wholesale applications of Classical principles to architectural design, as opposed to the 'superficial' use of Classical orders in palaces of more traditional plan such as Kirby Hall. The example was not widely imitated in the country, and can be seen as one cultural expression of the 'court/country' split that was one of the causes of the English Revolution. Another cause was financial and political crisis induced in part by royal expenditure; it is therefore appropriate that Charles I walked to his death on the scaffold in front of the Banqueting House.

certainly depended on Classical knowledge: central to its system is the way in which Classical citations and busts are deployed in both architecture and surrounding landscape in a way that is allusive to mythology and literature. It is also dependent on mathematical principles of symmetry and proportion.

It was this stylistic 'package' that Jones introduced into England in the earlier seventeenth century. It is striking that in this different context the Classical style took on very different meanings. The 'Court culture' of Inigo Jones's masques and such buildings as Whitehall Banqueting House (figure 6.10), and in particular the Catholic chapel built for Charles I's wife Henrietta Maria at Whitehall Palace, was not widely imitated in the 'Country', being identified with suspicious foreign practices and, in particular, popery. Jones's books on the Palladian style were not published until 1715–20; the redevelopment of Wilton House and Holkham Hall at this time were critical in reintroducing Palladian as an integrated style after a century (Bold 1988).

Cultivating Authority

Between the great house and the vernacular landscape beyond was the garden. At all periods gardens have been more than simply lawns and beds of flowers; gardens are about power as well as plants. Around the great house the gardens were planned as a mediation between the elite and the ordinary, as well as between Nature and Culture. The seventeenth-century antiquarian and philosopher Sir Thomas Browne in his essay on the quincunx turned a garden motif into a meditation upon the classical Ancients, and into a complex metaphor for life and death through the classification of plants and animals. For other early modern writers gardens had Utopian and Edenic associations. Evelyn's proposal for a Utopian college community was framed around a garden. Gardens could also constitute political agendas. Designs ranging from grandness and formality to simpler but more expansive designs had explicit connotations in the alternately absolutist and republican world of the seventeenth century (Parry 1992; Chambers 1992).

Medieval gardens were generally enclosed and inward-looking; they were used for both function and pleasure. The enclosure of large areas of space was not a specifically early modern phenomenon. Royalty and feudal lords enclosed large areas for use as deerparks, bounded by a park pale or wall or earthwork enclosure. The creation of such parks often swept away

earlier settlement, with whole villages being cleared away as at the sixteenth-century royal palace at Nonsuch (James 1990: 16). Complaints
against the iniquity of deerparks were as routine among sixteenth-century
rebels as those about enclosure were (Thirsk 1967).

Some writers have commented that medieval gardens were largely functional rather than for 'pleasure' before the sixteenth century (Platt 1994:
54); this view conflicts with the archaeological evidence. Chris Taylor for
example has surveyed Nettleham, Lincolnshire, and has suggested that 'the
whole site may be interpreted as an elaborate formal walled garden with
terraces, paths and flower beds set into the sloping ground and with a
separate compartment at the north-eastern end' (Taylor 1983: 38). Whatever the case, the development of large-scale formal parks and gardens as a
matter of routine around the great house goes along with the development
of the gaze in early modern elite landscapes. This can be seen most
markedly in the dissolution of medieval and sixteenth-century enclosed
gardens in favour of more extensive views and perspectives in the
seventeenth century. Kenilworth Castle in the early seventeenth century
was one of the first gardens to use large-scale terraces in the systematic
deployment of views (to the north of the keep in figure 6.2; see also figure
6.11).

Systematic development can also be seen in the form of symbolism
deployed within the gardens. Strong has termed the earlier sixteenth
century the age of the 'heraldic garden'. Heraldic emblems were displayed
within the enclosed courts, often as at Hampton Court on wooden posts.
Knots, emblems and 'devices' of various kinds continued to be deployed in
the time of Elizabeth with puzzle or riddle elements being especially
popular (figure 6.12).

The garden transformed the treatment of Nature. Trees and plants of all
kinds were brought under strict discipline before the eighteenth century:
they were clipped, shorn, 'tortured' into as unnatural a shape as possible,
while at the same time the yeoman farmers labouring in the fields of the
vernacular landscape disciplined Nature at an everyday level. At the same
time knowledge of the world beyond grew; where the Tudor garden
included largely domestic species, later gardens became a melange of
strange and exotic plants from all corners of the colonial world. An increasing number of alien species were imported from Europe, the Mediterranean
and North America. Jarvis counts a rise from 36 hardy woody alien species
before 1600 to 239 by 1700 (1979: 148 and 153).

The garden transformed the view of the house. Gardens had always been

Figure 6.11 Harrington, Northamptonshire: an elite landscape of medieval and late seventeenth-century date. In 1712 the now abandoned garden terraces, seen at the top left of the picture, were described thus by Morton: 'For a Descent of Garden Walks there is nothing so remarkable with us as that of the Walks of the Garden on the Northern Front of the Earl of Dysert's house' (Hunt 1986: 166). An 'eye-catcher' stood at the top of the terraces; traces of steps leading up to it are just visible. The survival of such terraces is rare, since most were swept away and replaced with more 'natural' curves by eighteenth-century landscape gardeners. The house stood immediately below the terraces, to one side of the sunken garden. The earthworks of a system of fishponds, and associated leats and sluices, survive below the house and garden; these are probably of medieval date. Cambridge University Collection of Air Photographs: copyright reserved.

part of the architecture of the house, the enclosed courts around the late medieval house merging into surrounding parks; but now this relationship was a mathematically proportioned one, the different elements being in clear and explicit relationship with each other, in which geometry was manipulated, explicitly sanctioned by invariant rules of proportion. House and landscape were most explicitly united in the *ferme ornee* (ornamental or villa farm), seen from the 1720s onwards in south-eastern England; this was imported from France where it had developed in response to Classical texts (Brandon 1979: 176).

Figure 6.12 Rushton Triangular Lodge, Northamptonshire, built from 1594–7 by Sir Thomas Tresham, a Catholic who spent time in prison for his beliefs. The Lodge is symbolic of the Trinity and thus refers to Tresham's religion. It has three sides with three three-lobed windows and three gables; there are three storeys and the building is topped by a three-

Concealing the Bounds

At the very height of the most elaborate, extensive formal gardens, a new style emerged in earlier eighteenth-century England: of the Palladian house combined with the 'English landscape garden'. Where gardens had been formal, aligned along straight lines, now they were to be irregular; where Nature had been clipped and shorn, now she was to be given free rein.

There is much debate over the specific historical origins of the 'English landscape garden'. Contemporaries and many subsequent commentators saw it as a distinctive statement of national identity (Lange 1992). Earlier styles of garden had often been imitative of Continental models. Hunt (1986: 180) argues that in fact the new style derived much from Italian models, but it is certainly true that within a few decades the style had become to be seen as distinctively English.

If landscape gardens were a statement of 'Englishness', they were a statement on the part of a specific group: the great paternal landlords who quite explicitly linked their claim to political power through their use and deployment of the 'correct' view of landscape (Cosgrove 1984: 189). John Barrell has argued that by the later eighteenth century polite culture asserted that correct 'taste' in architecture and landscape was intimately asociated with political authority; the latter 'is rightly exercised by those capable of thinking in general terms'. This ability to think in the general and abstract was produced by the correct education and an ability to spend one's time free of mechanical labour. It thus inevitably excluded women and the vulgar. Landscape appreciation was one test of taste, turning on the 'function of the panoramic, and ideal, landscapes on the one hand, and, on the other, actual portraits of views, and representations of enclosed, occluded landscapes, with no depth of view' (Barrell 1990: 20).

Eighteenth-century landscape parks can thus be viewed as a piece of ideology, of mystification of what was 'really going on' in the countryside. Such a view is reinforced by considering the relationship of the landscape style to contemporary vernacular landscapes and enclosure. At the very

---

(*continued*) sided chimney. Each side is 33–and-a-third feet long, and has symbols and inscriptions referring to one of the Holy Trinity; the inscription on each side is 33 letters long. Over the door is the inscription *Tres Testimonium Dant* which can mean either 'there are three that bear witness' or 'The Treshams bear witness'. Tresham also built but never finished a lodge in similar spirit at Lyveden, symbolizing the Passion.

time when enclosed agrarian landscapes were getting straighter, writers on parks and gardens were advocating the abandonment of straight lines (Franklin 1989: 145). Whereas boundaries within the park were transformed by the ha-ha (a wall set at the bottom of a small ditch to allow the illusion of an unbounded landscape), the boundary between the estate itself and the world beyond was reinforced with walls and the planting of groves of trees. The wall at Blenheim for example, built from 1727–9, was seven feet high and nine miles long (Green 1951: 314).

Addison, in articles in his magazine *The Tatler*, wrote of the landscape garden as being free from unnecessary constraints: his garden, envisioned in a dream, had the Goddess of Liberty and attendant statues representing the Arts and Sciences in her train; nearby the goddesses Plenty and Commerce were seated. Commerce 'was seated in a little island, that was covered with Groves of Spices, Olives, and Orange-trees; and in a Word, with the Product of every Foreign Clime'. Addison enjoyed his dream garden all the more 'because it was not encumbered with Fences and Enclosures' (Hunt and Willis 1975: 140).

The landscape garden in fact concealed its restraints rather than having none. Spence recommended the manipulation of perspective: how to 'unite the different parts of your garden gently together' by drawing distant objects close and close objects further away through the judicious use of narrowing and widening plantations of trees. Spence cited Pope who claimed that 'He gains all Ends, who pleasingly confounds, / Surprises, varies, and conceals the bounds' (Hunt and Willis 1975: 270–1). It was also full of allusion and complexity of meaning: again, principally to Classical sources, but also with follies of Druidic temples alluding to Britain's prehistoric glories. In the view of some great patrons the irregular wooded clumps and groves alternating with stretches of pasture were a return to Britain's 'natural' state before cultivation (Smiles 1994).

Along with the creation of the landscape garden went another discursive form: the emergence of landscape art. There is a profound silence of art on enclosed agrarian landscapes before the mid-eighteenth century. In contrast with the landscapes of the sixteenth- and seventeenth-century Dutch and Italians, English artists rarely portrayed everyday agrarian scenes (Fussell 1984: 4). Prince calls early eighteenth-century paintings 'escapist fantasies'. Thus for example the Duke of Bedford showed his interest in the agrarian landscape through his experimentation with new farming techniques, but he commissioned landscape paintings that are 'idyllic' and depict an ideal landscape without any such improvements (Prince 1988).

When Thomas Gainsborough portrayed Mr and Mrs Andrews in his

1748–9 painting, however, he showed them in the middle of an agrarian scene, as a newly married couple with a well-managed estate in the background. The position of the local church has been moved to be within the estate and the estate itself has been enclosed with improved methods. 'The wheat has been drilled, hawthorn hedges . . . are neatly cut and laid, a new-style five-barred gate gives entry to the field . . . and the sheep themselves are of the size and shape of breeds selected for feeding on turnips and artificial grasses' (Prince 1988: 103). Woodland also came to carry both authoritarian and radical meanings in such art (Daniels 1988). By the nineteenth century, landscape art had become a key idiom for representing national identity (Daniels 1993).

Conclusion

Jonson's praise of the great hall at Penshurst contrasts with the content and form of Pope's comments on Stanton Harcourt. Pope, who built himself a villa and landscape garden at Twickenham in the growing early eighteenth-century suburbs of London, wrote that of Stanton Harcourt: 'The great hall is high and spacious, flanked with long tables . . . In the hall, in former days, have dined Gartered Knights and Courtly Dames, with ushers, sewers, and seneschals; and yet it was but t'other night that an owl flew hither, and mistook it for a barn.' The kitchens were even worse, with their large ranges for the servicing of traditional feasting and hospitality:

> by the blackness of the walls, vast cauldrons, yawning mouths of ovens and furnaces, you would think it the forge of Vulcan, the cave of Polypheme, or the temple of Moloch. The horror of this place has made such an impression on the country people, that they believe the witches keep their Sabbath here, and that once a year the Devil treats them with infernal venison, a roasted tiger stuffed with ten penny nails (cited in Kelsall 1993: 69).

I have given an account in this chapter of the way the style and form of 'polite' architecture and landscapes related to an archaeology of authority. I have tried to draw attention to the way the landed elite created a legitimating image of themselves, to the way the workings of authority were encoded and mediated through the meanings of buildings and gardens. It is an account at once superficial and over-complex. It is superficial in the obvious sense that a huge amount of material and interpretation has been condensed into a very small space. It is particularly the case that a much deeper study is needed of the *coexistence* of styles. By the eighteenth century, a patron could choose between one of a number of different architectural and landscape styles. This degree of choice is important given the importance of demonstrating the possession of the right sense of 'taste' by this period. By the middle of the eighteenth century it was also possible to build in 'Gothick' taste: Castle Howard, for example, had big castle walls with bastions; 'follies' were often built in parks, mock ruins of castles or other structures. We often owe the survival of a ruined castle to its careful maintenance and preservation as part of a polite landscape. Such structures often had overt references to political triumphs and more subtly to the rights of landed property (Franklin 1989: 148 and 151).

At the same time, we need to know more about the houses and landscapes of the class immediately below the landed aristocracy: the gentry. The gentry were a distinctive social class whose self-definition was being transformed in the course of the early modern period, culminating in the emergence of self-definition through the articulation of style in the eighteenth century (Sinclair 1987). Did the gentry slavishly ape those above them in style, and if so what was the degree of time lag between their take-up of a style and its original introduction?

The 'gentry question' is one of the critical points about the styles of eighteenth-century architecture and landscape: their application as an organized system of ideas to houses and landscapes below the very top level of the social scale. Towards the end of our period, a gentleman or even a prosperous townsman or farmer in search of the latest fashions from London could buy a pattern-book with designs within it. Pope hinted at such a process of emulation in his praise of Lord Burlington's early eighteenth-century Palladian designs (figure 6.13), where he commented that Burlington's 'noble rules' published on architecture would

> Fill half the land with Imitating Fools,
> Who random Drawings from your Sheets shall take,
> And of one Beauty many Blunders make;
> Load some vain Church with old Theatric State;
> Turn Arcs of Triumph to a Garden-gate;
> Reverse your Ornaments, and hang them all
> On some patch'd Doghole ek'd with Ends of Wall,
> Then clap four slices of Pilaster on't,
> And lac'd with bits of Rustic, 'tis a Front . . .
> Conscious they act a true Palladian part,
> And if they starve, they starve by Rules of Art.
>   (Alexander Pope, 'Epistle to Lord Burlington')

Figure 6.13 Chiswick House, Lord Burlington's home outside London, built as a Palladian villa in the early eighteenth century. Chiswick House was surrounded by a garden that was central in the creation of the new 'landscape style'.

The account of changing styles that I have given in this chapter may also be over-complex. There may be less symbolism to some great houses and landscape gardens than meets the eye, both literally and metaphorically. The eighteenth-century landscape style did carry meanings of nationalism and the Whig settlement to a few elite patrons, but to many landowners its appeal may have been as much in its cheapness of upkeep compared to earlier ornamental gardens. Even the royal residents of Hampton Court, for example, found the expenses of the late seventeenth-century formal gardens too much to bear in the early eighteenth century.

Such a lack of concern with complex allusions may have been particularly true of its gentry imitators. For the first time the gentry could follow a national style of architecture through purchase of a Georgian pattern-book; for the first time also they could afford the upkeep of a fashionable garden, in which a few sheep or cattle could be kept, combining utility with adornment. Many eighteenth-century landscape parks were created not out of their ornamental predecessors, but directly from the result of the disparking of medieval deerparks (Brandon 1979: 172).

Similarly, what may have been at least as important to the patron was the process as much as the product of creating polite architecture and landscape. To clarify, it was important to be seen to be building, to be modifying, laying out new plantations and tinkering with old arrangements. Visitors to a great house in the eighteenth century would not just be shown round a wonderful house and garden, but would be equally impressed by the host's narratives of his illustrious ancestors, the historic past of the house, his accounts of planned improvements (all in the best possible taste), and by the pleasing and proper prospect of small groups of estate workers dotted around the landscape engaged in industry and improvement at a suitable distance from the house.

The medieval castle and the great house of the eighteenth century were both 'power houses'; they were both bound up with the polite culture of political authority and power in their respective ages. But in their different forms and meanings they were from utterly different worlds. It was the transition from an elite world and mentality of feudalism to one of aristocratic sensibility and great estates that was central to the moral and social constitution of rural capitalism.

7

Redefining the Domestic

We have seen in previous chapters how an archaeology of capitalism can be located in everyday social and cultural practices as much as in large-scale economic transformations. This chapter continues this theme by looking at aspects of the ordinary, vernacular and small scale. I shall examine the archaeology of the socially middling household and the members of this household. I shall suggest how, by redefining the domestic and its relations with public space, definitions of people and their relations with each other were also redrawn. The rise of the middling sort, and the changing relations within their households, are clearly integral to an archaeology of capitalism.

The very existence of a substantial class of socially middling households, members neither of the ruling elite nor of the labouring poor, and occupying a distinctive place in contemporary perceptions of social order, is itself worthy of comment. The 'middling sort', to use the common seventeenth-century term (Wrightson 1994: 25–73), existed as a defined group from the later middle ages onwards. The socially middling farmer was eulogized in Langland's later fourteenth-century poem *Piers Plowman* as one corner-stone of the social order. At the same time as the middling sort were entering the political consciousness of the time, their houses and material culture enter the above-ground archaeological record in the form of standing buildings.

Most structures dating from before AD 1300 and still standing today are 'polite' buildings: churches, palaces, castles, manor houses. From the fifteenth century onwards, large numbers of 'vernacular' houses survive, most still used as ordinary houses. It has long been assumed that their survival reflects the increasing economic fortunes of the middling sort, and thus their ability to build substantial houses capable of lasting the centuries (Mercer 1975; Smith 1970: 147). The date of the 'Vernacular

Threshold' in any given region of England and Wales is generally defined as the moment at which we have large numbers of ordinary surviving houses from a given region. It has thus been taken to reflect the rise of the middling sort, able for the first time to build 'permanent' houses. It implicitly suggests a move towards rural capitalism. The date of the Vernacular Threshold varies widely; as one might expect, it tends to be relatively early in the wood-pasture and cloth-producing areas of the south and east, and relatively late in many areas of the uplands of the north and west.

This interpretation of the Vernacular Threshold has come under attack recently, with scholars questioning both its very existence and the assumed link between house survival, periods of past economic prosperity and identification with middling social groups (Currie 1988; Johnson 1993: 9–10). It remains the case however that many areas of England and Wales possess literally thousands of surviving vernacular dwellings, dwellings that are neither one-hearth dwellings of the labouring poor on the one hand, nor elite structures on the other. For the archaeology of these dwellings to be fully understood, they must be placed in the context of the cultural values of households of the middling sort.

A Little Commonwealth

We have seen in chapter 2 how the unit of the household was seen by contemporary commentators and within legal discourse as constitutive of the State, a 'little commonwealth' whose relations between master and servant, husband and wife, adult and youth were seen as a microcosm of patriarchal political relations as a whole. The layout and form of the pre-industrial house was linked to this conception of household order, as mentioned in chapter 4.

Nevertheless the pre-industrial household was not a unit whose form was invariant and unquestioned, a mere 'building brick' from which the larger edifice of pre-industrial society was built. The form of the house and the social and cultural relations within it were continually renegotiated at both elite and vernacular levels. Many artefacts of this renegotiation of household relations survive as documents – the diaries often containing the agonized self-reflections of Puritan male householders (Wrightson 1982: 96–8), legislation and court cases concerning marital relations, the rare narrative of a servant or of a woman, the advice of a conduct book on manners or on the treatment of one's spouse, or instructions of a will on divisions of house and property (Johnson 1993: 155–7).

Social and cultural historians have used such information to sketch a complex picture of continuity and change in the marital, family and household relations prevalent among the 'middling sort' between the late medieval and early modern periods. It is unsurprising therefore to find continuity and change in the physical form of the house and the objects within it during this period. Architecture and material culture formed a critical area of social and cultural transformation and a key arena in the emergence of modern social relations. Despite being critical, this transformation was not one that was frequently explicitly commented upon by contemporaries. Written and popular complaints about enclosure and what were seen as its social consequences were endemic in the sixteenth and seventeenth centuries, as we have seen; discussions of ordinary houses and their inhabitants were more rare, partly due to their more implicit, everyday nature, and were thus framed according to different discursive rules. Precisely because vernacular architecture and material culture were 'silent', because their meanings did not necessarily rise to the level of the overtly articulated, they formed a key battleground in the framing of everyday assumptions, and thus for the dissolution of a medieval and the constitution of a modern way of life.

The house was not therefore a simple, private domestic retreat for 'people at home', away from the pressures and tensions of wider social and political forces. Those pressures and tensions existed as much within the household as outside it. At the same time the house served as the stage not just for the redefinition of relationships between people but also for the reformation of the people themselves. New ways of acting towards household and family brought with it new ways of acting towards oneself, of monitoring one's own behaviour, of fashioning and re-fashioning one's own individuality. If the household was a little State, it was also a body writ large. Redefining the domestic thus also involved redefining the self. A full account of the domestic must also include an account of the refashioning of the self: through clothing, hygiene, through the history of manners, the archaeology of death, and through the meanings and uses of material culture in general. These themes are closely related and will be treated in the next two chapters.

Harrison and the Great Rebuilding

One of the most quoted documentary sources for houses and furnishings in pre-industrial England is William Harrison's *The Manner of Building and*

Furniture of our Houses, part of his descriptive and topographic book on England as a whole (Furnival 1877). Written in 1587, Harrison's comments are often plundered selectively to buttress or to challenge particular views on housing and the domestic interior. The text deserves to be read in full, since many of the points made in earlier chapters about the embeddedness of different areas of pre-industrial life are made eloquently by Harrison himself. He draws distinctions, for example, between 'open champaign ground' and 'woody soils' in terms of a complex of criteria including settlement type, building layout and technique:

> for as in [wood-pasture], our houses are uncommonly strong and well timbered . . . so in the open champaign countries they are enforced for want of stuff to use no studs at all, but only frank posts, raisins, beams, prick posts, groundsels, summers (or dormants), transoms, and such principals . . . then cast it all over with thick clay to keep out the wind, which otherwise would annoy them . . . (Edelen 1968: 195).

Harrison also juxtaposes the three points discussed in detail below with three negative points: 'to wit, the enhancing of rents . . . the daily oppression of copyholders, whose lords seek to bring their tenants almost into plain servitude and misery, daily devising new means, and seeking up all the old . . . to the end they may fleece them yet more'; and the practice of usury (Edelen 1968: 202). Whether Harrison's perception is 'correct' or not, it acts as a fitting coda to the history of enclosure.

Harrison is at pains to emphasize the great improvement in housing and material living standards in sixteenth-century England. He asserts that 'in old time the houses of the Britons were slightly set up with a few posts and many raddles [rods], with stable and offices all under one roof, the like of which is almost to be seen in the fenny countries and northern parts unto this day' (Edelen 1968: 195). Since that time, and presumably also outside the fenny countries and northern parts, England has seen the replacement of wooden with glass windows, better framing techniques, and the increase and refinement of items of furniture.

The 'old men yet dwelling in the village where I remain [in Essex]' cite 'three things to be marvellously altered in England within their sound remembrance': the replacement of open hearths with chimney stacks; the 'great amendment of lodging' including the replacement of straw pallets with featherbeds, the use of a bolster or pillow instead of a 'good round log', and changes in furniture. The third element in this transformation is the exchange of wooden or 'treen' vessels and cutlery for those of metal, principally pewter – 'for so common were all sorts of treen stuff in old time, that a man should hardly find four pieces of pewter . . . in a good farmer's house' (Edelen 1968: 200–1).

Writers on traditional architecture have often turned to Harrison's comments as evidence of a major transformation in the building patterns and the domestic interior of the 'middling sort' in early modern England. W.G. Hoskins cited Harrison in his classic 1953 article 'The Rebuilding of Rural England, 1560–1640' as one piece of evidence for a major change in building and internal furnishings in the 80 years prior to the English Revolution. This rebuilding involved a rise in the comfort of domestic furnishings, building of new houses, and improvement of old ones. Hoskins's thesis has since been challenged and at the very least heavily qualified (Machin 1977; Johnson 1993), but its endurance is striking. Many documentary historians continue to cite Hoskins's article as evidence for domestic architectural improvement in preference to the many more substantive regional studies of traditional architecture that have been published more recently.

Recent scholars have been right to stress that Hoskins's Great Rebuilding has to be redated and seen as a much more drawn-out process, with much more regional variation in rates of rebuilding and the nature of any underlying social or economic transformation accompanying such a rebuilding. Harrison's comments have been reinterpreted as referring specifically to his Essex home, where as in many areas of the south and east rebuilding and associated changes in domestic comfort were earlier than the norm for England as a whole.

At this point, I want to draw attention to several aspects of Harrison's comments that I feel have been neglected by archaeologists. First, what he says is *unusual*. There are few such everyday written commentaries on material goods in ordinary households before this date. So just as material goods within the household were becoming more common and the household itself was being improved in terms of material comfort, so the domestic interior was increasingly the subject of overt and explicit comment below the uppermost social levels. This had not been the case in the Middle Ages. The rarity of medieval comments such as Langland's complaint about great men dining alone in parlours is shown by the way historians are forced to revert to quoting it again and again (for example Heal 1990: 40). The context of Harrison's comments is a topographical and antiquarian description of England of the sort discussed in chapter 5. There, the significance of such accounts of antiquities, great families and local geography in carving up the landscape mentally as it was being carved up physically was discussed.

Second, Harrison *merges the domestic and the public* in his discussion. At the same time it is *gendered*. His is very much a male account: it is clear which gender he is thinking of when he writes

> will the farmer, as another palm or date tree, think his gains very small towards the end of his term, if he have not six or seven years rent lying beside him, therwith to purchase a new lease, besides a fair garnish of pewter on his cupboard with so much more in odd vessel going about the house, three or four featherbeds, so many coverlets and carpets of tapestry, a silver salt, a bowl for wine, if not a whole nest, and dozens of spoons to finish up the suit (Edelen 1968: 202).

Harrison's text invites us to identify with a male yeoman farmer who sees the house as an extension of male pride, a physical embodiment of the prosperity of the farm. This was a typical attitude of a period when conceptions of masculinity were framed around conceptions of pride and honour (Fletcher 1994).

Third, Harrison sees material things – houses and the furnishings and objects within them – as *important*, worthy of comment. This ceases to be a statement of the obvious when we remember that this period saw a profound shift of attitudes towards domestic 'comfort' and material goods during time and between social groups. Chandra Mukerji (1983) has commented on the development of this new attitude, which she defines as materialistic, locates in the nascent capitalism of sixteenth-century Europe, and links to modern materialism. I am arguing here that this new set of attitudes can also be found in socially middling rural contexts in parallel with the development of agrarian capitalism. This long-term transformation related to shifts in perception and behaviour of different groups within the household and family that built and occupied the house and farmstead, rebuilt it or added new rooms and wings, and bought, used, passed on and inherited the material goods. It is this deeper social and cultural shift that I now want to explore.

The Household as Body

If the household was a little commonwealth, its borders had to be maintained. Like the State, there were threats of disorder and mayhem outside the household. The most classic threat was that of the witch. As a disorderly woman on the margins of society, the witch broke all the rules; it is not surprising, then, that witchcraft accusations see the witch entering the house through forbidden entries such as the chimney stack. Witchcraft precautions are known archaeologically in a variety of contexts.

In many cases witchcraft precautions and remedies are centred around the hearth, the physical and spiritual centre of the home, often treated as

Figure 7.1   a and b A witch-bottle and contents. The stoneware bottles were often German imports; they were filled with pins or nails and the victim's nails and urine. They worked on the principle that the witch had created a magical link between witch and victim, so that link could be used in reverse to harm the witch, forcing her to cut off the link or suffer or die herself. The bottle was buried below the hearth of the house, or thrown into the river; the heat from the fire agitated the pins and forced the witch to break off the link or be injured or killed herself. Photograph: Ralph Merrifield.

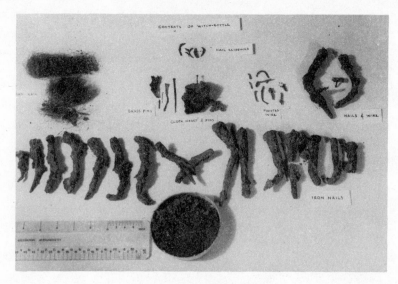

Figure 7.1   a and b *Continued*

its soul in early modern thought (Ewart Evans 1966: 74–81). Many 'witch-bottles' of imported stoneware have been found, often buried underneath the hearth; these were counter-measures to witchcraft (Merrifield 1987: 167–75; figure 7.1). The world outside the house was full of other dangers such as imps and spirits (Reay 1985a). These often punished offences against household order such as dirtiness, untidiness and lechery (Thomas 1983: 703).

The household being protected in this way was animal as well as human. In many areas of England and Wales, animals were kept under the same roof; certain classes of farm animal such as cows and horses were given names and even talked to. 'In many ways . . . domestic beasts were subsidiary members of the human community' (Thomas 1983: 98).

It is tempting to see this perception of outside threat to the household as one manifestation of the growth of privacy. The truth however is more complex. In the first place, the early modern household was a public domain, subject to court proceedings; window curtains were not common in rural middling households till at least the eighteenth century; so the tension was not simply one of privacy. It was also a tension between ideal and reality. The household may have been a little commonwealth, but it was never self-sufficient in terms of providing all its own subsistence needs (Weatherill 1988: 103–5). To understand the threats to the margins of the house, we must understand those threats as symptomatic of the tensions within the house itself.

Gender and Space in the Early Modern Household

As noted, Harrison's is a male account, viewing objects as emblems of male pride: to reiterate, in the old days,

> that if some one odd farmer or husbandman had been at the alehouse, a thing greatly used in those days, amongst six or seven of his neighbours, and there in a bravery to show what store he had, did cast down his purse and therein a noble or six shillings in silver . . . it was very likely that all the rest could not lay down so much against it (Edelen 1968: 202).

Women may well have viewed the changing structure of domestic space and furnishings in very different ways.

In the first place, patterns of movement associated with life in the pre-industrial farmstead suggest a very different ideal in which everyday experience of space was very different. Men, according to 'conventional' commentaries and advice books, were associated with the outside: they ran the farm, and were responsible for the public, overtly political face of the household. Women were enjoined to keep indoors; according to one writer who seamlessly links household and bodily discipline, they should stay at home behind doors just as they should keep their tongue firmly locked inside their mouth (Ingram 1994). A proverb published in 1670 stated that 'a maid oft seen, a gown oft worn/Are disesteemed and held in scorn' (Erickson 1993: 9). Again, for the much-read Gervase Markham in his advice book *The English Housewife*, man's 'Office and imployments are ever for the most part abroad, or removed from the house' while woman 'hath her most general imployments within the house' (Markham 1986: 5). Markham specified 'The inward and outward vertues which ought to be in a compleat woman' as:

> Physick, cookery, Banqueting-stuffe . . . Distillation, Perfumes, Wooll, Hemp, Flax, Dayries, Brewing, Baking and all other things belonging to an household (Markham, 1986: 1).

The contradiction is evident even here. In addition to a significant silence on the subject of motherhood, Markham's specifications indicate that in the course of their expected daily activities women went to market, met other women at the washhouse, bought and sold goods on the door-step, and so on. In any case, the role of woman as wife, mother and mistress of the household was not the only or even predominant one in the early modern period. Couples did not marry till well into their twenties, and a substantial proportion of both sexes remained unmarried throughout their lives. Many women outlived their husbands, the image of the 'merry widow' becoming another stereotype of fear and mysogyny.

Everyday experience of space was not therefore gendered in any straight-forward or binary way. There was an ideal linked to the inside/outside opposition, but the ideal itself concealed contradictions. Even if the male stereotype of disorderly women bore any relationship to the truth, women did not accept these injunctions. According to writers such as Richard Gough (discussed in chapter 5), disorderly women were regular frequenters of alehouses and other disreputable haunts, where they would engage in 'gossip' and 'tittle-tattle', an activity which in the male view would inevi-tably be peculiarly destructive of male self-esteem. Women in the male view were more lustful than men; they could be witches (Merchant 1980: 134–40); they were even seen as a mistake of Nature (Crawford 1981). Their disorderly activity could, however, be curbed by the use of charivari or the 'rough band' (Ewart Evans 1966: 115–19; Underdown 1985: 100–3) or the more formal use of the church courts (Ingram 1987).

Areas of the house could become specifically female spaces at specific moments. The parlour, for example, was normally a room for both master and wife, and was increasingly becoming a space for both to receive guests in the early modern period. Adrian Wilson has traced how the period of childbirth was marked by exclusion of men for periods of days or weeks from the the parlour where his wife lay in the marital bed, and the regular visits of women in order to bring gifts, to discuss and to receive food and hospitality in their turn (1990). One of the scenes in an early seventeenth century portrayal of gossiping women is labelled 'At the Childbed' (Kermode and Walker 1994).

If experience of space within and around the house was suffused with perceptions of gender, so the movable goods that adorned the house and defined the space within it were perceived differently. We have seen Harrison's link of pewter and silver goods with the urge to display, which he connects closely with the display of male pride through wealth in the alehouse. There is a general tendency among students of vernacular archi-tecture to interpret decoration, furnishings and precious items within pre-industrial households in terms of display and social emulation. This is undoubtedly part of their meaning, but I suggest that such a view may conceal a bias on the part of both contemporary commentators and modern scholars, an assumption that the developed sense of male pride and honour that characterized early modern England was uncritically shared or held in parallel terms by women. Carole Shammas, for example, has argued that at least part of the impetus behind the growth of domestic consumption within the household was due to this increasing desire to keep women within the house:

> the proliferation of knives and forks, glassware, ceramic dishes, and tea equipment throughout all social classes implied more sociability accompanying the taking of food and drink in the home . . . women whose work kept them more closely tied to the house and who because of their sex were less accepted in public places were a major force in promoting these enhancements to the domestic environment (Shammas 1990: 186–8).

If household order was both gendered and an area of public political concern, women could be prosecuted in the courts for threatening this order. David Underdown has suggested that the late sixteenth and early seventeenth centuries saw a crisis in household order, with male perceptions of women's threat to authority reaching a peak. The patriarchal response to this threat was a rise in prosecutions against scolds, witches, and rituals such as skimmingtons that subjected henpecked husbands to abuse (Underdown 1985: 100–3). There is a great deal of cultural complexity behind such a crisis. Ingram has looked more closely at the definition of the scold as a disorderly, loquacious woman, delineating the close links in patriarchal thought between household order, bodily discipline and silent submission (1994).

There were many ambiguities and contradictions between ideal and experience, and it is difficult to generalize between regions before a period when the world-view of the middling sort was not fully integrated within a national culture. We can generalize, however, that the household and its physical setting of the house and farmstead would be experienced in very different ways by women and men. It was also an arena perceived in different ways for masters and servants. Servants in pre-industrial England lived in the house: they would be apprenticed or hired during adolescence to a household. Service was thus as much an age grade as a social class; the majority of servants went on to marry, set up households of their own and even employ other servants.

The view of service expressed in the writings of literate masters was as co-option into the family. The master stood as head to all those under his roof. In this capacity he paid servants a cash wage, but also fed and clothed his employees. He was also responsible for their upbringing and moral well-being; masters could be held responsible by the courts for their servants' bad behaviour. Servants thus lived within an environment that was both their home and their place of work, where even their clothing was provided by someone else according to someone else's standards and cultural expectations. Like women, servants were perceived as potentially disorderly, prone to idleness and gossip. They required ceaseless monitoring and discipline, without which 'every man's house' would fall into disorder and ruin.

The Rebuilding of Rural Relations

Harrison's account of changes in ordinary housing, and the domestic sphere framed by that housing, is therefore in some sense also a social account: it impinges on ideas of household order as well as on levels of material affluence. How, then, is the transformation that Harrison describes seen within particular houses? And what does the changing architecture and domestic fittings of houses tell us of changing cultural attitudes in pre-industrial England?

Let us look at one house among many, and see how its narrative ties in with wider changes. I have deliberately chosen a house where we do not have documentary evidence for the name or social background of the original owner. The Lodge, in the village of Coney Weston, is a medium-sized house in the 'sheep-corn' landscape of north-west Suffolk (figures 7.2 and 7.3); it stands in the middle of the village. The name is probably relatively modern.

The first phase of The Lodge for which physical evidence survives was early sixteenth-century in date. Complete rebuilding, often after fire, was common at this time and there may have been a medieval house on the site that has completely disappeared. At this date it was a simple structure with two rooms on the ground floor; both rooms had ceilings, and there was a narrow loft space below the rafters of the roof above. In terms of size and ostentation, it was probably a yeoman's or prosperous husbandman's dwelling. It was of a relatively new and unusual plan, having no open hall with central hearth as was usual in the majority of houses of the middling sort at the time. Instead, the hall had a chimney stack and ceiling. The way the ceiling is constructed suggests the carpenter may not have been familiar with the technical procedure for timber-framing such a form.

The hall of The Lodge would have been a room of different purposes; the large hearth providing the only cooking facilities, meals being taken in that room, and many of the farm and household activities taking place there. The hall would therefore be 'charged with production': it would merge the worlds of work and the domestic. The parlour or solar

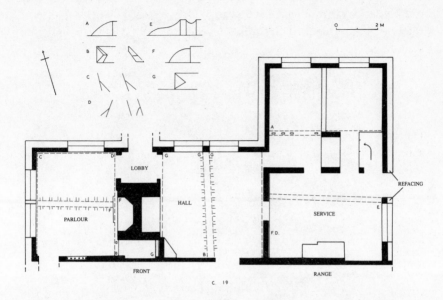

Figure 7.2 The Lodge, Coney Weston, Suffolk (after Johnson 1993: 73): the first phase of this timber-framed house was a two-cell house of hall and parlour, with chimney stack in the end wall of the hall. The hall cross-beam is jointed into its posts; there is, unusually, no cross-rail. The parlour, complete with fireplace and upper room, was probably added in the mid/later sixteenth century. Later, the extended service wing was added and the whole house heightened to two full storeys in the seventeenth century. The lobby entry may have been added at this point, creating a house of typical plan for seventeenth-century East Anglia. Later still, possibly in the early nineteenth century, a front range was added creating a double-pile house and the whole structure encased in brick, giving a 'Georgian' appearance and form to the whole building.

beyond, a private room for master and wife, was unheated. The general impression of the house to our eyes would have been basic and bare in the extreme.

Probably no more than one or two generations later, in the mid to late sixteenth century, a new parlour was built at the other end of the hall. This new parlour had a separate fireplace that was added to the rear of the former chimney-stack. The chamber above the parlour must have been used for some purpose, as the roof of this room was higher than that of the hall

Figure 7.3 The first floor of The Lodge, Coney Weston, showing successive wall heightenings.

(figure 7.3). Other houses of this time invariably had the bed on the ground floor, but may have used the upper room for storage, as a second bedroom, or for both purposes.

The old parlour would then have been turned into a service area, taking some of the life out of the hall. This was still unheated, so cooking and other activities would still have been centred in the hall. The master and his wife, however, may have been seen less in the hall during the course of the daily routine, now having a heated room to withdraw to. It is probable also at this point that a entry into a lobby by the side of the chimney-stack was created, making entry into the hall less direct.

The house was transformed again within one or two generations – possibly around 1600. In the first place, it was heightened, creating a house of two full storeys throughout. A tall, heated room with large windows was created above the parlour, probably being used as a bedroom and possibly leaving the parlour free for use purely as a private withdrawing room. In addition, circulation from one end of the house to the other was now possible at first-floor level. At the same time the service room at the other end of the house was extended into a large wing.

The house had a front range added and was encased in brick in the late eighteenth or nineteenth century. At the same time the roof was rebuilt at a lower pitch, turning it into what externally is a Georgian house. The naming of the house as The Lodge may well date to this remodelling.

The story of The Lodge is a not untypical one for houses in the wealthier, south-eastern half of England at this time. Through time, the house became increasingly segregated in terms of the provision of separate rooms for separate activities and people. The hall ceased to be the main living area and ultimately became one room among many. At the same time, the first floor became more than simply storage space; bedrooms became specialized areas and were increasingly moved upstairs. The increasing number of rooms in seventeenth-century houses had more specific functions attached to them; inventories of this period list ever-larger numbers of brewhouses, pantries, dairies, backhouses, and cheese houses (Johnson 1993: 95).

If the early modern house was getting larger, it was not simply because the household it accommodated was getting more numerous. The numbers of children in the household remained fairly steady after the earlier seventeenth century. Enlargement was also in response to the need to accommodate new activities, or activities such as entertainment which had previously taken place outside the house. The yeoman owners of the first house may have socialized in the local alehouse or on the village green on Sundays, taking part in popular outdoor rituals and sports alongside all levels of the local community. By the end of the seventeenth century, such scenes outside the house involving diverse social elements were becoming much less popular with the middling sort, particularly in socially and culturally 'progressive' areas such as East Anglia. By this time our yeoman farmer and wife may have invited and given hospitality to guests of their own social standing; and these guests would be invited in, not just to their house, but to the parlour, away from the service end of the house. There, they would be away from the smells of greasy servants and the everyday productive round, and could participate in polite conversation and civilized activities such as reading and playing music rather than the rough, crude jollity of popular outdoor culture.

The 'Rise of Comfort'

In sketching the transition between the medieval and modern house through one example, we have seen that domestic comfort is not a normal or natural thing. The middling sort were certainly becoming more prosperous from the later middle ages onwards; but in a world where the distinction between public and private was less than our own, and where much of everyday life took place outdoors, the expenditure of increased levels of wealth on more comfortable living within the domestic interior cannot be expected as inevitable. It would be one option among many for the expenditure of money by increasingly prosperous groups. In the Middle Ages it might be as advisable to spend money on one's future comfort, to contribute to the Church in the hope of ensuring a smoother passage for one's soul to Heaven. I suggest therefore that domestic comfort must be seen in the context of other cultural shifts of the time such as the secularization of culture, changing patterns of social display, and the rise of 'civility'.

Nevertheless the period 1400–1800 is marked by a transformation in domestic comfort and material affluence within the home. It is striking that historians of the fifteenth, sixteenth, seventeenth and eighteenth centuries all see 'their' century as the one when domestic interiors were transformed from bare, cold chambers at the beginning of the century, to well-furnished, comfortable rooms at the end. We can explore some of the complex ways in which such a transformation came about by looking at a range of material goods and domestic furnishings.

Most medieval peasant houses had wooden shutters for windows; there is no archaeological evidence for the tradition repeated by Harrison that these were often of horn. Glass had long been used in small quantities in higher-status medieval houses, but could only be afforded by the middling sort in increasing numbers after 1500. Sixteenth-century window glass often appears in probate inventories and records, on the grounds that glass was taken along if one moved house and was therefore a movable good; this practice was abandoned after 1599 (Godfrey 1975: 108). Window glass of this period was usually mounted in very small panes. Some houses in their concern for display were glazed on the front, and shuttered on the back (for example, see Johnson 1993: 75). Window curtains were rare at this time, only becoming common in households of the middling sort in the eighteenth century.

Many classes of household furnishing were moving away from fixed architectural settings to being movable goods – from being elements of the architectural frame to being commodities. The late medieval open hall in traditional houses was in many ways a smaller version of the great medieval halls discussed in the last chapter. It was largely defined as a piece of social space by fixed items: the raised dais end in larger and more elaborate halls, the canopy over the dais, benches along the sides, positioning of doors and bay windows at lower and upper ends of the hall respectively, even the lengthening of the upper bay of the hall by one rafter. By the end of the seventeenth century, the space within the hall and other rooms had become more commodified. To clarify, the space had become more neutral, less invested with meanings, with fewer fixed architectural signals. The meanings of the space were now defined by movable furniture, and were thus less fixed and more interchangeable. At the same time room divisions no longer corresponded to bay divisions within the physical structure of the house: the technical life of the house became detached from the social, and could be viewed in more 'rational', less traditional ways (Johnson 1993: 106–22).

Furniture was also moving in the direction of greater mobility and a lessening of architectural fixedness. Early beds, for example, were often fixed features within the house (figure 7.4). Fixed or not, they remained substantial four-poster affairs, usually the largest and most valuable item in the inventory. Later beds, like furniture more generally, were flimsier, of less value and more likely to be replaced within the lifetime of the farmer and wife.

The use of benches also declined over the centuries. The replacement of benches by stools and chairs has rightly been seen as a move in everyday

Figure 7.4   High Green, Mickleton: an eighteenth-century house in Teesdale, County Durham. The front façade of the house is laid out to Georgian principles; it now looks out over the back garden thanks to a change in road alignment. Within, however, this house is laid out in a traditional arrangement for this region of England, with a fixed ground-floor bed in the large central hall and an asymmetrical arrangement of rooms.

behaviour towards individualism, people now sitting separately. Equally it carried implications for the ease with which a room could be rearranged and the declining degree of material and cultural fixedness of the interior. Late medieval benches were sometimes fixed along the sides of the hall, running from upper to lower ends with the table between and thus again merging social and architectural space. Even where they were not fixed, however, their large size and weight meant that they were not easily moved around to redefine space.

As the architecture lost its traditional meanings, so the new forms of movable material goods acquired them. Inventories record more sophistication in the goods within houses. Pictures on walls became more common, especially at upper social levels; where mentioned in inventories, these seem to be of either landscape or portrait genres (Weatherill 1988: 207). In one set of rural probate inventories from the economically prosper-

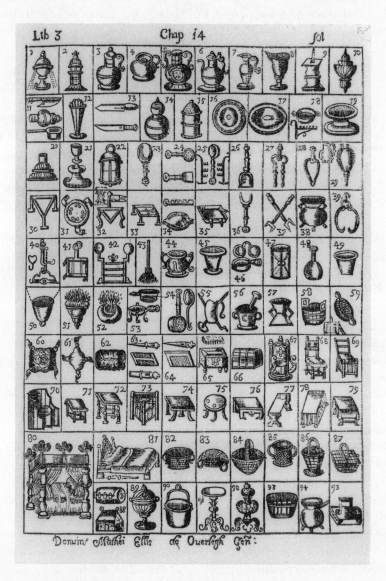

Figure 7.5 Depictions of different mid-seventeenth-century furniture types. Taken from Randle Holme *An Academic or Stone of Armony and Blazon*, Bodleian Library.

ous county of Essex (Steer 1969), we find increasing numbers of hangings and curtains; seats, mostly without upholstery, reserved for owner and guests till the eighteenth century, before which time benches are more common. Close-stools were first noted in 1682; desks appeared with increasing frequency from 1670 onwards, and looking-glasses from 1663; clocks were common from 1670, and hour-glasses from earlier still (Steer 1969: 14 and 20; figure 7.5).

The Meanings of Food

If domestic interiors were becoming more sophisticated arenas for interaction, so were the specific activities that took place within those spaces. The most obvious of these is food preparation and consumption. As an activity which started outside the home with cultivation, and involved processing in service areas culminating in consumption at the ritual of mealtimes in the hall, the meanings of food were bound up with the changing meanings of the house as a whole.

We have seen above how, in cultural terms, food was expected to be procured from Nature by men and preserved and prepared by women. Master and male servants worked in the fields; except at harvest-time when all labour was needed, female mistresses and servants were expected to 'keep indoors'. Though articulated within an ideology of male supremacy such a female role was far from being a passive one; in some households women had control over the household accounts and held domains of power through food preparation, for example through the activities of brewing and dairying (Amussen 1988).

Dairying was particularly important; evidence of its practice is again seen in distinctive pottery forms and in a range of objects such as churns, skimmers and troughs listed in household inventories (Johnson n.d.: 275–9). The production of butter and cheese was carried out within the household and production, sales and accounting were often handled by the mistress. Brewing was an equally important activity; weaker beer formed an important part of the caloric intake of labourers in particular. Larger households brewed their own beer, while widows and paupers often had the right to sell beer and run an alehouse reserved to them.

These channels of economic and cultural relations grouped around food preparation came together literally over the table, at mealtimes. Meals, however modest, had been important symbolic arenas in the later middle ages and this symbolism continued. Household inventories indicate that the master of the household had his own chair at mealtimes, while others sat on stools or benches. Grace would be said, and manners noted. At a time when servants were paid largely in kind the meal was also an important economic transaction between master and servant. Complaints from servants about the quality of the food were endemic and formed a medium for assertion of wider rights (Kussmaul 1981).

The central point here is that relations of power, authority, status and morality were entwined with the process of food production and consumption. Yet again, the political, economic and 'domestic' were bound up one with another. In Sahlins's terms the household was 'charged with production', but charged in a social and symbolic sense as well as an economic one. To explore this further we can look at how this pattern changed through the seventeenth and early eighteenth centuries. I am going to look at two aspects in particular.

First, a shift from the meal as a ritual stressing both communality and inequality within the household – that is, asymmetry of status between members of that commonwealth to difference and segregation in eating patterns between classes. As servants were increasingly paid less in kind and more in cash they spent less of their time outside work within the household and more of it 'out of doors', more often than not consuming beer and tobacco in the local alehouse. At the same time, as we have seen, masters and wives spent correspondingly less time out of doors. Specific occasions when food was consumed by the whole community also declined. The church ale, an occasion when the whole parish got together to raise funds, was 'reformed' as a frequent occasion of allegedly licentious and immoral behaviour (Hill 1964: 426). Increasingly, masters either stayed at home or did their drinking in a tavern of higher status to the alehouse, or if in town went to the coffeehouse to read one of the growing numbers of newspapers and hold a civilized discussion with their social peers.

This move towards different consumption patterns is more complex than a mere increase in order, symmetry and segregation. In the late medieval period diet variation was very high. What these changes refer to, rather, is a heightening of manners specific to social class, and a sharpening of class distinctions as opposed to those of status.

The specific form of the end product, the food itself, was changing in parallel directions. There was a shifting boundary between 'polite' and 'vernacular' forms of cooking, and through time the development of a more individualized style of cooking and eating. The medieval stews and soups were giving way to more differentiated patterns of food long before the process of 'Georgianization'. The seventeenth century saw the start of separate tastes in the cooking of the middling sort (Yentsch 1991: 29), while greater diversity in sauces and dishes varied the experience of eating among the middling sort well before the introduction of standardized eating patterns and tableware in the eighteenth century.

The second movement is one of increasing segregation between the activities of cooking and eating in both a spatial and social sense. In the sixteenth century house, food was both cooked and eaten in the large central hall. There could thus be minimal distinction between 'kitchen' and 'table' pottery forms, and it is difficult to see in the pottery assemblages of this period any such distinction. Again, inventories indicate the use of brass pots and pewter plates but there is little indication of the transfer of food from cooking vessels to serving dishes prior to consumption. Where such inventories give room-by-room accounts it is clear that when cooking equipment was listed outside the hall it was merely being stored.

By 1750 a very different pattern had emerged. Specialized kitchen ranges had always been present in higher-status households, but now middling houses had separate kitchens with their own chimney-stacks. These new kitchens often had more specialized cooking equipment. A variety of forms of spit had always been used for cooking joints of meat but these were now often automated with clockwork mechanisms. Increased control over heat was also given with the use of coal rather than wood and the introduction of ranges of ovens.

One of the key changes in this process was that the replacement of the central hearth open to the roof in the centre of the hall with the chimney-stack at one side in the sixteenth and seventeenth centuries was often followed or accompanied by a shift in cooking activities out of the hall into a separate kitchen. The hearth could now use jacks, pothooks, spits, ovens and side hobs; the cook could now hold skillets and posnets over the fire by hand. The excavation of spit-supports from non-elite social contexts in Wales (Redknap 1992), indicates a degree of wealth as well as sophistication in the cooking process in a supposed 'less advanced' rural area.

Another key change was the development of the 'double-pile' or two-room-deep house from the middle of the seventeenth century (Johnson 1993: 99). Now service activities, and with them servants and women, were no longer at one end of the house; they were relegated to the back, out of the way of the 'public face' of the hall and parlour. With the double-pile house came the development of 'front space' and 'back space' in the house, and a growing division between the production and cooking of food at the rear of the house and its consumption at the front.

So cooking became more complex and was moved out of the hall; at the same time the presentation of food came to deny its origins with a much clearer distinction between table and kitchen wares in pottery assemblages. This shift had started in the later middle ages with the replacement of large ceramic pots for cooking with metal receptacles as well as smaller pipkins, ceramic frying pans and dripping pans. Cisterns were used for storing water and beer; it has been suggested that the use of cisterns with bungholes allowed the straining-off of sediment.

Slipware plates and dishes became increasingly common after the middle of the seventeenth century while silver, pewter and glass became standard at table. Pewter in particular, being amenable to melting down and remoulding in the latest style, became an important new arena of fashionable consumption (Thirsk 1978: 106).

Thus, changes in seventeenth-century England prefigure and throw into perspective those discussed by Deetz and others in eighteenth-century New England and Chesapeake (Deetz 1977; Leone and Potter 1988): the irony is that the patterns these scholars consider to be 'medieval' or 'pre-Georgian' are from this perspective post-medieval or indicative of a move towards the flowering of Georgian principles.

There was thus an increasing division between different aspects of food preparation and consumption. At the same time as women's activities were moved out of the hall, their control over dairying and brewing was attacked. Both processes became centralized and 'professionalized' under the control of men. Amussen (1988) has noted how marginalization and separation of women from production in rural England contributed to developing patterns of inequality, while Howell has traced the move of urban production out of the home towards separate units and its effect of depriving women of economic power and status (Howell 1986).

Conclusion

By the later seventeenth century onwards we can see a divergence between the worlds of work and of the home; a marginalization of women's household activities; separation and segregation between different ends of the house; and a renegotiation of the household away from being a little commonwealth, a constituent unit of a greater polity subject to public interest and legislation, and towards a private domain. Such changes in everyday life were superficially very small ones, barely worth commenting upon in the view of many more traditional historians, or simple rises in comfort and convenience in need of no further explanation in the views of others. In the view presented here they occupied a key place in the genealogy of capitalism. Norbert Elias (1978) has described how such things as table manners changed through time, and how ideas relating to hygiene and civil behaviour related to changing notions of discipline and control over the body. The argument here is in parallel to Elias's. Through time, the pre-industrial household changed its physical form. Houses became more segregated and privatized, with more physical division between different areas of the house and the household and outside world. At the same time goods within the house became more numerous; the house became more comfortable. This marks a shift in relations between individuals; a development of distinctions between front space and back space; a notion of the house as domestic retreat rather than integral to the process of work. In this way, the house became more modern, more the place we know today; and the social relations of the household became so also.

In the eighteenth century regional traditions of vernacular architecture became subsumed under the national style and form of the Georgian house. Symmetrical in façade, ordered and segregated in plan, the two-room-deep layout of the Georgian house has been seen as the culmination of the processes of change sketched out above. Just as striking as the form itself is its repetition all over England in different building materials. The principle of the Georgian Order, however, was actively manipulated at the vernacular level and was by no means passively accepted (figure 7.4). To understand further the ways in which Georgian forms and styles were negotiated and formed we must first look at the world of goods, and at the individual. This is the task of chapter 8.

8

Thinking about Objects

A huge amount of academic labour is invested in the study of late and post-medieval artefacts – pottery, clay pipes, glass, pins, ornaments, trinkets, small things more easily forgotten than remembered. Within the accepted traditions of late and post-medieval archaeology, inferences are usually drawn from this material relating to the minutiae of economic and industrial history: production centres, markets, technical innovations. Such traditions of work have an obvious relevance to the rise of capitalism in a strictly economic sense.

In this chapter I want to suggest, however, that the meanings and interpretations of artefacts are necessarily more complex and difficult than this, and must be understood in a variety of different ways beyond the 'economic'. These different ways involve study of the very different meanings, ambiguous, subtle, changing, multiple, that artefacts carried and that were involved in their production and consumption.

Objects tend to be viewed by traditional economic historians purely as commodities, with a certain market value subject to the laws of supply and demand. In this view production and consumption are very separate analytical categories and the social life of things is underplayed. Their role of objects as commodities is an important aspect of their meaning and interpretation, but it must be a starting point rather than an assumption. To clarify, the view of objects as pure commodities is a distinctly capitalistic, modern one; to see where it came from, to trace its genealogy, we have to allow for very different contexts of consumption and meaning, very different origins in the pre-industrial past. To show how artefacts can be viewed in other, perhaps more rewarding, ways I shall first discuss three case studies of things being used actively in different social contexts relating to nascent capitalism.

Display and Honour in the Early Sixteenth-Century

Pleaseth your lordship to be ascertained that I have sent you by this bearer, Harry Drywry, first vj pair of hosen for your lordship; item, ij caps with ij under-caps, one of velvet another of satin, locked in a new cap-case whereof he hath the key; more, a yard and a half violet frisado fo Mr James; item iiij dozen staff torches; ij dozen quarriers; more, a chest containing therein jC/ j fine suger in xij loaves; ij lbs cinnamon; ij lbs ginger; j lb cloves; j lb maces; j lb sawndres [sandalwood], x lbs pepper; j lb tornsel . . . And for the viij dozen counterfeit [made of base metal or according to pattern] dishes, if it be posssible to have them in all London, I will have them this day, for yesterday Hugh Colton and I were about all London for them, but we could not speed above j dozen (John Husee to Lord Lisle, cited in St Clair Byrne 1983: 67).

The Lisles were an early sixteenth-century aristocratic family of traditional habit and attitudes. In 1533 Lord Lisle had been appointed as Governor of Calais, the sole remnant of England's French possessions after the Hundred Years War; there, as part of the duties of his office he was expected to live and keep house and hospitality in a style appropriate to his position. This obligation 'in banqueting and feasting of strange ambassadors and other foreign potestes and great personages' (St Clair Byrne 1983: 161) induced some financial strain as his repeated requests to the King for money testify.

The Lisles obtained many of their luxury goods from London. The quotation above is from their servant John Husee to Lord Lisle; it illustrates many of the characteristic values associated with the purchase and consumption of commodities among the elite in the early sixteenth century. It is striking that, as was the common practice in such great households, such consumption was done through private order through agents; and also that it was Lady Lisle who handled the majority of this business (the letter to Lord Lisle given above is exceptional).

Surprisingly to our eyes, the goods acquired by Lisle's agent for consumption in Calais did not need to be new; and there was a heavy and obvious emphasis on display at this elite level. Such display was directed both at social inferiors and at the social equals of the Lisles. Much of the social interchange between great families was accompanied by the giving and receiving of gifts. If much of the Lisles' purchase and consumption of material goods was done via agents through London, they exchanged gifts with other great families both back in England and with their French counterparts. These gifts were reciprocal in nature and involved an assertion of the code of civil manners of the time. Outard de Bies, the French seneschal of Boulogne and as such Lord Lisle's counterpart and potential opponent in diplomacy and war, invokes these civilities between two honourable knights of equal rank in a typical example. De Bies sends Lisle the head of a wild boar, all the more valuable and carrying so much more meaning given his account in the accompanying letter that the valiant boar had killed two of Bies's hunting dogs. Parallel exchanges took place between women: the daughter or wife of the captain of Tournehem in Flanders accepts 'the cramp ring and the codiniac that it hath pleased you to send me. And I send you a pentar upon which to hang your keys, which I pray you to accept' (St Clair Byrne 1983: 59 and 233).

Another gift that was exchanged between families at this time were the children of elite households. The Lisles sent their offspring to the households of aristocrats and royalty; others in sixteenth-century England sent their sons and daughters into service in great households of immediately superior rank to their own (McCracken 1983). Chapter 6 discussed how the deployment of numbers of servants, often in livery, around the great hall was used to emphasize rank and wealth.

It is too simplistic to see the Lisles' world and the place of material culture within it as one of a simple code of values of sub-medieval civility, patronage and chivalric honour. That world itself was shifting, as the Lisles' fall from grace in the hands of an assertive Tudor state was to show. Nevertheless the use of material goods is striking; it is clearly linked to their 'self-fashioning', their idea of themselves and their recreation of values and identities. At the same time the number and variety of new goods circulating combined with desire for elite display.

The increasing flow of new and exotic goods flowing into and through elite households at this time was a routine cause for complaint (Harte 1976: 141–3). Thus Sir Thomas Smith wrote in his *Discourse of the Commonweal of this weal of England* (1549) of such luxury:

> Of which sort I mean glasses as well looking as drinking as to glass windows, dials, tables, cards, balls, puppets, penhorns, inkhorns, toothpicks, gloves, knives, daggers, owches [buckles], brooches, aglets [pendants], buttons of silk and silver, earthen pots, pins, points, hawks' bells, paper both white and brown . . . For there is no man that can be contented now with any gloves than is made in France or Spain; nor kersey, but it must be made of Flanders dye; nor cloth, but French or frizado; nor owche, brooch, nor aglet, but of Venice making or Milan; nor dagger, sword, nor girdle, or knife, but of Spanish making or some outward country; no not as much as a spur, but that is fetched [bought] at the Milaners [milliners] (Dewar 1969).

Much tableware was produced apparently for use at one occasion only, as with the assemblage of fine wares excavated at Acton Court, apparently remnants discarded immediately after the visit of Henry VIII (Vince and Bell 1992). As late as 1617 Venetian ambassadors professed disgust at what they saw as the wilful and uncivilized smashing of glass at King James's court (Smuts 1987: 28).

The Lisles, like most elite families of the period, used objects to buttress their position in society. They fashioned an image of themselves through their clothing, the gifts they gave, and other artefacts. Their authority was not simply or solely one of fixed rank: it was defined and actively renego-tiated through the act of consumption.

Moving House and Reforming Manners

The Evetts family had lived in Warwickshire in the Midlands since the later fourteenth century; by the later seventeenth century they were well known as a reputable local family of the middling sort. They had lived in the Old Hall at Temple Balsall since 1660, as yeoman farmers and bailiffs of a local charity. In the late 1730s Thomas Evetts retired as bailiff and farmer; house and office of bailiff were taken over by his son Barlow Evetts. At the same time they moved house, from the Old Hall to the newly built Temple House.

It appears that during the move, or possibly a few years later upon the death of Thomas, all the pottery and glassware from the Old Hall was thrown out into a disused and derelict cellar in front of the house. Jugs, jars, glasses and bottles were thrown in armfuls from the top of the cellar steps, smashing on the floor below. Three generations of accumulated 'kitchen stuff' and tableware were thrown out in one event.

The material thrown out by the Evetts thus gives some impression of the kitchen and tableware of a yeoman family in the early eighteenth century. This pottery is of varying quality; the Evetts's pottery included brightly coloured slipware dishes, plates, shallow bowls and other vessels of various wares and designs. Several plates had been pierced to hang on the wall as ornaments. Drinking vessels included beer mugs of various sizes, as well as glasses and bottles for wine. Clay tobacco pipes were ubiquitous; cups and pipkins had been warmed by pushing up against the fire.

The assemblage is also striking in its omissions: in what was not thrown out. Very little newly fashionable pottery, such as white stoneware and English or Chinese porcelain, was found; this material may not have been used at the Old Hall, or more likely it was saved and taken to the Evetts's new home.

The Evetts were a prosperous and upwardly mobile yeoman family (Barlow Evetts was worth over £400 when he died in 1670, and his sons were called gentlemen; the accompanying faunal assemblage indicates a varied diet including oysters). In her report on the cellar assemblage from which this account is taken Eileen Gooder suggests that moving house was the moment at which the family had 'arrived' socially into the gentry class (1984: 153). They had moved from a traditional house of vernacular design to a new 'Georgian' building of the latest style (1984: 153). The Old Hall had irregularly set windows, and was one-room deep with a central hall and wing at one end; the latter had a symmetrical front and double-pile plan, with chimney-stacks discreetly placed at the rear and a 'Georgian' style and arrangement.

The pottery assemblage suggests a reformation of manners may have taken place alongside the Evetts's reformation of domestic space. Matched, mould-made sets of white porcelain were becoming increasingly popular in the middle of the eighteenth century; they went along with standardized place settings with knives and forks and more elaborate table furniture such as candlesticks (Sinclair 1987).

Increasingly refined, individualized table manners as part of what Norbert Elias has called the civilizing process (1978), producing new patterns of bodily and social discipline congruent with nascent capitalism (Shackel 1993). At the same time, the reformation of manners also marked a change in the nature of social class, a shift on the part of the middling sort to the values and ideas of polite culture. In the eighteenth-century, families of the middling sort had the levels of wealth to be able for the first time to buy and use such items as part of a 'package' of manners and lifestyle, as the parallel changes in architecture indicate. The way was open to emulate those above the middling sort on the social scale. And rather than be content with the 'solid sufficiency' of traditional patterns of eating and living, many families such as the Evetts seem to have been very willing to do so.

Clay Pipes and Cultural Disorder

Clay pipes are found in their thousands on any and every post-medieval site: tiny fragments of stem, the occasional bowl, all at first sight very much like one another (figure 8.1). Clay pipes do not appear to be a

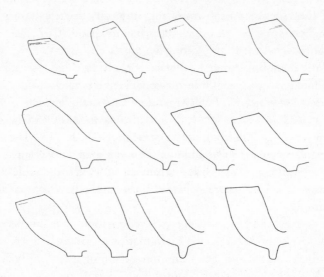

Figure 8.1   A selection of different clay pipe forms (after Helme 1978: 18). In general, the bowls of clay pipes get larger through time as the cost of tobacco decreases. The majority of bowls found on post-medieval sites are undecorated save for simple features such as milling around the rim.

promising ground for theoretical excursus. Most scholarship on this subject has concentrated on changing production centres, or on the vexed question of dating post-medieval sites from an analysis of the width of the bore-holes.

There is more to clay pipes than meets the eye, however. As artefacts of tobacco consumption, they are linked in to a very wide matrix of changes connecting production and consumption, authority and resistance, Old and New Worlds. Tobacco was imported into England; it was one of a number of New World commodities that excited the senses of the Old World and induced new patterns of expenditure and consumption (Elliott 1970). At first an expensive luxury product, tobacco smoking rapidly became popular at all social levels. King James I even felt moved to condemn the practice in his pamphlet *Counter-Blaste to Tobacco* (Knapp 1993: 273).

Among the middling sort and at lower social levels, a clay pipe of tobacco might be purchased and consumed at the alehouse along with a pot of beer (such stoneware tankards are themselves common finds, if less ubiquitous on post-medieval sites). Alcohol consumption was an integral part of the life of the early modern community: there was one licensed drinking establishment for 120 people in England (Clark 1983: 42–3; figure 8.2).

Alehouses were sources of concern to the authorities in early modern England and Wales. They were viewed not just as centres of drunkenness, 'whoredom' and disorderly behaviour, but as places of political dissent and radicalism. For ordinary people, they were sites of 'neighbourliness' as well as competition in drinking matches (Clark 1983: 114). They were used as places to receive stolen goods, and for illicit assignations; and as alternative centres of prostitution after the sixteenth-century crackdown on brothels. Puritans and others disliked alehouses and attempted to impose regulation with varying degrees of success.

Figure 8.2 A seventeenth-century alehouse scene (from Clark 1983). Alehouses were often no more than ordinary houses with a sign and 'ale-bench' outside. The apparent crudity of such depictions is belied by their complexity of allusion: Williams (1990) has explored how the simple forms depicted had many allusions to other stories and meanings.

Courtesy of York University History, © The British Library.

It would be interesting given this context of consumption of tobacco to know more about the iconography of the scenes and motifs often found on clay pipes. Many bear coats of arms and other symbols of Royal and lordly authority: can they therefore be viewed as evidence for the view that underlying the upheavals of the seventeenth century was a moral and political consensus spanning all social levels? Alternatively, is the distribution of particular decorative motifs between sites of different social classes at all significant?; do we find different symbols in drinking houses of different social statuses? Alehouses were found to be dirty and smoky by the gentry and mercantile classes, who increasingly preferred to drink wine rather than beer in inns and taverns, or to stay and entertain at home. Alehouses were regarded as male haunts, though Gough and other commentators made disapproving remarks about the disorderly behaviour of female clientele, and women's visits to alehouses are regularly attested to in court records; is the decoration of pipes gendered?

The paradox here is that the clay pipe is an artefact of colonialism as well as of popular resistance. Like many other commodities such as tea and sugar, the popularity of these items among ordinary people from the later seventeenth century onwards fuelled Imperial trade and colonial domination. Tobacco was produced in Virginia and the Chesapeake, colonies which at least in their early years were hugely reliant on imported goods from the Old World (Shammas 1990: 67). In the long term, tobacco production shifted from the use of indentured servants to slaves (Kulikoff 1986).

The Meanings of Things

I have started by discussing these three cases to show that objects are important in ways that are not simply economic, and also that their meanings are very complex and multifaceted. Most obviously goods are bearers and indicators of wealth, embodiments of material affluence; but they are other things than that. If 'credit' in the early modern world-view was a more complex concept than simply that of level of material wealth as discussed in chapter 4, so we must view objects in more complex ways.

For 'post-processual' archaeologists, material culture is active. To clarify, the meanings of objects are not fixed: they can be reclassified, renegotiated by people for different purposes and strategies. The seneschal of Boulogne made a boar's head mean so much more by wrapping a narrative of hunting around it; the head became an icon upon which values of gentility and civility were pinned. Further, through his offer of the head to Lisle, de Bies claimed that both he and Lisle were bonded by these shared values borne by the gift. Lisle, by accepting or rejecting the gift, could renegotiate the associated meanings in his turn. Neither, of course, would overtly articulate such values, which would be 'taken for granted'. Because people constantly renegotiate meanings at an implicit, 'taken-for-granted' level in this way, a simple, ordinary object like a clay pipe can come to bear many different and complex meanings. It is for these reasons that an archaeology of artefacts, an excavation of the often hidden and implicit social life of things, is one of the most exciting areas of an archaeology of capitalism.

Producing Objects

Up until very recently, the bulk of archaeological interest in late and post-medieval material culture was couched in terms of analysing production and distribution. In David Crossley's *Post-Medieval Archaeology in Britain* (1990) 103 pages out of 291 are taken up with the topic of extractive or manufacturing 'industry' of one form or another, while of the remainder of the text the sections on pottery and glass are almost entirely an account of changing wares and production centres. Crossley's summary accurately reflects the great emphasis on industrial and traditional artefact studies in medieval and post-medieval archaeology up until very recently.

Archaeological studies of production will continue to be important in writing the archaeology of capitalism. There was a transformation between 1450 and 1750 in industry and production of goods and commodities in England, and the impact of this transformation should not be underestimated. It was functionally linked to the new markets and trade networks of Empire, as well as to the rise in agricultural productivity during this period discussed in chapter 4 (Wrigley 1989; Kussmaul 1990). It was also linked to a massive rise in the volume and variety of internal trade between 1500 and 1750 (Chartres 1977), despite the fact that transport costs have been argued to be not significantly lower at this later date than in medieval England (Masschaele 1993 and 1994).

There is an archaeology of industry that needs to be explored here concerning the cultural context of these emergent technologies of production (Dobres and Hoffman 1994; Pacey 1974). For example, the emergence of new forms of machine technology was dependent on a mechanistic view of power. Such a view militated against older, more traditional forms of world-view and went hand-in-hand with a more mechanistic view of the universe (Mayr 1986). It has been argued that technological innovation in the early seventeenth century needs to be understood in terms of a Puritan ethic and world-view that combined new understanding of the natural world with the pursuit of the millenium (Webster 1975: 343–60). Whether Webster has overstated his case or not, it is certainly true that the technological and industrial developments of the seventeenth and eighteenth centuries need to be placed in their cultural context as an appropriation of Nature.

We also need to examine more closely the relationship between production, technology and consumption. I argued in *Housing Culture* that the technology used in the carpentry of houses, for example, changed radically between 1400 and 1700. I suggested that functional and decorative aspects of timber-framing were intertwined in medieval houses; a split between function and decoration was one feature of 'closure', making possible an opposition between 'economical' as opposed to 'decorative' carpentry methods. Thus a late medieval timber frame might well be lavish in its use of timber, whereas by the later seventeenth and eighteenth centuries the timber frame would be constructed as economically as possible before being rendered over; expenditure on decoration and display would go into the plasterwork or furniture within the closed house. More fundamentally, I suggested a shift between 'openness' and 'closure' in very tiny details of building technique.

One of the effects of this shift was to alter the relationship between producer and consumer, shifting the power to specify different forms into the hands of the owner of the house and away from the craft tradition (Johnson 1993: 115). Late medieval houses were prefabricated to the last detail in the builder's yard; by 1700, the detail of such prefabrication had lessened. The owner of the closed house, therefore, could specify in more detail the position of doors, windows and other fittings, rather than be guided by what was 'traditional'.

If other craft traditions followed related patterns, the contexts and categories of production and consumption may be more closely linked than we have previously allowed. We need more close studies of the way interaction between producer and consumer proceeded in an age when the operations of the market were not taken for granted.

The World of Consumption

Nevertheless, the most exciting work on material culture in recent years within both archaeology and history has centred around the theme of consumption: the different ways objects are bought, used, and eventually thrown away. A specific debate within social and economic history has centred around a suggested revolution in consumption in the century preceding the Industrial Revolution, with the implication that the birth of industrial capitalism was as much demand-led and small-scale as it was to do with the emergence of large-scale factory production. Attention has been drawn to the way in which even landless labourers changed their consumption patterns in the eighteenth century towards new goods such as tea and butter (Shammas 1990: 128–9) and to a 'Great Reclothing' of the countryside in parallel with Hoskins's Great Rebuilding, facilitated by the growing numbers of small traders and petty chapmen in the early modern period (Spufford 1984).

Such new choices in consumer goods were enabled by the more general rise in material affluence of the time, particularly among the middling sort, but were not necessitated by it. To clarify: people had more wealth and so were able to spend more, but could choose what they wanted to spend it on according to non-economic priorities. The choice of goods to consume is inevitably a cultural one, as Douglas and Isherwood have pointed out (1979). They thus raise the question: how do we theorize the consumption of goods in the late medieval and early modern periods?

We can start by drawing on Danny Miller's thinking about objects and meanings in his theoretical essay *Material Culture and Mass Consumption* (1987). Miller is interested in the way material culture comes to carry social meaning, and how the way things are produced and consumed within different historical circumstances affect the way it carries those meanings. In so doing he questions whether objects really are more 'material' than the ideas they carry: 'the very physicality of the object which makes it so immediate, sensual and assimilable belies its actual nature . . . material culture is one of the most resistant forms of cultural expression in terms of our attempts to understand it' (1987: 3).

For Miller, the material culture of modernity or of capitalism differs from that of other historical periods because the overwhelming majority of objects in our world are mass produced. Objects are already distant from us when we purchase and consume; we have no direct control over their form and nature except through consumer choice. In the modern world, then, objects come to give us identity partly through the act of consumption and partly through what Miller calls 'work'; the act of investing them with meanings through placing them in different contexts, within different narratives; the placing of a medieval glazed pot on a Georgian mantelpiece, or a gnome in a garden.

Miller's work is much more theoretically sophisticated than this account indicates, taking on Hegel and a number of other theorists. It is exciting because it suggests that objects play a very specific role in our world, not just in terms of their production but in terms of the way in which they come to signify meaning. Here, I want to encapsulate the way in which the relationship between object and meaning(s) changes with changing ideas of the self and others in the early modern world in the term 'commodification'.

Miller does not enter into a substantive discussion of how objects became commodified within concrete historical conditions; it is sufficient for his purposes to locate their origins within the changing relations of modern capitalism. This begs the question for our purposes of how, then, did material culture work within social and cultural relations in the early modern period?

I suggest that in the medieval world, popular culture was often immediately rooted in material forms: there was a close, embedded relationship between everyday activity, material culture and the meanings of goods. This does not necessarily mean that the meanings of vernacular material culture were simple or crude, or somehow less sophisticated than those of elite culture or of modernity; indeed, the thrust of this book has been to show how arenas such as fields, houses, and the church were invested with very complex meanings. Nevertheless, for the illiterate masses below elite level, experience of the world and places and objects within it was everyday, dramaturgical, embedded in practical activity. In such a world the consumption of objects was embedded in the everyday, and had a direct relationship to social standing.

Objects were few in such a world; the previous chapter discussed how the earliest inventories record domestic interiors that by our standards were bare, colourless and sparse. Lorna Weatherill's analysis of household expenditure suggests that spending on such objects came a poor fourth after food, clothing and shelter (1988: 114–33). This is not to say, however, that goods were not important: after land, movable goods were the main component of wealth in a peasant household. This was partly due to the greater durability of furniture and household objects; goods would be inherited, already carry meanings, be part of the immediate cultural background of the household. Thus, even as late as the seventeenth and early eighteenth centuries, families spent more on clothing than on furniture since the latter was infrequently replaced (Weatherill 1991: 298). If more goods were inherited, more were kept rather than being thrown away. Clothing, buildings, metals, and paper would all be reused rather than discarded (Woodward 1985).

It is in this context that we should understand the burgeoning of sumptuary laws in the later medieval and early modern periods. Sumptuary laws, which lay down prohibitions on different forms of consumption, were passed at different intervals between 1337 and 1603; thereafter they went into gradual abeyance, starting with the repeal of the 'statutes of apparel' governing clothing (Baldwin 1926). It is notable that the use of sumptuary laws declined much earlier in England than on the Continent.

The 1337 statute was concerned with food: the number of courses and kinds of meat allowed. By the sixteenth century sumptuary laws were principally though not exclusively concerned with clothing, forbidding, for example, men below a certain rank to wear certain materials and garments. A law passed after the main period of legislation in 1666 even specified that the dead must be buried in a woollen sheet (Harte 1976: 152), though the degree to which such laws were ignored is indicated in Pope's lines published in 1734:

> Odious! In woollen! 'twould a Saint provoke,
> (Were the last words that poor Narcissa spoke),
> No, let a charming Chintz, and Brussels lace
> Wrap my cold limbs, and shade my lifeless face:
> One would not, sure, be frightful when one's dead –
> And – Betty – give this Cheek a little red.
> (Alexander Pope, 'Of the Knowledge and Characters of Men'.)

There seem to have been very few prosecutions at upper social levels; in practice only the lower classes were prosecuted. In 1559 every master was ordered to see that servants were giving up forbidden items (Shammas 1990: 217).

The importance of sumptuary laws in this context is as an ideal statement. Sumptuary laws embodied the assumption that there were a series of more or less fixed statuses in society, and that one could tell a person's rank from the way he or she dressed, or more generally appropriated the world of goods. Further, that this mode of dress affected others: luxurious dress 'poisons and consumes others spiritually' (cited in Scattergood 1987: 272). It is not surprising therefore that they were principally aimed at men, the heads of households, in an age when men rather than women wore the more colourful clothing (Harte 1976).

Such laws could be locally imposed or even be a form of self-restraint. At Rye in Sussex, certain burial practices were confined to the upper classes of the town (Gittings 1984: 115). Lee Warley, a Kentish yeoman, was following the orthodoxy of social commentators when he wrote on the first page of his account and memorandum book that 'In our Expenses we should neither ape those that are placed in a more exalted sphere, nor . . . sink beneath our proper station' (Weatherill 1988: 196).

Others, apparently, did not follow Warley's self-restraint; the very passing of sumptuary laws was also an artefact of the contemporary perception that, whether or not it had ever existed, such a stable world in which a measured, invariate, unchanging conception of social rank and consumption went together was under threat. A person was defined by (fixed) social status in the medieval world; such definitions were threatened by the new luxuries and display of the fifteenth and sixteenth centuries.

The motivations behind sumptuary laws were more multi-stranded than simply an attempt to codify and protect social status. They were also designed to reduce imports and protect native industries. They nevertheless represented a way of looking at the world in terms of fixed ranks: put very simply, in which a way of dressing, eating or consumption generally was appropriate to social station, and in which the behaviour between individuals was broadly governed by notions of status rather than class.

Where was the threat to this conception coming from? Put very crudely, we see an explosion in the consumption of new forms of material culture from the later middle ages onwards, along with new forms of marketing and distribution. Behind this explosion was, I suggest, a new set of principles underlying the meanings of things, a set of principles closely related to the rise of capitalism.

Commodification

These new principles were not simply those of display. As the example of the Lisles made clear, display, or conspicuous consumption, had always been a feature of the upper ranks of society; one can use the analogy of Weber's point that there had always been material greed and acquisitiveness for thousands of years before the rational attitude to capital accumulation that he saw as being engendered by the Protestant ethic. What had emerged, however, by the eighteenth century, was a new system, a new order or set of discursive rules governing consumption of material goods.

One aspect of this new set of discourses was a new stress on fashion. The idea of fashion is not a cross-cultural universal (Wilson 1985: 47–66). It is intimately bound up with the rise of the middling sort, the constitution of the individual and the separation between public and private. To take clothing as an example, the more or less standard dress of the medieval peasant allowed immediate identification of social rank; conversely, its unvarying nature allowed little expression of individuality outside rank. Adoption by a newly affluent 'middling sort' of new and more diverse forms of clothing tied in both with new forms of individuality and with a threat to the social order of things.

Fashion within eighteenth-century polite culture was articulated around two features: first, a highly articulated idea of taste and style; and second, the co-option of the middling sort into this new system. This was a system whose social underpinnings were well understood by contemporaries, who saw it as having to do with the structuring of emulation within a ranked but fluid class system:

> In England the several ranks of men slide into each other almost impercep-
> tibly, and a spirit of equality runs through every part of their constitution.
> Hence arises a strong emulation in all the several stations and conditions to
> vie with each other; and the perpetual restless ambition in each of the
> inferior ranks to raise themselves to the level of those immediately above
> them. In such a state as this fashion must have uncontrolled sway. And a
> fashionable luxury must spread through like a contagion (Forster 1767,
> cited in McKendrick et al. 1982: 11).

This emergent discourse on style and taste was central to the new demand for consumer goods in the eighteenth century; it was this demand, for example, that Wedgwood catered for in basing his pottery on high prices, a mass market, and advertising. Wedgwood's pottery was fashionable to the point of being topical, having for example Antique fashions in the wake of interest in Pompeii and Herculaneum. It was also sensitive to differently perceived ideas of taste in other social classes and in terms of gender, draping nude classical figures to avoid 'offence to our delicate Ladies' in the middle-class market in particular (McKendrick et al. 1982: 113).

Anthony Sinclair's work on silver candlesticks (1987; see figure 8.3) has shown how the production of this luxury good for display on tables at mealtimes expanded after the later seventeenth century. The form of the candlestick being necessitated by function, its style changed rapidly and with reference to changing tastes. Sinclair places these artefacts in the context of an emergent discourse on style, linked in turn to the self-definition in terms of taste of the ruling classes.

A second aspect of commodification can be seen in Chandra Mukerji's delineation of patterns of modern materialism. Mukerji isolates the importance of the combination of capital accumulation and consumption after the Reformation in north-west Europe (1983: 5). This was more than a

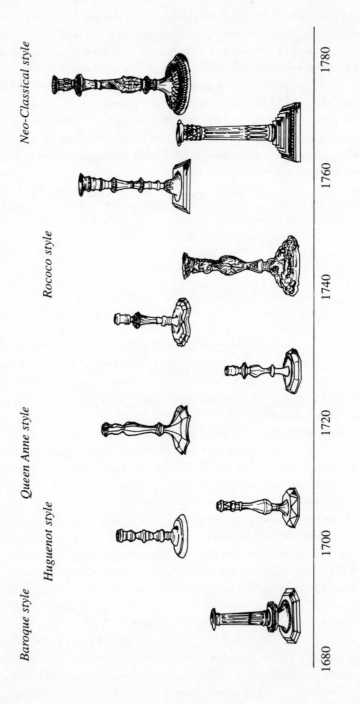

Figure 8.3 Changes in the form of silver candlestick made in England between 1680 and 1780 (after Sinclair 1987). Each style appears to rise and fall in a regular rhythm.

mere increase in the quantity of goods: it involved a newly articulated concern with their meanings. Mukerji highlights, for example, the creation of a mass market for maps, and stresses the relationship between new intellectual trends of scientific and materialist thought and new patterns of production and consumption of goods: independent study of the Bible, for instance, a central feature of Protestantism, was only possible given the printing press.

Obviously one way to examine commodification is through new artefacts of marketing. The trade token, for example, appeared after farthings and halfpennies were withdrawn by Parliament in 1644. The use of tokens declined after 1672 when farthings and halfpennies were reissued; they were mostly used by lower classes alongside formal and informal systems of credit, and reappeared again during the Industrial Revolution (Mathias 1962).

Marketing spread to new areas as one aspect of commodification. The elite, like the Lisles, had hitherto contracted for goods such as pottery or furniture. Less was produced within the household, thus widening the divorce between production and consumption: where the middling sort previously made their own clothes, they now could buy from the market (Shammas 1990: 200–3). The seventeenth and eighteenth centuries saw a rise of shops in smaller market towns and villages (Mui and Mui 1989). Before this time, the word 'shop' in a rural context often referred to a workshop, usually within the domestic household (Johnson 1993: 84). After 1660 shops would stock more than one good, including cloth, haberdashery, garments, and groceries. Shops of this kind were supplemented and preceded by petty chapmen and licensed pedlars, who sold books, pamphlets, and small trinkets on a door-to-door basis (Spufford 1984; Shammas 1990: 235 and 255).

A growing number of goods produced for and distributed via national markets, when linked to the new eighteenth-century practice of advertising, tied commodification into cultural centralization. Style books came out of London publishing houses, specifying what was fashionable or in good taste, while newspapers carried advertisements for a range of commodities. This expansion of media for the transmission of the meanings of objects was matched by a multiplicity of styles in which objects were made. Objects such as clocks and candlesticks went through rapid stylistic change (Sinclair 1987; Lucas 1995). In a wide range of areas from architecture through furniture to clothing, purchasers could now specify certain styles rather than what was available or traditional locally. This involved standardization of goods between different regions of England and Wales;

and increasing affiliation to a national pattern of dress and material culture rather than a sense of regional identity.

Commodification and Literacy

Commodification was also entwined with literacy in early modern England. I suggest that literacy went hand in hand with new views of the material world and objects within it. The growth of literacy also involved the elements of marketing, standardization and centralization.

As a whole, many more people could read and write in 1700 than two centuries earlier; and after the arrival of the printing press in England in the later fifteenth-century, books and pamphlets were increasingly available in large numbers. David Cressy estimates that in 1500 fewer than 10 per cent of the population were literate; by 1750 almost half the population had learned to read and write. Literacy was inevitably stratified socially, and in the long run was one way in which the middling sort could be co-opted into the values of an elite and national culture. According to Cressy, the elite could usually read and write in 1500; by 1700 they had been joined by almost all gentry and the majority of yeoman householders. Almost 80 per cent of husbandmen were illiterate, however (Cressy 1980: 156 and 176–7).

Literacy was inevitably biased towards London, the south and east, and away from 'dark corners of the land'. It was also gendered: many elite women could read and write, but it spread more slowly below this social level. Many more women could read than could write; women and those of lower social rank were forbidden to read the Bible until the later sixteenth century (Crawford 1993: 38–53).

It is important to understand literacy as representing a different way of relating a new set of social and cultural resources. Again, this was well understood by contemporaries, for example in their discussions of how to use and explain religious and political symbols in the church. Stephen Gardiner wrote of the importance of such symbols in 1547, suggesting that images were a text for the illiterate:

> The pursuivant carrieth not on his breast the king's names written in such letters as few can spell, but such as all can read be they never so rude, being great known leters in images of three lions and three fleurs de lis, and other beasts holding those arms. And he that cannot read the scripture written about the king's great seal . . . yet he can read Saint George on horseback on

the one side and the king sitting in his majesty on the other side (cited in Muller 1933: 274).

Royal proclamations were read from the pulpit; broadsheets, pamphlets and newsletters could be read aloud to one's illiterate friends in alehouses; friends could write a credit transaction.

Anthropologists, in particular Jack Goody, have emphasized that literacy is more than just another skill: it profoundly changed relationship between the self, others and the outside world. I suggest that it was thus tied in to the changing social meanings of material culture. Goody asserts that 'the shift from utterance to text led to significant developments of a sort that might loosely be referred to as a change in consciousness and which in part arose from the great extension of formal operations of a graphic kind' (1977: 75). In particular, he suggests that early writing systems were closely linked to lists and tabular thinking; it is striking that in the *Oxford English Dictionary* a list is also defined as a boundary. A list bounds its items: they cannot be put in different categories simultaneously as easily as they can in the thought of pre-literate societies or social groups.

So just as closure put new divides, fences, boundaries between fields, literacy put new divides between objects; allowed them to be sorted and classified by the middling sort in new ways such as the inventory. Fixed cash valuations, formal credit agreements and bonds, could all now be part of a world below that of the elite. The role of the implicit, the traditional and the customary was correspondingly reduced.

Literacy affected attitudes to the self. Puritans kept diaries; those of all faiths kept commonplace books. The act of writing itself, and the acquisition of literacy, required a profound form of bodily and mental discipline (Cressy 1980: 24).

One of the many new classes of commodities that sprang up in the early modern period was books and pamphlets for the middling sort. Chapter 4 discussed the agricultural treatise; pamphlets of all kinds, serious and trivial, were sold by petty chapmen (Spufford 1981 and 1984). The Bible fell steadily in price: Tyndale's New Testament cost three shillings where manuscript testaments had cost seven to eighteen times as much; in the 1650s an entire Bible cost 2s. to 2s. 4d. Cheap copies were bootlegged in from the Netherlands before 1640 (Hill 1993: 11 and 18). During the break in censorship of the English Revolution, there was a wide circulation of pamphlets dealing with politics, miracles, monstrosities and so on (Friedman 1993). Such documents developed into newspapers in the later seventeenth century.

A related aspect of commodification was that of the movement of the meanings of material culture away from the sacred and towards the profane. The growth of literacy meant the secularization of knowledge; writing was one potent source of symbols that was no longer the preserve of the Church. It is striking that very different classes of material culture move in parallel directions in the later sixteenth and seventeenth centuries. Within the medieval church, as Gardiner stressed, political authority rested on traditional images. When the iconoclasts swept many of the images and icons away, the lack of material resonance of what replaced them created the preconditions for English Revolution – images of the King and Church were replaced with those of God and Nation. At an elite level patronage of the arts was taken over by the secular nobility and gentry.

The development of a modern attitude to objects as commodities was thus dependent in turn on new mentalities shaped around the secularization of literacy and art. It is striking that at the moment when the church was becoming less colourful, secular popular culture was becoming more so. As churches were whitewashed and covered with the written word, domestic houses were being painted in new and more varied colours, with increasing numbers of brightly coloured slipwares on the table, more vessel glass of different colours, more tapestries and carpets on the wall, new materials and colours in clothing. Further research may suggest a vernacular 'secularization of colour' in the sixteenth and seventeenth centuries to accompany the secularization of other aspects of life.

Commodification and Gender

As with domestic space, attitudes to goods were gendered. Legally, women's property rights were very different. These have recently been summarized by Amy Erickson (1993), who has shown that the position of women was not a simple or unambiguous one. Legally, a woman gave up most of her property rights upon marriage. However, marriage settlements could be drawn up giving women more rights, and different regional practices often gave women certain rights, particularly in relation to movable goods.

Wills and inventories give some clue to gendered attitudes towards property. In particular, studies of wills have revealed that men usually gave land to their sons and household goods to their daughters (Erickson found that men in Yorkshire proved a notable exception to this rule). The majority of men died without leaving wills, whereupon the widow was entitled to one-third of movable goods, and courts often exercised flexibility to the widow's benefit (Erickson 1993: 61 and 180). Women also brought a dowry with them upon marriage, which was not insignificant even among the poor. Recent work has stressed the diversity of women's experiences in different situations (Kermode and Walker 1994).

As England was secularized, so the principles of common law came to dominate in the sixteenth and seventeenth centuries; so women lost property rights, having fewer rights under common law than under other forms. Women were active protagonists in the defence of their rights over property: when the Puritan William Gouge preached that women should not dispose of household goods without their husbands' consent he found that 'much exception was taken' in his congregation (Erickson 1993: 6 and 9). Walker (1994: 89) has suggested that underlying this legal complexity lay a very different attitude to goods: 'women had a more self-conscious, emotional investment in clothing, household goods, and personal effects, even when these were humble in origin and of little value'.

In such varied circumstances it is difficult to generalize about gendered attitudes towards material goods. Certain kinds of goods were specifically made by women and deserve further theoretically informed study as a form of covert or semi-covert discourse. Embroidery, for example, was a major activity of elite women, who often chose Biblical subjects for portrayal. Ruth Geuter has discussed embroidered depictions of the story of Esther, who had the temerity to petition her husband the King to save the Jews. Geuter comments that whereas most depictions by male artists in Bibles show Esther kneeling, embroideries often show Esther standing. Geuter places these embroideries in a mid-seventeenth-century context where individuals or groups of women caught on both sides of the English Revolution had a keen sense of 'an imperative to speak out', referring to the story of Esther in petitions submitted to Parliament and others (Geuter 1994).

Ceramic Revolutions

Commodification can also be seen in the very new forms and styles of material culture that appeared after 1500. One of these new forms and styles was a transformation in the nature of pottery and tableware. Medieval pottery had been generally low in status and of plain colours, unglazed cooking-pots and green-glazed jugs being the main forms; the disappearance of cooking-pots after the middle of the fourteenth century testifies to the growing ability to afford metal forms. In the fifteenth century, however, pottery changed its nature, becoming more varied and colourful. Many wares moved up-market to compete with pewter and brass. Rhenish stonewares, often with metal lids, and tin-glazed earthenwares appeared on the tables of the middling sort.

The century 1450–1550 has been termed the Post-Medieval Ceramic Revolution. Many new imports and a diversity of local wares were produced to meet the demands of a rising urban mercantile elite (Gaimster 1994). For the first time, also, pottery forms could change rapidly with fashion. The succeeding century saw increasing imports of stoneware tankards and jugs, and the first appearance of Oriental porcelain. Vessel glass was produced in England from the sixteenth century, and by the seventeenth century beer glasses of various colours were being produced, mainly being bought by inns and taverns.

By 1700 there were many more goods, both domestic and imported, in middling households. Porcelain was increasingly used for consumption of hot beverages also seen in inventories (Weatherill 1988: 28). There were also many more knives and forks. We know much less of the ceramic assemblages of rural households; most of the above information has come from urban excavations. It is probable that they followed similar trends at a slightly slower pace.

It was this varied and colourful set of ceramics and other tableware that was replaced in the eighteenth century by the mass-produced, mould-made sets of white tableware that appeared on the tables of the Evetts; and it is this replacement that has often been interpreted as constitutive of capitalism at the household level (Shackel 1993).

Conclusion

To summarize, then, commodification involved the placing of goods in secular rather than spiritual domains, giving freer rein to the acquisition and accumulation of goods; it thus 'de-spiritualized' the material world. Commodification also involved a new order imposed on the material world, through literacy; it had legal manifestations in the dominance of common law and the loss and gain of rights by women and men to property under that law. Commodification was thus much more than simply a rise in living standards or of numbers of commodities, just as closure was much more than a rise in agricultural productivity. It can nevertheless be seen archaeologically in the increase and variability of material things such as ceramics and glass in new forms and styles after 1500.

By 1725 the world of goods had been transformed, well before the 'Industrial Revolution'. Lorna Weatherill's analysis of inventories from a range of different social and regional backgrounds shows this transformation in its later stages in the later seventeenth and early eighteenth centuries (1988: 26–7). She notes a rapid expansion in 'frontstage' goods, particularly those involved in display at mealtimes: these included books, silver, table linen, pewter dishes and plates, looking glasses, earthenware of many different local and imported types, clocks, pictures, window curtains, and knives and forks. I suggested in chapter 7 that the contexts of 'frontstage' and 'backstage' were themselves architectural creations of the later seventeenth and eighteenth centuries.

Commodification was a process whose speed and direction were set within the urban context. The countryside, and the rural labouring poor in particular, were still not acquiring a greater range and variety of goods even by the earlier eighteenth century. In this sense the common perception of the eighteenth century as seeing 'the birth of a consumer society' has to be at least qualified (E.P. Thompson 1991). But if the process of commodification had not yet penetrated to many social groups, its origins lay, as we have seen, centuries before the Industrial Revolution. The genealogy of commodities has taken us back to the sixteenth century and beyond, and deep into a much more complex theorization of objects and cultures than simple reference to 'fashion' or 'emulation'.

Such an analysis is only the roughest of sketches, and needs many more case studies and theoretical elaboration. Different social classes responded in different ways to commodification: the 'solid sufficiency' of the yeoman ethic, for example, may have led to an environment in which 'small, new and decorative things were largely absent'; 'yeomen, at least those with agricultural occupations, were not inclined to be innovative in their household goods before the eighteenth century', although their surroundings were comfortable (Weatherill 1988: 172). The example of the Evetts, when seen in the light of the thousands of socially middling 'Georgian' houses erected by 1750 and the rising demand for new goods, suggests that this adherence to solid sufficiency had at least partly broken down by the middle of the eighteenth century.

If the current preoccupation with things that characterizes British and European archaeology is to be given any intellectual rigour, the changing social life of things within the feudal/capitalist transition must be addressed. In this chapter I have suggested some ways forward in tracing that life, through attention to the social and cultural context within which things were made, exchanged, consumed and thrown away.

9

Conclusion: Towards an Archaeology of Capitalism

In previous chapters I have tried to delineate some of the strands of an archaeology of capitalism. Agrarian change has been seen in cultural terms; an archaeology of closure has been drawn, seeing enclosure of the country-side as evidence of a much wider change in the landscape. The development of new orderings of the world through documents was interpreted in terms of new systems of discipline, and put in the context of new orderings of space and of people. These changes prefigured and were seen as part of the genealogy of a disciplinary society. Restructuring of architectural authority, of the homes of the middling classes and of the world of objects were all seen in terms of a move towards a more commodified mentality and world-view.

Many of these changes in the eighteenth century have been seen by other scholars in terms of the 'Georgian Order'. The Georgian Order can be seen as a consistent set of rules applied to architecture, material culture, and ways of living. Georgian houses are symmetrical in plan and elevation; internally, they are two rooms deep, divided between front and back, strictly segregated between master and servant and give a high stress to personal privacy in their layout. Rooms are assigned single functional uses; the hall is now an entrance vestibule rather than the bustling centre of a traditional house. The external façade is governed by rules of order (figure 9.1).

The Georgian Order has been linked by archaeologists to the development of capitalist relations in the American colonies (Leone 1988; Shackel 1993). In this view, the changes the Georgian Order brought to architecture applied equally to other areas of behaviour. The introduction of knives and forks, of standardized, individualized place-settings at table, and of new patterns of personal discipline generally, were all part of the stress on the individual and personal discipline that went hand in hand with the

Figure 9.1 A Georgian house: Marble Hill House, by the Thames. It was built for Henrietta Howard, Countess of Suffolk and mistress of George II, from 1724–9. It sat within a landscape garden terraced gently down to the Thames.

ideological base of capitalism. Where people had eaten with their hands or with a knife from common bowls and dishes, now they ate in a more refined, 'civilized' fashion that stressed the individual rather than the household.

If architecture and material culture became individualized, they also became standardized. Georgian architecture came out of a 'pattern-book'; its forms were repeated across the Atlantic world, from the North of England to plantations in the West Indies to New England. The new tableware, plates, dishes, tea-cups, were mass produced and standardized through the use of a mould. All these changes in everyday environment and patterns of living were congruent with the development of capitalism. Capitalism stressed standardization as part of mass production; placed the individual at the centre of its ideological base; relied on patterns of mass consumption; and required new systems of discipline in the workplace.

This view of the Georgian Order has been largely based on case studies from the eighteenth-century material culture and architecture of the American colonies. Its central linkages with the archaeology of capitalism are clear, and many of the ideas discussed in preceding chapters have drawn heavily on this work. The case studies in this book have also tried, however, to deepen and widen our understanding in various ways.

In particular, I have suggested that when one looks closely and critically at the antecedents of the elements that make up the Georgian Order as a 'package', however one defines that package, one finds that each has a long genealogy in social practices often stretching back to the later Middle Ages. This does not mean that any of the practices associated with capitalism have one true 'point of origin' or that they can only be 'properly understood' in earlier contexts.

It does mean, however, that an archaeology of such elements as agrarian practices, architecture, and material culture must place them back into those contexts and genealogies for a richer, more contextual understanding of how the archaeology of the Georgian Order is related to social practices related to capitalism. A final case with which to make the point is that of the Georgian Order's stress on 'the individual'.

Framing the Individual

The pre-industrial individual was seen in very different ways. Like the household, the individual was gendered, but in a very different sense to the notion of sexual difference generated by nineteenth-century medical thought. Laqueur (1990) has argued that medical ideology before the eighteenth century saw the body as having a single sex, the female sexual organs being smaller, 'hidden' versions of the male. Beliefs of gender inferiority thus hinged on analogical connections between moral and political order and the way this was mapped on to the body rather than on a clinical view of sexual difference.

If the body was gendered in different ways, it carried meaning in different ways also. Marcia Pointon has discussed how in eighteenth-century polite culture the body became a work of art: 'how one wore one's patches, how one held one's fan, the cut of one's clothes, the shape of one's wig – all these made of the body a mobile cluster of signifiers indicating party-political affiliation, class, gender and sexuality' (Pointon 1993: 44). I suggest that in broad terms the use of the body to carry complex meanings in polite culture had always been the case. We have seen the complex self-fashioning of elite Renaissance figures, most notably in the portrayal of Queen Elizabeth I. Vernacular culture equally acted as a cluster of signifiers around the body, redefining the body and the self in the process.

One of the ways in which this was done was through treatment of the body at death. Attitudes towards death in general have been interpreted by historians of mentality as bound up with changing attitudes to life, the body and the individual (Aries 1981; Elias 1985). Clare Gittings (1984) has examined the changing treatment of death in early modern England, arguing that varying attitudes towards death and their expression in the burial ritual reflect increasing stress on the individual among the elite from the later middle ages onwards, and among the middling sort well before the eighteenth century. In the later middle ages, people were crammed into cemeteries with few permanent markers for ordinary people. Among the upper classes, expenditure on the funeral was conspicuous; funerals and wakes were attended by the poor, who might receive alms, and occasionally by the horse of the deceased (Gittings 1984: 30).

Gittings suggests that the rise of the individual can be seen in a variety of ways. There was a growing separation from death by prohibiting burials in churches and reserving graveyards for interments only. Separation from the corpse was increased through the practice of embalming and by the body being coffined rather than wrapped in a cloth or 'winding-sheet'. Some coffins were even filled with bran to stop the sound of the corpse moving within (Gittings 1984: 115). Fewer wakes, games and ceremonies took place around the corpse, lessening the sense of community involved in burial. By the eighteenth century, attendance at many burials was confined to family members.

James Deetz's interpretation of varying attitudes towards death between the late seventeenth and early eighteenth century focuses on the changing design of gravestones, and his model of development in New England is broadly applicable to England itself. Deetz sees motifs such as death's heads and hour glasses as emphasizing the inevitability of death; through time, these are replaced by cherubs, urn-and-willow designs, and plain headstones (Deetz 1977).

Looked at from an earlier perspective however, the transition from death's head to cherub is the final stage of a long-term process. Few gravestones of the middling sort survive before the mid-seventeenth century; the very use of gravestones marks a rise in wealth and a diversion of resources away from transient rites of passage involving the community, such as the giving of gifts and the wake. The desire for the gravestone itself, a permanent memorial with the name of the deceased on, is similarly indicative of the 'rise of the individual'.

The eighteenth-century 'rise of the individual' was prefigured in other ways. The body, for example, was given increasing attention in the early modern period. There was a burgeoning vernacular medical literature in sixteenth-century England (Slack 1979). Bodily blemishes or deformity were taken as symptomatic of moral condition, most famously in the Shakespearian Richard III but also in contemporary medical ideology (Pelling 1986: 89). We must do more, therefore, than simply extend the history of the rise of the individual into previous centuries. We must look at very different configurations of the body, the individual, and social meaning, and understand the everyday, material context within which the idea of the individual was negotiated.

Genealogies of the Georgian Order

The genealogy of the individual, and the material expression of the individual in the archaeology of death, has been used as one final example of how elements of the Georgian Order have a genealogy and archaeology that need tracing in their own right rather than as part of a 'package'.

The central argument of this book, then, has been that the apparent unity of this set of eighteenth-century architecture and material culture is partly due to the perceived nature of its arrival as a 'complete package' in the context of the American colonies. Each element in fact has a genealogy several centuries old, and can be placed in disparate contexts, often within the patriarchal structure of early modern England. Let us take each area discussed in previous chapters in turn.

Transformation in agrarian practices must be traced back to enclosure in the later middle ages and the sixteenth century. Understood in cultural terms, enclosure opened the way to a commodification of the landscape through an erosion of the embeddedness of that landscape in the social and cultural values of the traditional community. Fields were now free to be treated in 'rational' ways. They were to be ordered through the hedge and the ditch, the view of the map, the agricultural treatise, and through the language of agricultural 'improvement' that was to become the common currency of the eighteenth century.

Ordering of the world through written discourse such as inventories, maps, and antiquarian and topographical accounts of the world must be seen within an early modern context in which such ordering was closely related to traditional conceptions of patriarchal authority, but which was being deployed in new ways. Here, new techniques of ordering people were first developed in the context of serving the old order.

Georgian architecture developed out of the introduction of Palladian and Baroque principles into architectural design; the use and social context of Palladian houses in early eighteenth-century England was sketched in chapter 6. But Palladian houses stood at the latter end of a long evolution of architectural forms. The great medieval hall and its values of hospitality and community had been reinvented to the end of the sixteenth century, and it was at that point that a critical rupture in the principles of spatial order underlying the style of the house and garden must be located. The principle of the gaze, the closure and commodification of the estate around the house, the new techniques of segregation inside the house, were all entwined with new self-definitions of elite social groups and were all constitutive of the 'rise of the great estates', another component of rural capitalism.

Similarly, the 'consumer revolution' of the eighteenth century, with its profusion of mass-produced, mould-made tablewares, knives and forks, needs to be placed in the context of several centuries of the emergent process of commodification. Chapters 7 and 8 showed how the archaeology of commodification must be traced back to at least the sixteenth century. Indeed many of the elements of Deetz's 'pre-Georgian' set of material culture – different forms of brightly coloured slipwares and other tablewares, substantial vernacular houses, forms of furniture – emerge in this longer-term account of antecedents as manifestations of the larger transition between feudal and capitalist mentalities and manners.

To understand the Georgian Order, then, we must trace the genealogy of a variety of practices in the archaeological record back to the sixteenth century and beyond. In such contexts we see such practices – the laying out of fields, the building of houses, the writing of documents – as the actions of real people, often having very different, if partial, understandings of the world around them and taking very different views of the changes in their world. Literate men like Richard Gough and William Harrison (chapters 5 and 7) are joined in an account of these understandings by others: by the women and men who consumed and threw away clay pipes in alehouses, who decided to retain a traditional house plan behind their symmetrical façade, who put up or pulled down hedges and ditches, who chose to throw out old pottery.

Many elements of the Georgian Order must also be understood as being dependent on a particular context within English society in the eighteenth century itself. The use of principles of geometry, harmonious proportions, and order in the landscape have been seen as an ideology of the ruling classes, the Whig aristocracy in particular: those free of mechanical labour were free also of sectional interest, limited experience of the world, and a preoccupation with material things. Barrell has summarized such an ideology thus:

> The successful exercise of the mechanical arts requires that material objects be regarded as concrete particulars, and not in terms of the abstract or formal relations among them. The man of independent means, on the other hand . . . will be released from private interest and from the occlusions of a narrowed and partial experience of the world, and from an experience of the world as material. He will be able to grasp the public interest (Barrell 1990: 20).

The Georgian Order, then, debarred those involved in 'the successful exercise of the mechanical arts' from the apex of the political body, and opposed the ideas of the abstract and the material where in the traditional world of custom they had previously been entwined.

There is a contradiction here that needs further exploration through case studies such as that of the Evetts in chapter 8. At the same time as it was stressing its social exclusivity, the new culture of eighteenth-century England was dependent on the co-option into the order of things of the gentry and the middling sort. Georgian houses, gardens, tableware, was now bought and used by the middling sort. The changes in dining practices and consumption of different artefact types were in part long-term shifts within certain social groups, in particular the move of the middling sort away from 'vernacular' towards 'polite' forms of material life and culture.

Standardization, then, was not simply about mass production: it was also about the relationship between vernacular and polite culture. One of the most striking aspects of 'Georgian' architecture is the uniformity with which the architectural system as seen in pattern-books applied, particularly in urban contexts, to houses of middling and upper social levels. Where street façades in seventeenth- and nineteenth-century towns might be varied, those of the eighteenth century were strikingly uniform (figure 9.2).

A prosperous farmer in, say, sixteenth-century County Durham was probably illiterate; lived in a vernacular house of regional style; and owed his most immediate and important affiliations to local patronage. By 1750 such a farmer would not only be much more materially affluent; he could live in a Georgian house of moderate size, specified out of a pattern-book published in London; he might well have visited London, and be aware of the latest styles in architecture and material culture through newspapers. In short, many upper and middling elements of society had been co-opted into a national culture, just as by 1750 many were now much more

Figure 9.2 Georgian façades at Durham City. The interiors of these houses are probably of a variety of seventeenth- and eighteenth-century dates, but in the eighteenth century were either rebuilt or given new façades as fashionable gentry town houses as towns such as Durham became important centres for the gentry and middling sort (Borsay 1989). Many are now used as student residences for the University, founded in the nineteenth century.

integrated into a national market and were also co-opted into national politics. Uniformity is easier to understand in this context.

Eighteenth-century material and mental landscapes were also dependent on a complex symbolic relationship between old spaces and new readings. It is easy to forget that many of the great medieval ruins that litter the landscape today have only survived due to careful and deliberate maintenance as ruins by eighteenth- and nineteenth-century landowners. Where ruins did not exist, great landowners would sometimes build follies in the form of ruins; medieval castles, then, enjoyed the paradoxical status of genuine follies. The medieval past played a continuing ideological role in post-medieval culture, from the Elizabethan cult of chivalry, through provincial architectural conservatism, to the eighteenth-century Gothick of Strawberry Hill, the rise of Romanticism, and the self-conscious medievalism of the Victorians. Every generation, it seems, gets the Middle Ages it deserves.

Such material and mental landscapes were also dependent on colonial relations, the archaeology of which has not been examined in this book. I

suggest that more work needs to be done on the way the changes delineated here interact with nascent colonialism, a topic briefly hinted at in
chapter 4. The estate and household of Austen's *Mansfield Park* rests on
income from plantations in Antigua; it also rests on a whole series of class
and status relations both within the Park and the estate, between the
female and male protagonists of the novel, and the countryside beyond.
Austen's silence on the subject of Antigua (the island is mentioned half a
dozen times in the novel) is rightly made much of by post-colonial critics;
Austen also fails to mention servants, enclosure, the labouring poor, and
the world of the countryside and growing urban centres beyond the estate
(Said 1993: 99–116). Indeed, Austen makes telling points about the lack
of social breeding of Fanny's 'other' family, somewhat inferior socially to
her adopted world at Mansfield Park, by referring to the way doors are left
open in the house, thus enabling the noise of the activities of the servants
to penetrate into the parlour. Colonial and class exploitation, and the way
these are materially negotiated and expressed, are thus bound up with one
another intellectually and morally.

One future avenue for an archaeology of capitalism is to link these
different scales of analysis together, from the level of the capitalist world-
system (Wallerstein 1974) through the circulation of commodities to the
individuals and households at either end of the chain, in the way hinted at
in the discussion of clay pipes in chapter 8. There should also be more
direct studies such as Evans's 1990 study of the Dutch East India Company, looking at how its architecture and iconography developed between
the seventeenth and nineteenth centuries. A related avenue is to look at
how things changed their meanings between contexts. We have seen, for
example, how the courtyard is a 'traditional' feature of English elite structures, deriving its architectural authority from the relative placing of great
hall, service and upper ends around its perimeter. Robert Blair St George
has traced how this was redeployed in a variety of colonial contexts ranging
from Ireland to New England, and how in the process it acquired a series
of new contexts and meanings (St George 1990).

Such a conclusion is rather diffuse: we need a bit more of this, a bit more
of that. But there is no one theoretical direction to impose on the study of
late and post-medieval archaeology. To repeat, this book is part of *an*
archaeology of capitalism; other understandings are possible and their
development should be encouraged. It is only through the clash of different
views that research moves forward. The only imposition I would suggest is
that late and post-medieval archaeology in England must address pressing
contemporary debates on both concrete historical issues and on wider

issues of theory. What archaeologists say about such issues is up to us as individuals, but we cannot duck the challenge if we wish our studies to gain any sort of respect and recognition from the intellectual world.

This stress on addressing historical debates is not a new assertion in some senses, at least within the field of English landscape history. W.G. Hoskins was well aware of the wider resonance of his work, in both a historical and ethical sense; his central theme was the rediscovery of a sense of community and provincial culture that he saw as being swept away by the Industrial and Agricultural Revolutions of the eighteenth and nine-teenth centuries. Such a sense of culture was, for Hoskins, locked into a sense of local topography and landscape, central to which was the way places and localities had a 'genius' and a subjective experience that was swept away by Parliamentary enclosure. Hoskins contrasted this sense of locality with the alienation, sameness and placelessness of modern culture (Phythian-Adams 1992: 152). It is difficult also not to perceive similar themes in the work of Richard Tawney. Tawney's specific model for the history of enclosure was criticized in chapter 3. His wider argument in *The Agrarian Problem in the Sixteenth Century* and in *Religion and the Rise of Capitalism* was that central to the transition between feudalism and capital-ism was a profound clash in mentalities, as pointed out at the start of chapter 4. Tawney's scholarship thus led directly to a call for a re-spiritualization of the present, a call to reintroduce ethics into modern economic life (1912: 409).

Both Hoskins and Tawney grasped the central need of listening to the past on its own terms, to 'hear the men and women of the past talking and working, and creating what has come down to us' (Hoskins 1967: 184). Tawney stood within a tradition of ethical socialism that is profoundly relevant to modern historical and social commentary. Such a tradition resonates with the need to see human faces in the past, to move beyond dry structural models of nascent capitalism to see people in the past actively hammering out their own future, and with a need to locate an ethics and morality in the present within an understanding of community. The modern archaeologist and historian with any sense of the moral context of his or her work cannot ignore his achievement. Both Hoskins and Tawney also grasped the central need to forsake the record office for the field, to put one's pen away and to don a stout pair of boots; to attend to the physicality of things, to the importance of putting documentary history in a material and landscape context. I suggest that these concerns for the physical landscape, the need for a modern sense of community, and attention to women and men in the past are intimately related.

We cannot return to the past; we can only read scraps of documents in the unearthly silence of record offices, excavate and painstakingly record bits of pottery, fragments of metalwork and glass, run hand-tapes along the decaying walls of great and small buildings, argue about clay pipes and cultural conflict in library tea rooms, try to write about castles and inventories as best we can. But we must never forget that in all that we do, however mundane or tedious, we are trying to write human histories. Behind the often unpromising fragments that we study we can see women and men in the past thinking and acting, in ways that made sense to them and that we must appreciate and understand on their terms as well as on ours. We must never forget that we try to write in a present that is the creation of all those past lives; a present whose turbulence and tensions can be traced back to the concerns and conflicts of those past lives; and also a present whose sense of its own history, identity and social and moral dimensions are re-cast by us in the way that we think, write and act.

Glossary

Arminianism: an early seventeenth-century interpretation of Christian doctrine that influenced the beliefs and organization of the Anglican Church

Bailey: courtyard of a castle

Bargeboards: timbers running up the angled sides of a gable, often with carved decoration

Bovate: a measure of land between 10 and 18 acres (also 'oxgang')

Carpet: cloth to lie upon a cupboard or table

Chapbook: small book or pamphlet sold by chapmen

Chapmen: itinerant small traders of the early modern period

Commensality: eating together

Consistory: a church court

Copyhold: land held of the lord; often a less secure form of tenure than some forms of freehold

Coverture: the proposition that a husband and wife were one person and that the one was the husband, the woman thus having no independent legal identity at common law

Crenel: the upright part of a castle battlement between two embrasures; also used in decorative contexts

Crenellation: battlements. A 'licence to crenellate' was permission to fortify a dwelling

Corn: in English usage, wheat

Cupboard: either a table upon which items were placed, or similar to a sideboard; often readily movable; often with a carpet on it, used for storing/displaying goods such as vessels

Dais: the raised upper end of a hall

Device: heraldic emblem

Diocese: the area administered by a bishop

Double-pile: house plan two rooms deep

Early modern: in this book, AD 1500–1750

Fine: a payment made to the lord – for example on inheritance

Formalism: a school of economic theory which holds that the formal assumptions applied by modern economists to economic behaviour under modern capitalism can be applied to other cultures and periods

Freehold: a form of land tenure, usually reasonably secure

Gentry: a class of 'substantial landowners and agents of government' below the aristocracy

Hundred: a grouping of parishes for administrative purposes

Ha-ha: a park fence placed at the bottom of a ditch, thus hidden and leaving an uninterrupted view

Husbandmen: a class of small farmers, below that of yeomen

Jack: device to make the spit revolve automatically, or a large leather container

Jetty: projection of the upper storey of a building over that below

Joined: of furniture made by a joiner

Keep: the central element of some castles, often of tower form, often providing residence for the lord

Lintel: horizontal timber over an opening or fireplace

Livery: clothing, often marked with the device of the lord

Marches: border areas, often controlled in the Middle Ages by feudal magnates who had special liberties in return for maintaining border security

Medieval: in this book pre-1500, differing in usage from that of American historical archaeologists

Motte: an earthen mound that is often topped by the keep of a medieval castle

Mullion: an upright dividing a window into lights

Newel stair: a spiral stair with the steps framed into the central post

Passage: in medieval and sub-medieval houses, the area between two opposed doors at the lower end of the hall: a screens-passage where the passage is divided from the hall by screens, a cross-passage where they are not

Polite: of architecture or material culture that is elite, upper class, and national or international in fashion

Portion: either the property a child inherits from a parent or the property a bride takes into marriage (also dowry)

Rebus: an image containing the name of a patron in riddle form

Rendering: plaster covering

Scantling: dimensions of a timber

Severalty: land held in exclusive ownership, as opposed to that subject to common rights

Skillet: shallow bowl or frying-pan with three legs

Solar: withdrawing room at the upper end of the hall

Spit: bar or series of bars attached to joint of meat to turn it over the fire, often mechanically

Stack: abbreviation of 'chimney-stack'

Sumptuary laws: laws passed prohibiting consumption of certain goods, for example the wearing of certain kinds of cloth or fur, often in an attempt to limit consumption to a specific social rank

Tenement: a property or holding

Tithes: taxes on land or produce paid to the Church

Tithe maps: drawn up in the 1840s when tithes were abolished and the Church compensated by being given a share of the land

Tenure: form of landholding from an owner, of various forms and degrees of security and with different conditions attached. Freehold and copyhold by inheritance were reasonably secure forms

Tie or tie-beam: the horizontal timber of a truss at wall-plate level connecting the tops of the posts

Transom: an intermediate bar across a window

Treen: an early modern word for wood

Vernacular: of architecture or material culture that is ordinary, regional in tradition, common and small in scale

Waste: unbounded land not under cultivation. The term is potentially misleading since 'waste' could be used by individuals or the community for various purposes

Weald: an area of countryside in Kent and Sussex, formerly forested and with a dispersed settlement pattern

Yeomen: a socially middling class of tenant farmers of reasonable security and wealth

Bibliography

Addleshaw, G.W.O. and Etchells, F. 1948. *The Architectural Setting of Anglican Worship*. London: Faber and Faber.

Airs, M. 1975. *The Making of the English Country House, 1500–1640*. London: The Architectural Press.

Allen, R.C. 1992. *Enclosure and the Yeoman*. Oxford: Clarendon Press.

Amussen, S.D. 1988. *An Ordered Society: Gender and Class in Early Modern England*. Oxford: Blackwell.

Andersson, H. and Wienberg, J. (eds) 1993. *The Study of Medieval Archaeology*. Stockholm: Almqvist and Wiksell.

Andrews, J.H. 1970. Geography and government in Elizabethan Ireland. In Glasscock and Stephens (eds), 178–91.

Anglo, S. 1992. *Images of Tudor Kingship*. London: Seaby.

Appleby, A.B. 1979. Diet in sixteenth-century England: sources, problems, possibilities. In Webster (ed.), 97–116.

Appleby, J.O. 1978. *Economic Thought and Ideology in Seventeenth-Century England*. Princeton: Princeton University Press.

Aries, P. 1981. *The Hour of Our Death*. London: Allen Lane.

Astill, G. 1993. The archaeology of the medieval countryside – a forty-year perspective from Britain. In Andersson and Weinberg (eds), 131–48.

Aston, M. 1994. *The King's Bedpost: Reformation and Iconography in a Tudor Group Portrait*. Cambridge: Cambridge University Press.

Aston, M., Austin, D. and Dyer, C. (eds) 1989. *The Rural Settlements of Medieval England*. Oxford: Clarendon Press.

Aston, T.H. (ed.) 1987. *Landlords, Peasants and Politics in Medieval England*. Cambridge: Cambridge University Press.

Aston, T.H. and Philpin, C.H.E. (eds) 1985. *The Brenner Debate: Agrarian Class Structure and Economic Development in Pre- Industrial Europe*. Cambridge: Cambridge University Press.

Austin, D. 1989. The 'proper study' of medieval archaeology. In Austin and Alcock (eds), 9–35.

Austin, D. and Alcock, L. (eds) 1990. *From the Baltic to the Black Sea: Studies in Medieval Archaeology*. London: Unwin.

Austin, D. and Thomas, J. 1990. The 'proper study' of medieval archaeology: a case study. In Austin and Alcock (eds), 43–78.

Baechler, J., Hall, J.A. and Mann, M. (eds) 1988. *Europe and the Rise of Capitalism*. Oxford: Blackwell.

Baillie, H.M. 1967. Etiquette and the planning of the State Apartments in Baroque palaces. *Archaeologia* 101, 169–200.

Baker, A.R.H. and Biger, G. (eds) 1992. *Ideology and Landscape in Historical Perspective*. Cambridge: Cambridge University Press.

Baker, A.R.H. and Billinge, M. (eds) 1982. *Period and Place: Research Methods in Historical Geography*. Cambridge: Cambridge University Press.

Baldwin, F.E. 1926. *Sumptuary Legislation and Personal Regulation in England*. Johns Hopkins University Studies in History 44. Baltimore: Johns Hopkins Press.

Barker, F., Hulme, P. and Iversen, M. (eds) 1991. *Uses of History: Marxism, Postmodernism and the Renaissance*. Manchester: Manchester University Press.

Barker-Benfield, G.J. 1992. *The Culture of Sensibility: Sex and Society in Eighteenth-Century Britain*. Chicago: University of Chicago Press.

Barnes, T. and Duncan, J. (eds) 1992. *Writing Worlds: Discourse, Text and Metaphor in the Representation of Landscape*. London: Routledge.

Barrell, J. 1990. The public prospect and the private view: the politics of taste in eighteenth-century Britain. In S. Pugh (ed.) *Reading Landscape: Country–City–Capital*, 19–40. Manchester: Manchester University Press.

——(ed.) 1992. *Painting and the Politics of Culture: New Essays on British Art 1700–1850*. Oxford: Oxford University Press.

Barton, K.J. 1992. Ceramic changes in the western European littoral at the end of the Middle Ages: a personal view. In Gaimster and Redknap (eds), 246–55.

Beier, A.L. 1985. *Masterless Men: The Vagrancy Problem in England, 1560–1640*. London: Methuen.

Beier, A.L. and Finlay, R. (eds) 1986. *London 1500–1700: The Making of a Metropolis*. London: Longmans.

Beier, A.L., Cannadine, D. and Rosenheim, J. (eds) 1989. *The First Modern Society: Essays in English History in Honour of Lawrence Stone*. Cambridge: Cambridge University Press.

Belsey, A. and Belsey, C. 1990. Icons of diversity: portraits of Elizabeth I. In Gent and Llewellyn (eds), 11–35.

Ben-Amos, I.K. 1994. *Adolescence and Youth in Early Modern England*. Yale: Yale University Press.

Bender, B. 1994a. Stonehenge: contested landscapes. In Bender (ed.), 245–80.

——(ed.) 1994b. *Landscape: Politics and Perspectives*. Oxford: Berg.

Beresford, G. 1975. *The Medieval Clay-Land Village: Excavations at Goltho and Barton Blount*. Monograph 6. London: Society for Medieval Archaeology.

Beresford, M. 1954. *The Lost Villages of England*. Lutterworth: Lutterworth Press.

Beresford, M. and St Joseph, J.K. 1958. *Medieval England: An Aerial Survey*. Cambridge: Cambridge University Press.

Beresford, M. and Hurst, J.G. 1990. *Wharram*. London: Batsford.

Blades, B.S. 1986. English villages in the Londonderry plantation. *Post-Medieval Archaeology* 20, 257–69.

Bois, G. 1984. *The Crisis of Feudalism: Economy and Society in Eastern Normandy c.1300–1550*. Cambridge: Cambridge University Press.

Bold, J. 1988. *Wilton House and English Palladianism: Some Wiltshire Houses*. London: Her Majesty's Stationery Office.

Borsay, P. 1989. *The English Urban Renaissance: Culture and Society in the English Provincial Town, 1660–1770*. Oxford: Clarendon Press.

Bowden, M. 1992. The invention of American tradition. *Journal of Historical Geography* 18, 3–26.

Bowie, G.G.S. 1987. Watermeadows in Wessex: a reevaluation for the period 1640–1850. *Agricultural History Review* 35, 151–58.

Boyer, P. and Nissenbaum, S. 1974. *Salem Possessed: The Social Origins of Witchcraft*. Cambridge: Harvard University Press.

Braudon, P.F. 1979. The diffusion of designed landscapes in south-east England. In Fox and Butlin (eds), 165–87.

Braudel, F. 1973. *Capitalism and Material Life 1400–1800*. London: Weidenfeld and Nicolson.

Brenner, R. 1985. The agrarian roots of European capitalism. In Aston and Philpin (eds), 213–27.

Brewer, R. 1989. Bourgeois revolution and transition to capitalism. In Beier et al. (eds), 271–304.

Bristol, M. 1985. *Carnival and Theatre: Plebeian Culture and the Structure of Authority in Renaissance England*. London: Methuen.

Britnell, R.H. 1993. *The Commercialisation of English Society, 1000–1500*. Cambridge: Cambridge University Press.

Brooks, C. and Barry, J. (eds) 1994. *The Middling Sort of People: Culture, Society and Politics in England, 1550–1800*. Basingstoke, Macmillan.

Bryson, A. 1990. The rhetoric of status: gesture, demeanour and the image of the gentleman in sixteenth and seventeenth-century England. In Gent and Llewellyn (eds), 136–53.

Burke, P. (ed.) 1991. *New Perspectives on Historical Writing*. Oxford: Polity.

——1992. We, the people: popular culture and popular identity in modern Europe. In Lash and Friedman (eds), 293–308.

Butlin, R.A. 1979. The enclosure of open fields and common rights in England, circa 1600–1750: a review. In Fox and Butlin (eds), 65–82.

——1982. *The Transformation of Rural England, 1580–1800: A Study in Historical Geography*. Oxford: Oxford University Press.

——1990. Drainage and land use in the Fenlands and fen-edge of northeast Cambridgeshire in the seventeenth- and eighteenth-centuries. In Cosgrove and Petts (eds), 54–76.

Cain, T.G.S. 1992. The visual arts and architecture in Britain 1625–1700. In Cain and Robinson (eds), 107–50.

Cain, T.G.S. and Robinson, K. 1992. *Into Another Mould: Change and Continuity in English Culture 1625–1700*. London: Routledge.

Cameron, D.K. 1984. *The Cornkister Days: A Portrait of a Land and its Rituals*. London: Gollancz.

Canny, N. 1986. Protestants, planters and apartheid in early modern Ireland. *Irish Historical Studies* 25, 105–15.

Carter, C.H. (ed.) 1965. *From the Renaissance to the Counter Reformation: Essays in Honour of Garrett Mattingly*. New York: Random House.

Chambers, D. 1992. 'Wild Pastoral Encounter': John Evelyn, John Beale and the renegotiation of pastoral in the mid-seventeenth-century. In Leslie and Raylor (eds), 173–94.

Chapman, J. 1993. Enclosure commissioners as landscape planners. *Landscape History* 15, 51–5.

Charles, L. and Duffin, L. 1985. *Women and Work in Pre-Industrial England*. London: Croom Helm.

Chartier, R. 1977. *The Order of Books*. Cambridge: Cambridge University Press.

Chartres, J. 1977. *Internal Trade in England 1500–1700*. London: Macmillan.

Chartres, J. and Hey, D. (eds) 1990. *English Rural Society, 1500–1800: Essays in Honour of Joan Thirsk*. Cambridge: Cambridge University Press.

Clark, K. 1993. *Landscapes of Industry*. London: Routledge.

Clark, P. 1983. *The English Alehouse: A Social History, 1200–1830*. Harlow: Longman.

Clarke, H. 1984. *The Archaeology of Medieval England*. London: British Museum.

Cockburn, J.S. 1977. The nature and incidence of crime in England 1559–1625: a preliminary survey. In Cockburn (ed.), 49–71.

——(ed.) 1977. *Crime in England 1550–1800*. London: Methuen.

Coleman, D.C. and John, A.H. (eds) 1976. *Trade, Government and Economy in Pre-Industrial England: Essays Presented to F.J. Fisher*. London: Weidenfeld.

Coope, R. 1984. The gallery in England: names and meanings. *Architectural History* 27, 446–55.

Cosgrove, D. 1984. *Social Formation and Symbolic Landscape*. London: Croom Helm.

——1985. Prospect, perspective and the evolution of the landscape idea. *Transactions of the Institute of British Geographers* 1, 45–62.

——1993. *The Palladian Landscape: Geographical Change and Its Cultural Representations in Sixteenth-Century Italy*. Leicester: Leicester University Press.

Cosgrove, D. and Daniels, S. (eds) 1988. *The Iconography of Landscape*. Cambridge: Cambridge University Press.

Cosgrove, D. and Petts, G. (eds) 1990. *Water, Engineering and Landscape: Water Control and Landscape Transformation in the Modern Period*. London: Belhaven.

Coulson, C. 1979. Structural symbolism in medieval castle architecture. *Journal of the British Archaeological Association* 88, 73–90.

——1982. Hierarchism in conventual crenellation: an essay in the sociology and metaphysics of medieval fortification. *Medieval Archaeology* 26, 69–100.

——1993. Specimens of freedom to crenellate by licence. *Fortress* 18, 3–15.

Coulson, M., Magas, B. and Wainright, H. 1982. 'The Housewife and her Labour under Capitalism': a critique. In Malos, E. (ed.) *The Politics of Housework*. London: Allison and Busby, 182–97.

Crawford, P. 1981. Attitudes to menstruation in seventeenth-century England. *Past and Present* 91, 47–73.

——1993. *Women and Religion in England 1500–1720*. London: Routledge.

Cressy, D. 1980. *Literacy and the Social Order: Reading and Writing in Tudor and Stuart England*. Cambridge: Cambridge University Press.

Cronon, W. 1983. *Changes in the Land: Indians, Colonists, and the Ecology of New England*. New York: Hill and Wang.

Crossley, D. 1990. *Post-Medieval Archaeology in Britain*. Leicester: Leicester University Press.

——1994. Early industrial landscapes. In Vyner (ed.), 244–63.

Currie, C. 1988. Time and chance: modelling the attrition of old houses. *Vernacular Architecture* 19, 1–9.

Dahlman, C.J. 1980. *The Open Field System and Beyond: A Property Rights Analysis of an Economic Institution*. Cambridge: Cambridge University Press.

Daniels, S. 1988. The political iconography of woodland in later Georgian England. In Cosgrove and Daniels (eds), 43–82.

—— 1993. *Fields of Vision: Landscape Imagery and National Identity in England and the United States*. Oxford: Polity Press.

Davison, A. 1988. *Six Deserted Villages in Norfolk*. East Anglian Archaeology Report No. 44. Gressenhall: Norfolk Archaeological Unit.

Deetz, J. 1977. *In Small Things Forgotten: The Archaeology of Early American Life*. New York: Anchor.

Dewar, M. (ed.) 1969. *A Discourse of the Commonweal of this realm of England, attributed to Sir Thomas Smith*. Charlottesville: University of Virginia.

Diller, H.-J., Kohl, S., Kornelius, J., Otto, E. and Stratmann, G. (eds.) 1992. *Englishness*. Heidelberg: Heidelberg University Press.

Dixon, P. 1988. The donjon of Knaresborough; the castle as theatre. *Chateau Gaillard* 14, 121–40.

Dobres, M. and Hofmann, C.R. 1994. Social agency and the dynamics of prehistoric technology. *Journal of Archaeological Method and Theory* 1 (3), 211–58.

Dodgshon, R.A. 1985. *The European Past: Social Evolution and Spatial Order*. London: Macmillan.

Douglas, M. and Isherwood, B. 1979. *The World of Goods*. London: Allen Lane.

Dyer, C.C. 1980. *Lords and Peasants in a Changing Society: The Estates of the Bishopric of Worcester, 680–1540*. Cambridge: Cambridge University Press.

—— 1982. Deserted medieval villages in the West Midlands. *Economic History Review*, second series, 35 (1), 19–35.

—— 1989. *Standards of Living in the Later Middle Ages*. Leicester: Leicester University Press.

—— 1990. Dispersed settlements in medieval England. A case study of Pendock, Worcestershire. *Medieval Archaeology* 34, 97–121.

Dymond, D. and Martin, E. (eds) 1988. *An Historical Atlas of Suffolk*. Ipswich: Suffolk County Council.

Edelen, G. (ed.) 1968. *The Description of England by William Harrison*. Ithaca: Cornell University Press.

Egan, G. and Pritchard, F. 1991. *Dress Accessories c.1150–1450*. London: Her Majesty's Stationery Office.

Elias, N. 1978. *The Civilising Process. Volume One: The History of Manners*. Oxford: Blackwell.
—— 1985. *The Loneliness of the Dying*. Oxford: Blackwell.

Elliott, J.H. 1970. *The Old World and the New, 1492–1650*. Cambridge: Cambridge University Press.

Emmison, F.G. 1965. *Some Types of Common Field Parish*. London: National Council of Social Services.

Erickson, A.L. 1993. *Women and Property in Early Modern England*. London: Routledge.

Evans, C.C. 1990. 'Power on silt': towards an archaeology of the East India Company. *Antiquity* 64, 643–61.

Ewart Evans, G.E. 1966. *The Pattern Under the Plough: Aspects of the Folk-Life of East Anglia*. London: Faber.

Falk, L. (ed.) 1991. *Historical Archaeology in Global Perspective*. Washington: Smithsonian Institution.

Ferguson, A.B. 1993. *Utter Antiquity: Perceptions of Prehistory in the Renaissance*. Duke University Press.

Finberg, H.P.R. (ed.) 1967. *The Agrarian History of England and Wales. Volume Four, 1500–1640*. Cambridge: Cambridge University Press.

Fildes, V. (ed.) 1990. *Women as Mothers in Pre-Industrial England*. London: Routledge.

Fletcher, A. 1986. *Reform in the Provinces: The Government of Stuart England*. New Haven: Yale University Press.

——1995. *Gender, Sex and Subordination in England 1500–1800*. London: Yale University Press.

Fletcher, A. and Stevenson, J. (eds). 1985. *Order and Disorder in Early Modern England*. Cambridge: Cambridge University Press.

Ford, W. 1993. The problems of literacy in early modern England. *History* 78, 22–37.

Foucault, M. 1972. *An Archaeology of Knowledge*. London: Tavistock.

——1979. *Discipline and Punish: The Birth of the Prison*. Harmondsworth: Penguin.

Fox, Alan 1985. *History and Heritage: The Social Origins of the British Industrial Relations System*. London: Allen and Unwin.

Fox Sir Cyril, and Raglan, Lord 1951. *Monmouthshire Houses: A Study of Building Techniques and Smaller House-Plans in the Fifteenth to Seventeenth Centuries*. Cardiff: National Museum of Wales.

Fox, H.S.A. and Butlin, R.A. (eds) 1979. *Change in the Countryside: Essays on Rural England, 1500–1900*. Special Publication No. 10. London: Institute of British Geographers.

Franklin, J. 1989. The liberty of the park. In Raphael, F. (ed.) *Patriotisms: The Making and Unmaking of British National Identity*. London: Rontledge.

Friedman, J. 1993. *Miracles and the Pulp Press During the English Revolution: The Battle of the Frogs and Fariford's Flies*. London: University College London Press.

Fussell, G.E. 1972. *The Classical Tradition in West European Farming*. Rutterford: Fairleigh Dickinson University Press.

——1984. *Landscape Painting and the Agricultural Revolution*. London: Pindar.

Gaimster, D. 1994. The archaeology of post-medieval society, *c*.1450–1750: material culture studies in Britain since the war. In Vyner (ed.), 293–312.

Gaimster, D. and Redknap, M. (eds) 1992. *Everyday and Exotic Pottery from Europe: Studies in Honour of John G. Hurst*. Oxford: Oxbow.

Gent, L. and Llewellyn, N. 1990. *Renaissance Bodies: The Human Figure in English Culture c.1540–1660*. London: Reaktion.

Geuter, R. 1994. Reconstructing the context of seventeenth-century English figurative embroideries. Paper presented at the Material Culture and Gender conference, University of Exeter, July.

Giddens, A. 1971. *Capitalism and Modern Social Theory: An Analysis of the Writings of Marx, Durkheim and Weber*. Cambridge: Cambridge University Press.

Girouard, M. 1978. *Life in the English Country House: A Social and Architectural History*. London: Yale University Press.

——1981. *The Return to Camelot: Chivalry and the English Gentleman*. Yale: Yale University Press.

——1983. *Robert Smythson and the Elizabethan Country House*. London: Yale University Press.

Gittings, C. 1984. *Death, Burial and the Individual in Early Modern England*. London: Croom Helm.

Glasscock, R. (ed.) 1992. *Historic Landscapes of Britain from the Air*. Cambridge: Cambridge University Press.

Glasscock, R. and Stephens, N. 1970. *Irish Geographical Studies in Honour of E. Estyn Evans*. Belfast: Queens University Dept. of Geography.

Glassie, H. 1975. *Folk Housing in Middle Virginia: A Structural Analysis of Historic Artifacts*. Knoxville: University of Tennessee Press.

Glennie, P. 1987. The transition from feudalism to capitalism as a problem for historical geography. *Journal of Historical Geography* 13, 296–302.

—— 1992. Late Tudor and Stuart Britain: *c*.1540–*c*.1714. In Glasscock (ed.), 125–53.

Godfrey, E.S. 1975. *The Development of English Glassmaking 1560–1640*. Oxford: Clarendon Press.

Gooder, E. 1984. The finds from the cellar of the Old Hall, Temple Balsall, Warwickshire. *Post-Medieval Archaeology* 18, 149–250.

Goody, J. 1977. *The Domestication of the Savage Mind*. Cambridge: Cambridge University Press.

—— 1982. *Cooking, Cuisine and Class: A Study in Comparative Sociology*. Cambridge: Cambridge University Press.

—— 1986. *The Logic of Writing and the Organization of Society*. Cambridge: Cambridge University Press.

Grafton, A. and Blair, A. (eds) 1990. *The Transmission of Culture in Early Modern Europe*. Philadelphia: University of Pennsylvania Press.

Graves, P. 1989. Social space in the English medieval parish church. *Economy and Society* 18 (3), 297–322.

Gray, H.L. 1915. *English Field Systems*. Cambridge: Harvard University Press.

Green, D.B. 1951. *Blenheim Palace*. London: Country Life.

Greenblatt, S. (ed.) 1982. *The Power of Forms in the English Renaissance*. Norman: Pilgrim.

—— (ed.) 1993. *New World Encounters*. Berkeley: University of California Press.

Gregory, D. 1991. Interventions in the historical geography of modernity: social theory, spatiality and the politics of representation. *Geografiska Annaler* 73B, 17–44.

—— 1994. *Geographical Imaginations*. Oxford: Blackwell.

Gregory, D. and Urry, J. (eds) 1985. *Social Relations and Spatial Structures*. London: Macmillan.

Gurevich, A.J. 1985. *Categories of Medieval Culture*. London: Routledge.

Habbakuk, H.J. 1987. Review of The agrarian history of England and Wales: regional farming systems and agrarian change, 1640–1750. *Economic History Review* 40, 281–96.

Hall, M. 1991. Fish and the fisherman, archaeology and art: Cape Town seen by Bowler, D'Oyly and De Meillon. *S.-Afr. Tydskr. Kuns- Argit.-gesk* 2, 78–88.

—— 1992. Small things and the mobile, conflictual fusion of power, fear and desire. In Yentsch and Beaudry (eds), 373–97.

Harley, J.B. 1988. Maps, knowledge and power. In Cosgrove and Daniels (eds), 277–312.

—— 1992. Deconstructing the map. In Barnes and Duncan (eds), 231–47.

Harrington, P. 1992. *The Archaeology of the English Civil War*. Princes Risborough: Shire.

Harte, N.B. 1976. State control of dress and social change in pre-industrial England. In Coleman and John (eds), 132–65.

Harvey, P.D.A. 1980. *The History of Topographical Maps: Symbols, Pictures and Surveys*. London: Thames and Hudson.

—— 1989. Initiative and authority in settlement change. In Aston et al. (eds), 31–44.

—— 1993. Estate surveyors and the spread of the scale-map in England 1550–80. *Landscape History* 15, 37–50.

Heal, F. 1984. The idea of hospitality in early modern England. *Past and Present* 102, 66–93.

———1990. *Hospitality in Early Modern England*. Oxford: Clarendon Press.

Helgerson, R. 1986. The land speaks: cartography, chorography and subversion in Renaissance England. *Representations* 16, 50–85.

Heller, L. 1984. *Everyday Life*. London: Routledge.

Helme, D. 1978. *The Clay Tobacco Pipe*. Durham: Hewison.

Heppell, E. and Clack, P.A.G. 1991. The enclosures of the Townfields of Sherburn and Shadforth. *Durham Archaeological Journal* 7, 135–41.

Hervey, F. (ed.) 1902. *Suffolk in the Seventeenth Century: the Breviary of Suffolk by Robert Reyce, 1618*. London: Murray.

Hey, D. 1974. *An English Rural Community: Myddle under the Tudors and Stuarts*. Leicester: Leicester University Press.

———(ed.) 1981. *The History of Myddle*. Harmondsworth: Penguin.

Hill, C. 1964. *Society and Puritanism in Pre-Revolutionary England*. London: Secker and Warburg.

———1965. The many-headed monster in late Tudor and early Stuart political thinking. In Carter (ed.), 296–325.

———1972. *The World Turned Upside Down: Radical Ideas During the English Revolution*. London: Temple Smith.

———1993. *The English Bible and the Seventeenth-Century Revolution*. London: Allen Lane.

Hilton, R.H. 1973. *Bond Men Made Free: Medieval Peasant Movements and the English Rising of 1381*. London: Methuen.

———1975. *The English Peasantry in the Later Middle Ages*. Oxford: Clarendon Press.

———1985. *Class Conflict and the Crisis of Feudalism: Essays in Medieval Social History*. London: Hambledon.

Hodder, I. (ed.) 1982. *Symbolic and Structural Archaeology*. Cambridge: Cambridge University Press.

———(ed.) 1987. *The Archaeology of Contextual Meanings*. Cambridge: Cambridge University Press.

Hodges, R. 1982. *Dark Age Economics*. London: Duckworth.

———1989. *The Anglo-Saxon Achievement*. London: Duckworth.

Hodgson, R.I. 1979. The progress of enclosure in County Durham, 1550–1870. In Fox and Butlin (eds), 43–64.

Holmes, C. (ed.) 1970. *The Suffolk Committees for Scandalous Ministers, 1644–46*. Suffolk Records Society 13. Ipswich.

Honeyman, C.H. and Hunter Blair, H.L. 1990. *Warkworth Castle and Hermitage, Northumberland*. London: Her Majesty's Stationery Office.

Hooper-Greenhill, E. 1989. The museum in the disciplinary society. In Pearce (ed.), 61–72.

Hoskins, W.G. 1953. The rebuilding of rural England, 1560–1640. *Past and Present* 4, 44–59.

———1967. *Fieldwork in Local History*. London: Faber.

Howard, M. 1987. *The Early Tudor Country House: Architecture and Politics 1490–1550*. London: George Philip.

———1990. Self-fashioning and the classical moment in mid sixteenth-century architecture. In Gent and Llewellyn (eds), 180–217.

Howell, M.C. 1986. *Women, Production and Patriarchy in Late Medieval Cities*. London: University of Chicago Press.

Hoyle, R.W. 1990. Tenure and the land market in early modern England. *Economic History Review* 43, 1–20.

Hughes, A. (ed.) 1980. *Seventeenth-Century England: A Changing Culture. Volume One: Primary Sources*. London: The Open University.

Hunt, J.D. 1986. *Garden and Grove: The Italian Renaissance Garden in the English Imagination 1600–1750*. London: Dent.

Hunt, J.D. and Willis, P. 1975. *The Genius of the Place: The English Landscape Garden 1620– 1820*. London: Elek.

Hunt, L. (ed.) 1989. *The New Cultural History*. Berkeley: University of California Press.

Ingram, M. 1985. The reform of popular culture? Sex and marriage in early modern England. In Reay (ed.), 129–65.

——1987. *Church Courts, Sex and Marriage in England, 1570–1640*. Cambridge: Cambridge University Press.

——1994. 'Scolding women cucked or washed': a crisis in gender relations in early modern England? In Kermode and Walker (eds), 48–80.

Isaac, R. 1983. *The Transformation of Virginia, 1760–1820*. Chapel Hill: University of North Carolina Press.

——1988. Ethnographic method in history: an action approach. In St George (ed.), 39–62.

James, M. 1986. *Society, Politics, Culture: Studies in Early Modern England*. Cambridge: Cambridge University Press.

James, N. 1994. The middle and south barrier banks of the Fens. *Archaeological Journal* 150, 503–7.

James, T.B. 1990. *The Palaces of Medieval England, c.1050–1550: Royalty, Nobility, The Episcopate and their Residences from Edward the Confessor to Henry VIII*. London: Seaby.

Jarvis, P.J. 1979. Plant introductions to England and their role in horticultural and sylvicultural innovation, 1500–1900. In Fox and Butlin (eds), 145–64.

Jennings, S. 1982. *Eighteen Centuries of Pottery from Norwich*. East Anglian Archaeology 3. Norwich.

John, A.H. 1976. English agricultural improvement and grain exports, 1660–1765. In Coleman and John (eds), 45–67.

Johnson, M.H. 1989. Conceptions of agency in archaeological interpretation. *Journal of Anthropological Archaeology* 8, 189–211.

——1991. The Englishman's home and its study. In Samson, R. (ed.) *The Social Archaeology of Houses*. Edinburgh: Edinburgh University Press, 245–58.

——1993. *Housing Culture: Traditional Architecture in an English Landscape*. London: University College London Press (published in USA by Smithsonian Institution, Washington, DC).

——n.d. A contextual study of traditional architecture in western Suffolk, 1400–1700. University of Cambridge Ph.D. dissertation.

Kelley, D.R. 1990. 'Second nature': the idea of custom on European law, society and culture. In Grafton and Blair (eds), 131–72.

Kelsall, M. 1993. *The Great Good Place: The Country House and English Literature*. New York: Columbia University Press.

Kermode, J. and Walker, G. (eds) 1994. *Women, Crime and the Courts in Early Modern England*. London: University College London Press.

Kerridge, E. 1967. *The Agricultural Revolution*. London: Allen and Unwin.

——1969. *Agrarian Problems in the Sixteenth Century and After*. London: Allen and Unwin.

Knapp, J. 1993. Elizabethan tobacco. In Greenblatt (ed.), 272–312.

Knowles, D. 1974. *Bare Ruined Choirs: The Dissolution of the English Monasteries*. Cambridge: Cambridge University Press.

Kubovy, M. 1986. *The Psychology of Perspective and Renaissance Art*. Cambridge: Cambridge University Press.

Kulikoff, A. 1986. *Tobacco and Slaves*. Chapel Hill: University of North Carolina Press.

Kussmaul, A. 1981. *Servants in Husbandry in Early Modern England*. Cambridge: Cambridge University Press.

——1990. *A General View of the Rural Economy of England, 1538–1840*. Cambridge: Cambridge University Press.

Lange, B.P. 1992. The English garden and the patriotic discourse. In Diller et al. (eds), 49–70.

Laqueur, T. 1990. *Making Sex: Body and Gender from the Greeks to Freud*. Cambridge: Harvard University Press.

Lash, S. and Friedman, J. (eds) 1992. *Modernity and Identity*. Oxford: Blackwell.

Lefebvre, H. 1991. *The Production of Space*. Oxford: Blackwell.

Leone, M. 1982. Some opinions about recovering mind. *American Antiquity* 47, 742–60.

——1984. Interpreting ideology in historical archaeology: the William Paca Garden in Annapolis, Maryland. In Miller and Tilley (eds), 25–35.

——1988. The Georgian Order as the order of capitalism in Annapolis, Maryland. In Leone and Potter (eds), 235–62.

Leone, M. and Potter, P. (eds) 1988. *The Recovery of Meaning in Historical Archaeology*. Washington: Smithsonian Institution.

Leslie, M. and Raylor, T. (eds) 1992. *Culture and Cultivation in Early Modern England: Writing and the Land*. Leicester: Leicester University Press.

Levine, D. 1984. *Proletarianisation and Family History*. Orlando: University of Florida Press.

Lindley, K. 1982. *Fenland Riots and the English Revolution*. London: Heinemann.

Little, B. (ed.) 1992. *Text-Aided Archaeology*. Ann Arbor: CRC Press.

Lucas, G. 1995. The changing face of time: a study of English domestic clocks from the seventeenth to the nineteenth century. *Journal of Design History* 8 (1) (forthcoming).

Macculloch, D. 1986. *Suffolk and the Tudors: Politics and Religion in an English County, 1500–1600*. Oxford: Clarendon Press.

McCarthy, M. and Brooks, C.M. 1988. *Medieval Pottery in Britain AD 900–1600*. Leicester: Leicester University Press.

McClellan, D. (ed.) 1977. *Karl Marx: Selected Writings*. Oxford: Oxford University Press.

McCloskey, D.N. 1979. Another way of observing the open fields. *Journal of Historical Geography* 5, 426–9.

McCracken, G. 1983. The exchange of children in Tudor England: an anthropological phenomenon in historical context. *Journal of Family History* 8, 303–13.

Macfarlane, A. 1978. *The Origins of English Individualism*. Oxford: Blackwell.

——1988. The cradle of capitalism: the case of England. In Baechler et al. (eds), 185–203.

McGuire, R. and Paynter, R. (eds) 1991. *The Archaeology of Inequality*. Oxford: Blackwell.

Machin, R. 1977. The Great Rebuilding: a reassessment. *Past and Present* 77, 33–56.

McKendrick, N., Brewer, J. and Plumb, J.H. 1982. *The Birth of a Consumer Society*. London: Hutchinson.

Macrae, A. 1992. Husbandry manuals and the language of agrarian improvement. In Leslie and Raylor (eds), 35–62.

Mah, H. 1991. Suppressing the text: the metaphysics of ethnographic history in Darnton's Great Cat Massacre. *History Workshop Journal* 31, 1–20.

Mann, M. 1988. European development: approaching a historical explanation. In Baechler et al. (eds), 6–19.

Manning, R.B. 1988. *Village Revolts: Social Protests and Popular Disturbances in England 1509–1640*. Oxford: Oxford University Press.

Martin, J.E. 1983. *Feudalism to Capitalism: Peasant and Landlord in English Agrarian Development*. Basingstoke: Macmillan.

Markham, G. R. 1986. *The English Housewife*. Edited by M.R. Bert. Montreal: McGill-Queen's University Press.

Markus, T. 1993. *Buildings and Power: Freedom and Control in the Origin of Modern Building Types*. London: Routledge.

Masschaele, J. 1993. Transport costs in medieval England. *Economic History Review* 46, 266–79.

——1994. The multiplicity of medieval markets reconsidered. *Journal of Historical Geography* 20 (3), 255–71.

Mathias, P. 1962. *English Trade Tokens: The Industrial Revolution Illustrated*. London: Aberlard-Schuman.

Mayr, O. 1986. *Authority, Liberty and Automatic Machinery in Early Modern Europe*. Baltimore: Johns Hopkins University Press.

Mercer, E. 1975. *English Vernacular Houses: A Study of Traditional Farmhouses and Cottages*. London: Her Majesty's Stationery Office.

Merchant, C. 1980. *The Death of Nature: Women, Ecology, and the Scientific Revolution*. London: Harper and Row.

Merrifield, R. 1978. *The Archaeology of Ritual and Magic*. London: Batsford.

Mertes, K. 1988. *The English Noble Household: Good Governance and Public Rule*. Oxford: Blackwell.

Miller, D. 1987. *Material Culture and Mass Consumption*. Oxford: Blackwell.

Miller, D. and Tilley, C. (eds) 1984. *Ideology, Power and Prehistory*. Cambridge: Cambridge University Press.

Mitchison, R. and Roebuck, P. (eds) 1988. *Economy and Society in Scotland and Ireland 1500–1939*. Edinburgh: John Donald.

Mitson, A. 1993. The significance of kinship networks in the seventeenth century: south-west Nottinghamshire. In Phythian-Adams (ed.), 24–76.

Moore, H. 1985. *Space, Text and Gender*. Cambridge: Cambridge University Press.

——1988. *Feminism and Anthropology*. Cambridge: Cambridge University Press.

Moran, M. 1989. Re-erecting houses in Shropshire in the late seventeenth century. *Archaeological Journal* 146, 538–53.

Morris, C. (ed.) 1949. *The Journeys of Celia Fiennes*. London: Cresset.

Moss, A. 1993. Commonplace-rhetoric and thought-patterns in early modern culture. In Roberts and Good (eds), 49–60.

Muchembled, R. 1978. *Culture populaire et culture des elites dans la France moderne (15e–18e siecles): essai*. Paris. (English translation 1985. *Popular Calture and Elite Culture in France*

1400–1750. Baton Rouge: Louisiana State University Press.)

Mui, H. and Mui, L.H. 1989. *Shops and Shopkeeping in Eighteenth-Century England.* Kingston: McGill–Queen's University Press.

Mukerji, C. 1983. *From Graven Images: Patterns of Moden Materialism.* Columbia: Columbia: University Press.

Muldrew, C. 1993. Interpreting the market: the ethics of credit and community relations in early modern England. Social History 18 (2), 163–83.

Muller, J.A. (ed.) 1933. *The Letters of Stephen Gardiner.* Cambridge: Cambridge University Press.

Nisbet, R. 1967. *The Sociological Tradition.* London: Heinemann.

O'Dowd, M. 1988. Land and lordship in sixteenth and early seventeenth-century Ireland. In Mitchison and Roebuck (eds), 17–26.

Ormond, D. 1984. R.H. Tawney and the origins of capitalism. *History Workshop Journal* 18, 138–59.

Pacey, A. 1974. *The Maze of Ingenuity: Ideas and Idealism in the Development of Technology.* London: Allen Lane.

Parker, K.L. 1988. *The English Sabbath: A Study of Doctrine and Discipline from the Reformation to the Civil War.* Cambridge: Cambridge University Press.

Parry, G. 1992. John Evelyn as hortulan saint. In Leslie and Raylor (eds), 130–50.

Patterson, A. 1989. *Shakespeare and the Popular Voice.* Oxford: Oxford University Press.

Payling, S.J. 1992. Social mobility, demographic change and landed society in late medieval England. *Economic History Review* 95 (1), 51–73.

Peacock, J. 1990. Inigo Jones as figurative artist. In Gent and Lewellyn (eds), 154–79.

Pearce, S.M. (ed.) 1989. *Museum Studies in Material Culture.* Leicester: Leicester University Press.

Pelling, M. 1986. Appearance and reality: barber-surgeons, the body and disease. In Beier and Finlay (eds), 82–112.

Phillips, J. 1973. *The Reformation of Images: Destruction of Art in England, 1535–1660.* Berkeley: University of California Press.

Philo, C. 1989. 'Enough to drive one mad': the organisation of space in nineteenth-century lunatic asylums. In Wolch and Dear (eds), 258–91.

Phythian-Adams, C. 1987. *Re-Thinking English Local History.* Dept of English Local History Occasional Papers, Fourth Series, 1. Leicester: Leicester University Press.

——1992. Hoskins's England: a local historian of genius and the realisation of his theme. *Transactions of the Leicestershire Archaeological and Historical Society* 66, 143–59.

——1993a. Local history and societal history. *Local Population Studies* 51, 30–45.

——(ed.) 1993b. *Societies, Cultures and Kinship, 1580–1850: Cultural Provinces and English Local History.* Leicester: Leicester University Press.

Platt, C. 1969. *The Monastic Grange in Medieval England.* London: Batsford.

——1976. *The English Medieval Town.* London: Secker and Warburg.

——1978. *Medieval England: A Social History and Archaeology from the Conquest to 1600 AD.* London: Routledge.

——1981. *The Parish Churches of Medieval England.* London: Secker and Warburg.

——1994. *The Great Rebuildings of Tudor and Stuart England: Revolutions in Architectural Taste.* London: University College London Press.

Pointon, M. 1993. *Hanging The Head: Portraiture and Social Formation in Eighteenth-Century England.* New Haven: Yale University Press.

Polanyi, K. 1944. *The Great Transformation: The Political and Economic Origins of Our Time.* Boston: Beacon.

Pollock, A. 1987. *A Lasting Relationship: Parents and Children Over Three Centuries.* London: Fourth Estate.

Pred, A. 1985. The social becomes the spatial, the spatial becomes the social: enclosures, social change and the becoming of places in Skane. In Gregory and Urry (eds), 137–65.

Prince, H.C. 1982. Modernisation, restoration, preservation: changes in tastes for antique landscapes. In Baker and Billinge (eds), 33–43.

——1988. Art and agrarian change, 1710–1815. In Cosgrove and Daniels (eds), 98–118.

Prior, M. 1990. Wives and wills 1558–1700. In Chartres and Hey (eds), 201–26.

Purvis, J.S. 1948. *Tudor Parish Documents of the Diocese of York: A Selection with Introduction and Notes.* Cambridge: Cambridge University Press.

Quaife, G.R. 1979. *Wanton Wenches and Wayward Wives.* London: Croom Helm.

Quimby, I.M.G. (ed.) 1984. *The Craftsman in Early America.* New York: Winterthur.

Razi, Z. 1987. Family, land and the village community in later medieval England. In Aston (ed.), 377–93.

Reay, B. 1985a. Popular religion. In Reay (ed.), 91–128.

——(ed.) 1985b. *Popular Culture in Seventeenth-Century England.* London: Croom Helm.

Redknap, M. 1992. Post-medieval brick spit-supports or stands found in Wales. In Gaimster and Redknap (eds), 45–58.

Reed, M. 1984. Enclosure in north Buckinghamshire, 1500–1750. *Agricultural History Review* 32, 133–44.

Relph, E. 1981. *Rational Landscapes and Humanistic Geography.* London: Croom Helm.

Richeson, W. 1966. *English Land Measuring to 1800: Instruments and Practices.* Cambridge: Massachusetts Institute of Technology Press.

Robbins, R. (ed.) 1972. *Sir Thomas Browne: Religio Medici, Hydriotaphia and The Garden of Cyrus.* Oxford: Clarendon Press.

Roberts, M. 1994. *Durham.* London: Batsford.

Roberts, R.H. and Good, J.M.M. 1993. *The Recovery of Rhetoric: Persuasive Discourse and Disciplinarity in the Human Sciences.* Bristol: Classical Press.

Robinson, P.S. 1983. 'English' houses built at Moneymore, County Londonderry, c.1615. *Post-Medieval Archaeology* 17, 47–63.

——1984. *The Plantation of Ulster: British Settlement in an Irish Landscape, 1600–1760.* New York: St Martin's Press.

Said, E.W. 1993. *Culture and Imperialism.* London: Chatto and Windus.

St Clair Byrne, M. 1983. *The Lisle Letters.* Chicago: University of Chicago Press.

St George, R.B. 1984. Fathers, sons and identity: woodworking artisans in south-eastern New England, 1620–1700. In Quimby (ed.), 89–125.

——(ed.) 1988. *Material Life in America 1600–1860.* Boston: Northeastern University Press.

——1990. Bawns and beliefs: architecture, commerce and conversion in early New England. *Winterthur Portfolio* 25 (4), 241–87.

——n.d. The erotics of property in historical thought. Unpublished paper in possession of author.

Samuel, R. (ed.) 1989. *Patriotism: The Making and Unmaking of British National Identity.* London: Routledge.

Saunders, T. 1990. The feudal construction of space: power and domination in the nucleated village. In Samson, R. (ed.) *The Social Archaeology of Houses*, Edinburgh: Edinburgh University Press, 181–96.

Scattergood, J. 1987. Fashion and morality in the later Middle Ages. In Williams (ed.), 225–72.

Schama, S. 1987. *The Embarrasment of Riches: An Interpretation of Dutch Culture in the Golden Age*. London: Collins.

Schmied, D. 1992. The countryside – ideal and reality. In Diller et al. (eds), 71–82.

Schrire, C. (ed.) 1991. The historical archaeology of the impact of colonialism in seventeenth-century South Africa. In Falk (ed.), 69–96.

Shackel, P. 1992. Probate inventories in historical archaeology: a review and alternatives. In Little (ed.), 205–16.

—— 1993. *Personal Discipline and Material Culture: An Archaeology of Annapolis, Maryland, 1695–1870*. Knoxville: University of Tennessee Press.

Shammas, C. 1990. *The Pre-Industrial Consumer in England and America*. Oxford: Clarendon Press.

Sharp, B. 1980. *In Contempt of All Authority: Rural Artisans and Riot in the West of England, 1586–1660*. Berkeley: University of California Press.

Shaw, C. and Chase, M. (eds) 1989. *The Imagined Past: History and Nostalgia*. Manchester: Manchester University Press.

Simpson, J. 1986. God's visible judgments: the Christian dimension of landscape legends. *Landscape History* 8, 53–8.

Sinclair, A.G.M. 1987. 'All Styles are Good, save the tiresome kind'. In Hodder, I. (ed.) *The Archaeology of Contextual Meanings*. Cambridge: Cambridge University Press.

Slack, P. 1979. Mirrors of health and treasures of poor men: the uses of the vernacular medical literature of Tudor England. In Webster (ed.), 237–74.

Smiles, S. 1994. *The Image of Antiquity: Ancient Britain and the Romantic Imagination*. New Haven: Yale University Press.

Smith, J.T. 1970. The evolution of the English peasant house to the late seventeenth-century: the evidence of buildings. *Journal of the British Archaeological Association* 33 (third series), 122–47.

Smuts, M.R. 1987. *Court Culture and the Origins of a Royalist Tradition in Early Stuart England*. Philadelphia: University of Pennsylvania Press.

Snell, C. 1986. *An Inventory of Nonconformist Chapels and Meeting-Houses in Central England*. London: Her Majesty's Stationery Office.

Spufford, M. 1981. *Small Books and Pleasant Histories: Popular Fiction and its Readership in Seventeenth-Century England*. London: Methuen.

—— 1984. *The Great Reclothing of Rural England: Petty Chapmen and Their Wares in the Seventeenth-Century*. London: Hambledon.

—— 1990. The limitations of the probate inventory. In Chartres and Hey (eds), 139–74.

Starkey, D. 1982. Ightham Mote: politics and architecture in early Tudor England. *Archaeologia* 107, 153–63.

Steer, F. 1969. *Farm and Cottage Inventories of Mid-Essex 1635–1749*. London: Phillimore.

Stone, L. 1965. *The Crisis of the Aristocracy*. Oxford: Clarendon Press.

—— 1983. Interpersonal violence in English society, 1300–1980. *Past and Present* 101, 22–33.

Stone, L. and Stone, J.C. 1984. *An Open Elite? England 1540–1880*. Oxford: Clarendon Press.

Strong, R. 1977. *The Cult of Elizabeth: Elizabethan Portraiture and Pageantry*. London: Thames and Hudson.

——1979. *The Renaissance Garden in England*. London: Thames and Hudson.

Tawney, R.H. 1912. *The Agrarian Problem in the Sixteenth Century*. London: Longmans.

——1926. *Religion and the Rise of Capitalism*. London: Murrary.

Tawney, R.H. and Power, E. 1924. *Tudor Economic Documents*. London: Longmans.

Taylor, C.C. 1983. *The Archaeology of Gardens*. London: Shire.

Taylor, C.C., Everson, P. and Wilson-North, R. 1990. Bodiam Castle, Sussex. *Medieval Archaeology* 34, 155–7.

Thirsk, J. 1967. Enclosing and engrossing. In Finberg (ed.), 200–40.

——1978. *Economic Policy and Projects: The Development of a Consumer Society in Early Modern England*. Oxford: Clarendon Press.

——1992. Making a fresh start: sixteenth-century agriculture and the classical inspiration. In Leslie and Raylor (eds), 15–34.

Thomas, K. 1971. *Religion and the Decline of Magic: Popular Beliefs in Sixteenth- and Seventeenth-Century England*. London, Weidenfeld and Nicolson.

——1983. *Man and the Natural World: Changing Attitudes in England 1500–1800*. London: Allen Lane.

Thompson, E.P. 1963. *The Making of the English Working Class*. London: Gollancz.

——1967. Time, work-discipline and industrial capitalism. *Past and Present* 38, 56–97.

——1977. *William Morris: Romantic to Revolutionary*. London: Merlin Press.

——1991. *Customs in Common*. London: Merlin Press.

Thompson, M.W. 1991. *Kenilworth Castle*. London: English Heritage.

Thompson, R. 1984. Adolescent culture in colonial Massachusetts. *Journal of Family History* 9 (2), 127–44.

Thrower, N.J.W. (ed.) 1978. *The Compleat Plattmaker: Essays on Chart, Map and Globe Making in England in the Seventeenth and Eighteenth Centuries*. Berkeley: University of California Press.

Tribe, K. 1978. *Land, Labour and Economic Discourse*. London: Routledge.

——1981. *Genealogies of Capitalism*. London: Macmillan.

Turner, J. 1979. *The Politics of Landscape: Rural Scenery and Society in English Poetry 1630–1660*. Oxford: Blackwell.

Turner, V. 1968. *The Drums of Affliction: A Study of Religious Processes among the Ndembu of Zambia*. London: Hutchinson.

Underdown, D. 1985. *Revel, Riot and Rebellion: Popular Politics and Culture in England 1603–1660*. Oxford: Oxford University Press.

——1992. *Fire from Heaven: Life in an English Town in the Seventeenth Century*. London: Harper Collins.

Upton, D. 1986. *Holy Things and Profane: Anglican Parish Churches in Colonial Virginia*. Cambridge: Massachusetts Institute of Technology Press.

Vince, A. and Bell, R. 1992. Sixteenth-century pottery from Acton Court, Avon. In Gaimster and Redknap (eds), 101–12.

Vyner, B. (ed.) 1994. *Building on the Past: Papers Celebrating 150 Years of the Royal Archaeological Institute*. London: Royal Archaeological Institute.

Walker, G. 1994. Women, theft and the world of stolen goods. In Kermode and Walker (eds), 81–105.

Wallerstein, M. 1974. *The Modern World-System: Capitalist Agriculture and the Origins of the European World-Economy in the Sixteenth Century*. London: Academic Press.

Warmington, A. 1989. Frogs, toads and the Restoration in a Gloucestershire village. Midland History 14, 30–42.

Warner, P. 1987. *Greens, Commons and Clayland Colonisation: The Origins and Development of Green-side Settlement in East Suffolk*. Leciester: Leicester University Press.

Watson, R.C. 1989. 'According to the custom of the province of York'. *Lancashire Local History* 5, 5–14.

Weatherill, L. 1988. *Consumer Behaviour and Material Culture in Britain, 1660–1760*. London: Routledge.

——1991. Consumer behaviour, textiles and dress in the late seventeenth and early eighteenth centuries. *Textile History* 22.

Weber, M. 1947. *The Theory of Social and Economic Organisation*. Oxford: Oxford University Press.

——1958. *The Protestant Ethic and the Spirit of Capitalism*. Translated by Talcott Parsons. New York: Scribner.

Webster, C. 1975. *The Great Instauration: Science, Medicine and Reform 1626–1660*. London: Duckworth.

——(ed.) 1979. *Health, Medicine and Mortality in the Sixteenth Century*. Cambridge: Cambridge University Press.

White, H. 1987. *The Content of the Form: Narrative Discourse and Historical Representation*. Baltimore: Johns Hopkins University Press.

Wilks, A. 1980. Pioneers of topographical printmaking: some comparisons. *Landscape History* 2, 59–69.

Williams, D. (ed.) 1987. *England in the Fifteenth Century: Proceedings of the 1986 Harlaxton Symposium*. Woodbridge: Boydell.

Williams, T. 1990. 'Magnetic Figures': polemical prints of the English Revolution. In Gent and Llewellyn (eds), 86–110.

Williamson, T. 1988. Ancient landscapes. In Dymond and Martin (eds), 40–1.

Williamson, T. and Bellany, L. 1986. *Property and Landscape: A Social History of the English Countryside*. London: Allen.

Wilson, A. 1990. The ceremony of childbirth and its interpretation. In Fildes (ed.), 68–107.

Wilson, E. 1985. *Adorned in Dreams: Fashion and Modernity*. London: Virago.

Wolch, J. and Dear, M. 1989. *The Power of Geography: How Territory Shapes Social Life*. London: Unwin Hyman.

Wood, D. 1993. *The Power of Maps*. London: Routledge.

Woodward, D.A. 1978. English cartography, 1650–1750: a summary. In Thrower (ed.), 159–94.

——1985. 'Swords into ploughshares': recycling in pre-industrial England. *Economic History Review* 38, 175–85.

——1990. 'An essay on manures': changing attitutdes to fertilization in England, 1500–1800. In Charters and Hey (eds), 251–78.

Wordie, J.R. 1983. The chronology of English enclosure, 1500–1914. *Economic History Review* 36, 483–505.

Wrathmell, S. 1980. Village depopulation in the seventeenth and eighteenth centuries: examples from Northumberland. *Post-Medieval Archaeology* 14, 113–26.

——1994. Rural settlements in medieval England: perspectives and perceptions. In Vyner (ed.), 178–94.

Wright, S.M. 1976. Barton Blount: climatic or economic change? *Medieval Archaeology* 20, 148–52.

Wrightson, K. 1981. Alehouses, order and reformation in England, 1590–1660. In Yeo and Yeo (eds), 1–27.

——1982. *English Society 1580–1680*. London: Hutchinson.

——1994. The language of sorts in early modern England. In Brooks and Barry (eds), 1994.

Wrightson, K. and Levine, D. 1979. *Poverty and Piety in an English Village: Terling, 1525–1700*. New York: Academic Press.

Wrigley, E.A. 1989. *Continuity, Chance and Change: The Character of the Industrial Revolution in England*. Cambridge: Cambridge University Press.

Wrigley, E.A. and Schofield, R.S. 1981. *The Population History of England 1541–1871*. Cambridge: Harvard University Press.

Yates, N. 1991. *Buildings, Faith and Worship: The Liturgical Arrangement of Anglican Churches 1600–1900*. Oxford: Clarendon Press.

Yeo, E. and Yeo, S. (eds) 1981. *Popular Culture and Class Conflict 1590–1914: Exploration in the History of Labour and Leisure*. Brighton: Harvester.

Yelling, J.A. 1977. *Common Field and Enclosure in England 1450–1850*. London: Macmillan.

Yentsch, A. 1991. Chesapeake Artefacts and their cultural context: Pottery and the food domain. *Post-Medieval Archaeology* 25, 25–73.

Yentsch, A. and Beaudry, M. (eds) 1992. *The Art and Mystery of Historical Archaeology: Essays in Honour of James Deetz*. London: CRC.

Index

Italics have been used in page numbers to denote a figure. Titles are also in italics.